World Wisdom
The Library of Perennial Philosophy

The Library of Perennial Philosophy is dedicated to the exposition of the timeless Truth underlying the diverse religions. This Truth, often referred to as the *Sophia Perennis*—or Perennial Wisdom—finds its expression in the revealed Scriptures as well as in the writings of the great sages and the artistic creations of the traditional worlds.

Samdhong Rinpoche, Uncompromising Truth for a Compromised World: Tibetan Buddhism and Today's World appears as one of our selections in the Spiritual Masters: East and West series.

Spiritual Masters: East & West Series

This series presents the writings of great spiritual masters of the past and present from both East and West. Carefully selected essential writings of these sages are combined with biographical information, glossaries of technical terms, historical maps, and pictorial and photographic art in order to communicate a sense of their respective spiritual climates.

SAMDHONG RINPOCHE
Uncompromising Truth
for a **Compromised World:**

Tibetan Buddhism
and Today's World

Conceived, Recorded, and Edited by
DONOVAN ROEBERT

Foreword by
His Holiness the 14th Dalai Lama

World Wisdom

Library of Congress Cataloging-in-Publication Data

Rinpoche, Samdhong.
  Samdhong Rinpoche : Uncompromising truth for a compromised world : Tibetan
Buddhism and today's world / conceived, recorded, and edited by Donovan
Roebert ; foreword by His Holiness the 14th Dalai Lama.
     p. cm. -- (Spiritual masters--East and West series)
  Includes index.
  ISBN-13: 978-1-933316-20-8 (pbk. : alk. paper)
  ISBN-10: 1-933316-20-9 (pbk. : alk. paper) 1. Rinpoche, Samdhong--Interviews.
2. Tibetans--India--Interviews. 3. Political refugees--India--Interviews. 4. Lamas--
India--Interviews. I. Roebert, Donovan, 1959- II. Title. III. Title: Uncompromising
truth for a compromised world : Tibetan Buddhism and today's world. IV. Series:
Library of perennial philosophy. Spiritual masters--East and West series.
DS432.T5R49 2006
294.3'420423--dc22

                                                                                2006017303

Printed on acid-free paper in Canada.

For information address World Wisdom, Inc.
P.O. Box 2682, Bloomington, Indiana 47402-2682
www.worldwisdom.com

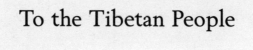

To the Tibetan People

CONTENTS

Foreword by H.H. the Dalai Lama   *xi*
Preface   *xiii*
Acknowledgments   *xix*
The Venerable Samdhong Rinpoche   *xxi*

PART I: THE LONG ROAD TO NOW
Introduction   3
The Dialogues: 7
    Origins   7
    Biological Evolution   9
    Societies   12
    Culture   16
    Governance   18
    Economies   20
    Industry and Commerce   23
    Law   25
    Philosophy   30
    Religion   34
    Morality   38
    Spirituality   41
    Science   43
    Art   45
    Complexity and Escapism   48
    Civilization and Decline   53
    The Future in Prospect   56

PART II: THE MODERN INDIVIDUAL
Introduction   63
The Dialogues   67

**PART III: HUMANKIND IN SAMSARA, ON EARTH,
AND IN THE UNIVERSE**
Introduction   79
The Dialogues: 80
    The Gap between Governments and the Governed   80
    Law as Moral Sufficiency   82

Environmental Destruction   85
International Influence and Expansionism   89
Power   93
Violence and War   96
America and the Superpower Principle   98
Toothless International Law   102
The Ideal   103
A View on This Millennium   104

PART IV: TIBET—THE MODERN WORLD'S HIDDEN TRAGEDY

Introduction   115
The Invasion and Occupation of Tibet   116
Tibet at the United Nations   117
The Cultural Revolution   117
Post-Maoist Policies   118
The Scope of Abuse   122
Religious Persecution   124
Two Statements from April 2003   125
Plunder and Destruction for China's Benefit   126
Population Transfer: China's "Final Solution" for Tibet   131
The Status of Tibet   132
What Tibetans Want   133
The Response from Beijing   135
The Dialogues: 137
   The Karma of Tibet   137
   Tibet and Taiwan: Contrasting Stances   141
   Preserving Dharma and Buddhist Culture in Tibet   142
   The Future Vision of Tibet   144
   Losing Patience With Non-Violence   155

PART V: SATYAGRAHA AND AHIMSA (TRUTH-INSISTENCE AND NON-HARMFULNESS)

Introduction   163
The Dialogues   167

PART VI: THE FOUNDATIONAL VIEW—BUDDHADHARMA

The Life of Siddhartha Gotama   181
The First Noble Truth: The Truth of Suffering   182

The Second Noble Truth: The Truth of the Causes of Suffering 183
The Third Noble Truth: The Truth of the Cessation of Suffering 184
The Fourth Noble Truth: The Eightfold Path 184
Karma 188
Rebirth 189
Interdependent Origination 189
Impermanence, Suffering, Not-Self 190
The Five Aggregates 190
Compassion 191
Wisdom-Compassion and the Six Perfections 192
Bodhicitta and Skilful Means 192
The Bodhisattva 193
The Inner and Outer Lama 193
Study and Practice 194
The Vajrayana 194
View, Conduct, Meditation 195
Taking Refuge 196
The Dialogues 197

Conclusion 233
Glossary of Terms 237
Biographical Notes 239
Index 241

His Holiness the 14th Dalai Lama

THE DALAI LAMA

FOREWORD

Samdhong Rinpoche is someone I hold in high regard. He belongs to the last generation of Tibetans who reached adulthood and accomplished a part of their monastic training before leaving Tibet. Then, having come into exile in India, he both completed his traditional Tibetan monastic studies and acquainted himself well with modern approaches to education. Rinpoche first taught at our Central School for Tibetans in Shila and Darjeeling as a spiritual and cultural teacher in the early sixties and later became the Principal of our school in Dalhousie. His subsequent long and effective career in education as Principal and later as the Director of the Central Institute of Higher Tibetan Studies in Sarnath was distinguished. Having reluctantly entered into political affairs, he has become an Influential Chairman of the Kashag or Council of Ministers in the Central Tibetan Administration.

Despite his genuine qualities and accomplishments, I have always found Samdhong Rinpoche to be an abstemious, reserved man. Consequently, his firm views on many issues may not be widely known outside the Tibetan community. Considering the important position he now occupies, I believe the editor of this book has done a public service in preparing this selection of Rinpoche's observations and opinions. Of course, Rinpoche and I share a similar outlook on many issues, not only because we are both Tibetan Buddhist monks, but also because we have both been impressed by contemporary advocates of non-violence such as Mahatma Gandhi.

I think we both believe that there is an urgent need for ethics or spiritual values in the world of politics and economics. For example, we live in a world in which most human beings have to engage in some kind of economic activity to ensure their survival. They need goods and services to meet the essential requirements of existence, not to mention those things that bring dignity and comfort to human life. Yet for all the innovation and creativity of our economic activity we have not succeeded in securing these essentials for all human beings everywhere. We have to ask ourselves whether something is wrong with our choice of goals or with our motivation or with both. A social system that perpetuates and accentuates the kind of disparities we witness today can only be kept alive through violence and injustice. Violence provokes more violence. Peace, on the other hand, can only be achieved if we implement compassion.

On a personal level, if you practice tolerance and compassion, you will immediately discover that these qualities are causes of happiness. There is no machine that can produce inner peace; there is no shop that sells inner peace. No matter how rich you are, there is no way you can buy inner peace. It is something that has to come from inside, through mental practice. From a wider point of view, an interdependent community, such as the increasingly globalized world in which we live, has to be a compassionate community, compassionate in the choice of goals, compassionate in the means of cooperation or the pursuit of goals.

I feel quite sure that readers interested in these issues will find much in this book to stimulate them and I hope they may be encouraged by what they read to take practical steps according to their own circumstances to contribute to making the world in which we live a happier, more peaceful place.

January 24, 2006

PREFACE

I first met Venerable Professor Samdhong Rinpoche briefly during the 2003 conference of Tibet Support Groups held in Prague. Throughout the four days of that conference I observed his unassuming modesty and essential humility, qualities very rare among the accomplished, even rarer among political leaders. As Kalon Tripa, or Prime Minister, of the Tibetan Exile Government I expected to see him being served and attended by his subordinates. Instead, I noticed him quietly take his place in the buffet queue, help himself to a modest vegetarian meal, and find a seat, like everyone else, at any available table. In no way in any of the conference activities did Rinpoche seem to expect special consideration or deference to his position.

Of course, in my mind this made him stand out all the more. Moving quietly about, clad in the maroon and yellow robes of a Tibetan Buddhist monk, he seemed to me to emanate, even from a distance, the energy of a wisdom that is completely at peace with itself, that has no need of being fed by submissive attention. I felt myself deeply drawn to him. In Tibetan Buddhism, as in all other religions, there is at least as much sham as there is authenticity; in Tibetan politics, as in all politics, there is duplicity. It was clear to me that Rinpoche, both as a spiritual teacher and as a politician, was completely authentic, transparent, and conformed to the truth in himself.

It was only when Rinpoche delivered his speech on Satyagraha (Truth-Insistence) that I became aware of the real nature of his uncompromising views. That short speech, delivered with unshakeable self-confidence and an unexpected power, rippled through the conference more like a call to a new way of life rather than only an approach to the problem of Tibet. It brought home to me with a painful suddenness the distance between the way our world is run and the way it can be run. It infused me with hope.

On the last evening of the conference I mustered up the courage to approach Rinpoche and, taking hold of his hand, to thank him for what he had given me. As I blurted out my inarticulate words of appreciation he gazed at me with a slightly surprised and amused detachment. How could he know what powerful seeds of revolution he had planted in my own thinking?

From that point on I became driven by an impulse to bring Rinpoche's total view to the attention of a much wider audience. It didn't matter whether everyone who heard his truth became immediately influenced by it or not. Truth has its own power, its own potential to grip those who are alive to it, but also to lie like a patient seed in the deep mind of those who are not yet ready to acknowledge it. The important thing is that it be sown.

At another level, I was surprised that Rinpoche's views had not yet been gathered and disseminated to the wider world. This fact, I subsequently discovered, was again due to his modesty. Indeed, Rinpoche had been approached many times by writers who wanted to convey his story to the world, but their requests had been refused. In my own case, he agreed to many hours of interviews on the understanding that these should focus on his ideas and not on his life or his achievements. He conveyed to me his belief that it is the truth itself, and not the individual who speaks it, that has the power to work transformatively. In the end, having badgered Rinpoche relentlessly and having pulled all the strings at my disposal, I had my reward. But by what Karmic working this great reward finally came to me remains beyond my comprehension.

During my 21 days in Dharamsala, the seat of the Tibetan Exile Government, and during the more than 20 hours of dialogue with Rinpoche, I was treated with the utmost kindness and consideration. I was accommodated at the Men Tsee Khang, the Tibetan Institute of Medicine, in an apartment adjacent to Rinpoche's modest quarters, with a breathtaking view over the mountains of this northernmost corner of India and across the settlement of Tibetan exiles.

In this environment, beautiful though it was, and surrounded by the happy, peaceful flow of Tibetan life in exile, I found myself struggling with an immense sense of sorrow and loss on behalf of a people who have been driven from their country and traditional way of life by a callous and unrepentant giant.

Transcribing our recorded dialogues in the afternoons, I became dismayed by the sense that Rinpoche's views might be too idealistic, too out of touch with the stubborn realities of our modern world order and its pragmatic orientation. Having expected something perhaps more worldly-wise, I found myself confronted with simple truth.

It was only after my return to South Africa, when I began to look deeply into the nature of Rinpoche's view, to study it and allow it to penetrate the layers of my own Western conditioning, that I discovered its power to challenge and to corner me. It was because I forced myself to take the leap, not of faith but of simple logic, that my deep-seated Graeco-Roman worldliness was in the end subdued.

And I hope that this may serve as a warning to the reader. No doubt there are those more open and wiser than myself who will easily find within their own minds an immediate and authentic accord with Rinpoche's ideas. For those who might struggle with them as I did, I can only appeal to my own experience, which is that this book repays constant rereading and determined delving, both into its contents and into the conditioning of one's own mental outlook. For some of us Truth comes as a shock to which we have to adjust gradually.

My gratitude to Samdhong Rinpoche is boundless. Through sharing with me the fruits of decades of a life lived in wisdom-compassion, I have found my own thinking transformed and my insights radically reshaped. My hope is that this book will bring the same transformation to all those who approach it with honesty.

The topics which we covered in discussion were those which I believe to be most directly relevant to a fundamental understanding of ourselves and of our world. And I was not seeking an intellectual response but a spiritual one. I wanted Rinpoche to shed a clearer light on those aspects of our existence that have lost their obvious meaning in an ocean of ultra-intellectual analysis. It is in that ocean of detail that we have lost our balance, and I wanted Rinpoche to simplify or to resimplify the issues and problems that are central to our collective sanity, but which have become complicated beyond the grasp of the ordinary person. In fact, they have become complicated to the point where even the experts can give no ultimate answers. Having outrun ourselves to the extent that most of our lives are bounded by question marks rather than a clear way forward, I felt it would be more than sufficient to concentrate on grounded basics.

For that reason, this book is not for those seeking intellectual titillation or mere mental entertainment, as it were. It is for those who are seeking groundedness in a view that appeals as much to common-sense as it does to our innate spirituality. It is a reminder of what we know deeply but have largely expelled from our shallow consciousness and distracted approach to life.

We can trace fairly accurately the path that has led us from the cave to the now. This route has been the subject of thesis upon thesis and does not need to be revisited in detail here. What we need to focus on is where we find ourselves today in terms of our spirituality, philosophy, self-view, and world-view, because these views shape our motivation and actions.

Even a cursory glance at these aspects would reveal that we have settled for a position of compromise. Our spirituality has dried up into a religious tradition or gone over the edge into emotional escapism. In either case we have allowed ourselves to compromise with the latent violence in our minds. What should be an ultimate refuge and an ultimate stronghold of goodness has degenerated into an attempt to balance our wholesome tendencies with our unwholesome drives. In consequence of this "modernization" of our spiritual vision, authentic spiritual life has become a rarity, almost an eccentricity.

Our philosophy has washed up on the shores of Existentialism. It keeps us trapped as subject-in-the-world, and although it expresses a genuine truth, it falls short of admitting our capacity to completely transcend ourselves and our world. Of course it has been stretched to the formulation of an existentialist spirituality, but again it will not allow us room to overcome the immediate experience of the subjective "I." And again we must settle for a compromise.

Our self-view and world-view are so compromise-laden that we barely notice the fact. Actually, we cannot imagine how it could possibly be any other way. In this regard our politics have played the major indoctrinating role, closely followed by the new gurus of the West, the psychological and neuropsychological theorists. Their doctrine is easy to grasp and easy to practice: in order to arrive at solutions, in order to live with Truth, some compromise is necessary.

Anyone who rejects this doctrine is branded a radical or a fundamentalist—either dangerous to the social order, or just plain ridiculous. The very words "radical" and "fundamental" have in this context been compromised in their meaning. Is it ridiculous or dangerous to make it one's goal to get to the root of a problem or to take a stand on the foundation of one's Truth? Yes, it is both ridiculous and dangerous in a compromised world.

Still, it would be wrong and even ignorant to stress only the shortcomings in our aspirations and achievements, many of which are in their essence spectacular and admirable and hugely beneficial to all living beings. How much more marvelous they would be, though, had they not all fallen prey to the doctrine of compromise which in every case forces us to ask: "Beneficial at what cost?"

It is a tenet of Existentialist ethics that no deed can be absolutely good or absolutely righteous. Somewhere down the line a deed that has benefited one party will bring harm to another. If we admit this as Truth, we are at the same time compelled to ask the question whether it is not ourselves, the acting subjects, that have made it Truth. In other words, is compromise an inescapable part of the way it is, or have we made it so?

This may well be the most crucial question for our time and for our survival. We need to assess with a sense of urgency where our compromises have brought us. If we think about it clearly, I believe that a radical and fundamental view might reveal itself not only as valid but as vital.

The view of Samdhong Rinpoche is both radical and fundamental. In its simplicity we can find the remedy for our apparent helplessness. All that is needed is an open mind.

And, finally, we must distinguish between the kind of radicalism and fundamentalism that is sane and that which is not. The formula is again very simple: non-violent, non-harmful, and compassionate thoughts, words, and deeds are the sane expression. As long as we adhere to these principles our radical and fundamental view needs no bounds. In the enlightened Mind these qualities are considered as existing without limit. They destroy the roots of self-centeredness, fear, and ignorance, and liberate us into the potential to benefit other living beings.

May this book bring benefit to many.

ACKNOWLEDGMENTS

For preparing the way to these dialogues my thanks are due to Mr. Jampal Chosang-la, Representative of H.H. the Dalai Lama in South Africa; to Tashi Wangdu-la of the S.A. Office of Tibet; and to Penpa Tsering-la MP, Jigmey Namgyal-la, and Wangchuk Phasur-la. My special thanks are also due to Kasur Lodi Gyari Rinpoche, Special Envoy of H.H. the Dalai Lama.

For preparing my mind to understand the Dharma my profound gratitude goes to all my precious teachers, both those who have instructed me indirectly through their writings and those from whom I have received oral teaching.

My special thanks go to the Most Venerable Professor Samdhong Rinpoche for making the time to grant me the many hours of dialogue that make up the important element of this book. No amount of sincere gratitude can ever hope to repay the kindness of one's heart teacher.

For his teaching and practice of boundless compassion I thank H.H. the Dalai Lama, the emanation of Avalokiteshvara in this realm.

For keeping my nose to the grindstone and my feet on the path, I thank my wife Merriel and my daughter Naomi. I thank them also for their intelligent criticism of the work in progress.

Although I have not reached the fullest altruistic potential,
I have no intentions of harming others.
The means of achieving freedom of Tibet for others,
I feel rests on us without relying on others.

This is the thought of an insignificant man,
Who was first conceived and born in the Land of Snow,
But I have spent most of my life in India's holy land.
Although I entered into a spiritual life,
The karmic forces have thrown me into politics.

Neither expecting power nor position,
Nor do I have enemies to defeat or friends to protect,
I, the drifter, have no need of politics.
Yearning for world-peace, I have blurted out these words.

                                        Samdhong Rinpoche

THE VENERABLE SAMDHONG RINPOCHE

Obtaining a full account of the life of Venerable Professor Samdhong Rinpoche is an impossible task. Although I persistently applied to Rinpoche for more intimate and revealing biographical details, my requests were politely but equally persistently denied. As he wrote me in the period before the dialogues were held: "The person is not important; only ideas are important." My protests that his reticent modesty in this regard would deprive readers and students of a deeper insight into the background which formed his views were also met with a steady silence. I therefore had to rely on information from other sources and content myself with a general outline of his life and achievements.

Samdhong Losang Tenzin was born on November 5, 1939, in Nagduk village in the old Tibetan province of Kham. At the age of five he was recognized, according to Tibetan custom, as the reincarnation of the Fourth Samdhong Rinpoche and enthroned in Gaden Dechenling Monastery. At seven years he took the Getsul vows from Khenchen Dorjichang Kyabje Sangbhum Rinpoche, and at nine years received preliminary teachings from the Buddhist scholar Ngawang Jinpa. He commenced his monastic studies in 1951 at the great Drepung Monastery in Tibet and, after taking refuge in India in 1959, continued studying at the newly established Drepung Monastery in India.

In 1970 he obtained his Geshe Degree (the Tibetan equivalent of a Doctorate in Buddhist Philosophy) at Gyuto Monastery, Dalhousie, Himachal Pradesh, India. From 1970 to 1973 he was Vice-President of the Tibetan Youth Congress (TYC). In 1971 he was appointed Principal of the Central Institute of Higher Tibetan Studies (deemed university) and was appointed Director of the Institute in 1988.

From 1991 to 1995 Rinpoche was appointed by H.H. the Dalai Lama as a member of the Assembly of Tibetan Peoples' Deputies and was later unanimously elected as its Chairman. Since 1994 he has been a member of the Standing Committee of the Association of Indian Universities (AIU), and later held the Vice-Presidency. He was elected President of the AIU for the year 1998.

By appointment of H.H. the Dalai Lama he is a member of the Central Tibetan Schools' Administration and Deputy Chairman of the Library of Tibetan Works and Archives, Dharamsala.

By appointment of the Indian Government he is a member of the Executive Board of the Indian Council for Philosophical Research and a member of the Executive Board of the Asiatic Society, Kolkata.

Rinpoche is also a member of the Executive Board of the Krishnamurti Foundation in India, a Counselor at the World Peace Council (U.S.A), and a Trustee Member of the Foundation for Universal Responsibility of H.H. the Dalai Lama, New Delhi. He is also a lifelong member of the Theosophical Society.

On August 20, 2001, Venerable Professor Samdhong Rinpoche was elected Kalon Tripa (Prime Minister) of the Tibetan Government-in-Exile, receiving 84.5% of the popular exile vote. Rinpoche's self-view and approaches to his accomplishments are perhaps best summed up in the acceptance speech which he delivered on his election as Kalon Tripa:

> As you all know, I have served the Tibetan community in various capacities for four decades. Although I served to the best of my ability under the guidance of H.H. the Dalai Lama, I was not at all satisfied with my contribution. Then my age and numerous other factors led me to a decision not to assume a rank or position in the exile establishment. Thereafter, as I set out to lead a reclusive life in order to begin my efforts for the cause of non-violence, I was informed against all my anticipations that an unexpectedly large number of voters had nominated me as a candidate for the Chairperson of the Kashag.
>
> I was incredulous and filled with anxiety. In a democracy every citizen has the fundamental right to either contest elections or to withdraw one's name from the nominations. In line with this I desired to withdraw my name and stick to my earlier decision. This is why I did not respond when the Tibetan Election Commission requested me to send my resume and photograph.
>
> Meanwhile I received a large number of requests from most exile Tibetan communities, telling me that it would not be right to withdraw my name. A number of messages to this effect came from Tibet as well. This moved me very deeply, forcing me to contemplate the matter more thoroughly. I normally believe that if there were a clash of interests between a large number of people and a few, it should be the majority's will that must prevail. As I thought

over this matter more closely, I realized that if I ignored the will of 30,000 voters and insisted on exercising my own right, I would be acting against my own belief.

I also realized that my refusal to participate in the election would deal a blow to the very first democratic exercise of this kind among the exile community. It was thus that I abandoned my earlier plan and participated in the elections.

I have now assumed this responsibility, following the final election's mandate. It is, of course, a mammoth responsibility. However, I will bear this responsibility as an opportunity to serve the Tibetan people and H.H. the Dalai Lama at a critical juncture when Tibetan identity is under threat of extinction. I have made a firm commitment to toil sincerely and selflessly. Whether I am able to produce results or not is another matter.

Of course, much more can be said about this deeply spiritual Lama, accomplished scholar, and reluctant but committed politician. In keeping with Rinpoche's wishes I will not here repeat some of the many personal accounts which have been given to me by various religious and lay people in the exile community, except to say that they all confirm my strong impression of his personal integrity, huge capacity, and spaciousness of mind, and of his unfaltering humility.

The Venerable Samdhong Rinpoche

PART I:

THE LONG ROAD TO NOW

INTRODUCTION

In the first section of our dialogues I wanted Rinpoche to address the questions around the various aspects of human endeavor that have brought us to the way we live today. The way we live today is the total result of all that has gone before. Our technocratic society of pragmatism, compromise, and violence is seldom considered in all its complexity by the very busy average person of today.

We live together in growing confusion on this small planet and more often than not we are confused without knowing it. Our leaders, our mentors, and the media plaster over the cracks of our confusion with swift indoctrination and plain deceit, and even though something in our minds sees through it all with a sense of unease, we allow ourselves to be pacified by the misguided belief that the saner section of humanity still has things under control. In a time of deepening crisis we want ourselves to be lied to. After all, if we were brought to face the truth plainly, wouldn't we at the same time be confronted with our own powerlessness to do anything about it?

Our ignorance has led us to this point. Our ignorance is the void which swallows up our power to act correctly, to speak correctly, to think correctly. Because our view is distorted by our ignorance we are forced to endure rather than to live. And when we find that we can no longer endure, we escape more deeply into our ignorance. We withdraw; we go along with it all; we give up. We're only human.

We need not go very deep to realize how complex we have made this world and our individual lives in it. We call this process of ever-increasing complexity "cultural evolution" and because we think that evolution is a synonym for progress—a way of saying that things are getting better and better all the time—we naturally think that we are better off than we were a hundred or a thousand years ago. We need only switch on an electric light or send off an email to confirm us in this view.

We are vaguely aware that we are surrounded by a plethora of clutter which makes life more difficult and more stressful. We know that we are caught up in systems from which there seems to be no escape. We have few choices. We allow ourselves to be swept along in this stream of systematic complexity, and it is a rough ride. One has to be tough to endure.

We have to become tough because the system is tough. It is unforgiving and relentless. Our view becomes fragmented because there is so much complexity to contend with. Nothing is straightforward; we have to be able to embrace several points of view at once. Shifting opinions and double standards have become the norm and the result is that anything goes. It goes, whether we embrace it, view it askance, or helplessly accept it.

The ordinary person, living so completely within the system's confines and taking for granted the inescapable complexity which surrounds them and influences their mental and physical life at so many points, is generally too distracted to try to unravel the threads. For most of us the daily routine, with its time-consuming and exhausting busy-ness, leaves little over for a clearer consideration of where we stand in it all and how we have arrived at this place.

When we do pause to look at it, we tend to do so only at the shallowest levels: the levels of insight that are churned out by the media, by our politicians, and by the few experts who are allowed their minute or two on television from time to time. The sense again arises that we are being kept in the dark.

Whether or not there is a tacit conspiracy to keep us in the dark is not important. There is sufficient access to information and counter-information to help us make the crucial decisions about the way the world is run and our role in it. But dredging up this information is a difficult, time-consuming task and we are too tired, too pressed for time, or just too lazy to attempt this complicated jigsaw puzzle, this fugue of points and counterpoints. So we live on what is fed to us by politically correct theorists and experts, and now and again we may be refreshed by an alternative point of view which prods us for a short while into thinking differently. Then the system and its complexity take over again, and we surrender.

Yet the way out is actually not beyond our capacity, even though it requires the cultivation of understanding, courage, and a willingness to act. All we really have to grasp is the truth of what we are and why we are not living in conformity with that truth. Because it is this very non-conformity with our true nature that causes us to sink under the complexity of our modernness and to be enslaved by its systems.

4

What we really are is much more than we conceive ourselves to be. Looking deeply into ourselves, we know that there is an unsatisfied part of our total mind, an aspect of our mental life which, yearning for joy and love, plagues us instead with guilt, anxiety, and depression. Whether we call this aspect of our mental continuum spiritual or not is irrelevant. All we have to do is face it honestly and find out what it wants us to be.

It was Dilgo Khyentse Rinpoche, a great Tibetan Master, who said, "In joy we live," and the corollary is obvious: outside of joy we do not live. If we look outwardly into our society and inwardly into ourselves how much natural joy do we find? Because we find so little of it we are compelled to seek escape routes away from this misery of the world and the misery in ourselves. But this only leads us deeper into ignorance and self-destruction because the essence of escapism is avoidance of truth and avoidance of conformity to truth.

I am no expert on all the elements which make up the complexity of our modernity or the inner workings of our systems. I only know that it is unhealthy and inadequate to allow oneself constantly and irremediably to be baffled by them. And I believe there are millions of others who have had enough of having the wool pulled over their eyes.

The recognition of human spirituality is not based only on mystical experience, but on an undistorted insight into the true nature of our minds or spirits, and to bring the way we live into conformity with this truth. The route to its discovery as presented by Samdhong Rinpoche is simple, authentic, and elegant; almost matter-of-fact. And the discovery of the true nature of our minds is not only a personal education: it has impactful connotations for the way we conduct ourselves in the smaller and wider contexts of our total human society; in our families, with our friends and enemies, in our communities and in the universal community of living beings.

In the first section of our dialogues I wanted Rinpoche's views on how we have arrived at our present state. I wanted to address subjects concerning the central aspects of human history. Accordingly, the dialogue proceeds along a complex historical path.

Of course, not every aspect has been considered. A brief glance at the multitudinity and diversity of only the scientific disciplines would be sufficient to discourage the attempt to cover all of it. If we consider the prolific aspects of philosophy, religion, culture, the arts—to mention only a few of the elements that have developed in concourse to bring us to the now—the task becomes impossibly cumbersome.

So I decided to lift out those elements which play most directly on our daily lives and contribute most directly to form the modern conception of what we are, what human society is, and how we view our planet and all its living beings and phenomena.

The following subjects seemed most relevant:

Origins
Biological Evolution
Societies
Culture
Governance
Economies
Industry and Commerce
Law
Philosophy
Religion
Morality
Spirituality
Science
Art
Complexity and Escapism
Civilization and Decline
The Future in Prospect

All of these aspects Rinpoche addressed with characteristic straightforward honesty and openness. And this is perhaps the appropriate place to remind the reader one more time that Rinpoche's views are deeply informed by his many years of study and practice of Buddhism. Yet it doesn't take a great leap to see the common sense and the universal wisdom of his uncompromising radicalism.

The Dialogues

ORIGINS

DR: Science insists that matter precedes mind and that mind is nothing more than the function of increasingly complex molecular interactions. How can we convincingly prevent meaning, purpose, destiny, and morality from being undermined by these increasingly commonly held scientific theories of chaos and randomness? For, if we are the result of random origins, we are entitled to justify the absurd in our thinking about ourselves and our universe and to express this absurdity in our speech and conduct.

RINPOCHE: This is a very big question. I don't know how to answer it appropriately. One issue is the nature of mind and matter and their relationship, the other is a question of origins.

I always wonder and question myself: why do scientists insist that mind arises from matter? This is an unconvincing statement. If mind arises from matter, then there should be mind arising from all matter. Why does some matter give rise to mind and other matter not?

In India there was an ancient philosophical tradition which did not believe in rebirth. They believed that certain combinations of matter, combinations of elements—earth, water, air, fire—created conditions in which mind could arise; that is, created conditions through which a body could arise, and from this body mind could arise. Then this body would decay, and with this body the mind also would decay. This theory is quite similar to that of modern science.

But the question remains unanswered: how can matter be converted into mind? Matter can be a supplementary cause but it cannot be the main cause. For instance, gold is the main cause of various forms of gold jewelry, but many supplementary causes are needed to produce rings, bracelets, and so forth. The goldsmith, various tools, a furnace are some of these supplementary causes. Again, wood is the main cause of ashes. We may perceive the fire, the heat, as supplementary causes, but the main cause of ashes is wood. It is wood that is perceptibly converted into ashes.

But even non-perceptible things can be inferred by logic. You can infer that this or that entity works in such and such a sequence. In this case scientists must feel the need to prove that matter is the cause of mind, and they use conjecture in the attempt. But the scientific age is not an age where speculation suffices as proof: scientists are not convinced by theory but by experiment and observation—and since this is for them an age of experiment, scientists should be able to show by experiment how matter is converted into mind. Then we can all accept it as true; otherwise it remains an assumption.

In Buddhist doctrine mind has existed from beginningless time, whereas matter has a finite beginning. This also means that matter can come to an end but mind cannot; mind will always exist. It has its own nature of continuity—it is not a continuous and unchanging flux—it has its impermanent and discontinuous moments, but these will follow each other without ever ending.

Therefore Buddhists definitely believe in a form of continuity of mind, even while various universes are coming into and going out of existence. Some universes are in decay, others in a state of evolution due, in both cases, to the quality of the collective karmic force of the beings which inhabit these universes.

This is somewhat different from the majority of religions in our world, which believe in some form of Creator, either personal or impersonal, say, a creative force. Only the Buddhists believe in a collective karmic force rather than in some absolute Creator principle. But in my view these things only represent a difference in language, a different way of saying the same thing. All major religions believe in some form of Karma: consequences for good and bad actions, speech, and thought.

However, regarding the all-important question whether or not mind arises from matter, there is no absolute answer available which is beyond dispute.

The human mind is completely conditioned. We need to move beyond the limitations of our conditioning in discussing these matters. We must realize that our instruments are limited and in speaking of "Divine" issues, we must realize that our limited minds can only go so far, since these are matters of wisdom, which are discoverable only by wisdom and not by our limited intellect and language.

We might speak of God as "Unlimited Mind," but this remains only a relative expression, related to our concept of limitedness. The real Absolute is not in that category. All we can do in this regard, both religion and science, is to establish a definition of mind (which would per se be limited) and then we could enter into discussion around that definition. But of course this would not bring us nearer to a true understanding of the Absolute.

Note: With regard to Rinpoche's question, "If mind arises from matter, then there should be mind arising from all matter. Why does some matter give rise to mind and other matter not?," it is important to note that Rinpoche is here referring to mind which can understand, realize, and transcend itself—mind which can attain to Enlightenment.

Teilhard de Chardin posited a "within-ness" of particles, by which he meant a form of unconscious life-mind. Theoretical physicists echo Teilhard in their theories of information, in terms of which matter bears an informational imprint which causes particles to exhibit their inherent qualities. Even if we consider these theories to postulate a rudimentary form of "mind," they are not of the nature of mind to which Rinpoche is referring here. On the other hand, biologists would argue that mind can only arise in organisms which have nervous systems. But Rinpoche is also not referring to the mind which arises solely in dependence on neuronal activity.

BIOLOGICAL EVOLUTION

DR: The central dogma of evolutionary theory is "natural selection of chance mutations." What this means in familiar language is that any changes caused to my body by the environment in which I live, such as the darkening of my skin in a sunny climate, will not be genetically heritable by my offspring. The only genetic changes which are heritable are those which occur by chance in the sequence of bases in a nucleic acid molecule, and any such chance mutations will only survive in the species if they prove adaptive to the environment. This is the scientific view.

Of course such random "chance mutations" affect not only our bodies but also our brains. Our mental formation and, indeed, the very existence of our minds is again relegated to the operation of sheer chance. How can we find meaning and purpose while regarding ourselves as the product of a series of random preconditions giving rise to cause and effect which result in the processes of evolution?

Exponents of evolutionary theory believe that throughout the phases of our biological evolution we see humankind passing through increasingly complex stages of physical and mental development, but always carrying genetic traces of our animal ancestry.

Is evolutionary theory correct in its assumptions about the purely biological and genetic nature of humanity?

RINPOCHE: I don't think we can put an end to this debate. It is also a debate within the conditioning and limitations of our thoughts. But the basic question is about biological composition and the processes of mind: how much they depend on each other and how much possibility there is of separation of the two—perhaps in this context "separation" is not an appropriate word. What is the possibility of making the mind independent of biological preconditioning, of the "random accidents" which compose the body?

I can make the presumption or I can state that the genetically evolved material body has its own limitations, and there are limits on the extent to which it can be evolved or transmuted—but the Mind is completely independent of this body, and it can evolve to complete Enlightenment.

Of course at this moment the Mind hires this body as a boat or as a temporary residence, but the awakening of this Mind does not depend on the genetic inheritance of the body; it is neither limited by it nor will it be helped by genetic imperatives for the awakening of Mind.

So I think in this way I can very confidently say that the awakening of Mind or transcending the mind can never depend on biological factors. I think this is quite clear to our own perceptions and experiences. There is a small degree of interrelatedness: due to genetic inheritance one may be more short-tempered or perhaps more tolerant, but that is a temporary manifestation. You can get freedom of the mind, freedom from all the mental defilements, despite your biological inheritance or evolutionary factors, whatever they may be.

The mental defilements can be removed by exercising mind only, without dependence on the state of the evolution of the biological body or genetic inheritance. I think this is very clear. So once this is established, the biological or genetic factors are only secondary helpers, not the principal causes or conditions for mental development.

DR: There are people who are born mentally defective, and we can ask three questions about this fact: Why are they born this way? What are their chances of mental development towards awakening the mind? And what can we do to bring such people to a state of health sufficient to allow them the ability for mental development?

RINPOCHE: Yes, this is a good question. I have been speaking about normal people. In the case of the mentally underprivileged there is much greater dependence, a much greater interdependence, between mind and body.

For example, you might have a stream of consciousness within you but your physical body does not have an eye organ. Your consciousness cannot see an object without the existence of an undamaged eye organ. You need an undamaged, clear eye organ in order for your consciousness to make contact with colors or shapes: seeing depends on an eye organ, hearing depends on an ear organ—and so forth.

Organs are biologically developed or evolved things and they differ from person to person according to their bodily health or unhealth. A child is born mentally defective because the body is not sufficiently equipped to help the mind to function normally.

In this case the extent to which we can repair the impaired or damaged instrument of the body depends on how developed our technology is, and it is possible that modern technology can reach to such an extent that it can bring the person to a point where they can sufficiently exercise the mind towards mental development.

Once mental normalcy is restored, the mind does not need to stop at that level; the mind can develop itself separately from the physical organism and it can grow separately, and in this case the development of mind may function to improve the organism as well.

For example, you can develop your power of consciousness and power of seeing so that you can see hundreds of kilometers far, and that development is independent of your eye organ. But if your eye organ does not function, if your body has no eye organ, then of course you cannot see objects at such a long distance; you can only realize them in your thoughts or in your inner consciousness, not seeing it as we see it. So there is a certain degree of dependence, yet there is a lot of independence of the mind.

DR: In the case of people who are born or become mentally or physically handicapped, would Buddhism ascribe this purely to Karma? Would such a person have the opportunity in other lifetimes to begin again?

RINPOCHE: Karma will give its result and no force can stop it. Karma has the power to bring about a result but if the result is not yet manifested, then you can remedy it.

But if, for example, a child is born without an eye organ, you cannot create a new eye organ by any means. A child who is born with an eye organ which is defective or having a certain weakness, in this case karmic force is not yet giving the full result. In such a case, if you get treatment in time, perhaps the eye organ can be improved or repaired. If you cannot get timely treatment it may end up in complete blindness.

In that period during which Karma is in the process of bringing about a result but the result is not yet completed, there is the possibility of a remedy. This does not mean that the Karma has become less potent; it may give its full result at some other time unless you have completely removed it by positive forces. So in the process of Karma producing its result there can be alterations to that result. But once the karmic forces have produced their complete result, then you have to experience it fully.

In the case of human evolution by "natural selection of chance mutations," Buddhism would certainly relegate such mutations to the functioning of karmic forces rather than the operation of sheer chance. No effect is causeless, and in the case of our own evolutionary development the causes are the operation of collective and individual karmic forces.

SOCIETIES

DR: Evolutionists and anthropologists tell us of stages in the evolutionary development and formation of societies: the nuclear family expands into the clan, then clans unite to form tribes, which in turn become amalgamated into nations. This is of course a simplistic outline, but this kind of development has continued to the point to which our societies have evolved today, manifested in multi-ethnic and multi-cultural societies which have proven to be problematic.

Is this pattern of development necessarily leading to a more tolerant and compassionate social order in the world or has it left us more conflicted because of the increasing intermingling of races and cultures with widely differing and often conflicting cultural, religious, and moral values.

Is there not a point at which the increasing integration of global society becomes the root of conflict? In this regard, what is the role of the individual in our increasingly globalized society? What can I do to make the world a more compassionate place?

RINPOCHE: I don't know much about this subject. I also do not know whether the notion of the expansion of clans into tribes and so forth into multi-ethnic nations is a truthful interpretation.

But we believe with a rational basis that, with very few exceptions, each creature is a social creature, and there are only small differences in the essential organization of their groups. Very few creatures can survive without a group.

Basically the human being is a social animal. They need to live in groups of at least ten individuals, without which the continuity of the human race cannot survive. The human community is not like microbial life-forms which take bodies everywhere: human birth needs parents and without parents the human race cannot go on.

Therefore the human race necessarily depends on family and the family depends on the community, and we have made the community dependent on nations. This dependence on nations is an artificial dependence. Family and community, however, are in natural dependence on each other without which neither the family nor the community can survive.

DR: When you speak of an artificial dependence on nations, what do you mean by that? In what sense is this dependence artificial?

RINPOCHE: The nations are all "thought creations"; there is no real necessity for nationhood. If people are left in small communities with diverse systems there is no need for a more complex, larger organization—this is an unnecessary step. Even though we consider the organs of nationhood indispensable, they are all unnecessary creations. They have become "necessary" through gradual imposition, and have now become seemingly indispensable.

Otherwise as few as five families can constitute a community. My birthplace had 11 families and it was not less than 20km away from the next community, and our population made up of 11 families numbered about 120.

These 120 people were completely self-sufficient. We made our clothes in our homes, fashioned our tools and instruments at home, and we cultivated all our own food, and then we had our own priests for spirituality. So these 11 families living together in a corner of a beautiful landscape were not dependent on any nation or government. No government was providing any of our needs. So we just sometimes paid a tax to a distant government representative and apart from that there was no dependence on each other.

Of course being there together, all the members of our community were interdependent; all the families were dependent on each other. Community life is necessary even for spiritual development, for education, for health, for many things which we recognize as necessary. But communities need not be as big as nations or ethnic groups. It can be a small or a big community: there is not much difference.

DR: Do I understand correctly that you have a negative view towards expansion into nationhood, that nationhood is an unnecessary encumbrance (let's not use the word "evil")—but that it is an unnecessary obstacle to our development as human beings? Nationhood is not the best way?

RINPOCHE: Yes. Yes. Nationhood, nationalism divides the community.

DR: So if I ask if there is not a point at which the increasing integration of global society becomes the root of conflict. . . ?

RINPOCHE: Yes, I am coming to that. There are many different kinds of integration. What we believe is that each community of human beings should be self-sufficient and self-supporting, and that excess, surplus, should be shared with others.

And the basic thing is that you should not live on the production of others. To live on the production of others, to live off the labor of others, means that you are exploiting others. And when you are exploiting others your life, your existence, is simply a form of violence: so it is not an integration but a disintegration.

Merely coming together and living together is not the real meaning of integration. Integration means bonds of affection and bonds of love, people coming together to help rather than to exploit each other.

So localization of professions and localization of materials is the way to true integration. Otherwise it is simply crowding together and exploiting each other.

DR: What can I do to make the world a more compassionate place?

RINPOCHE: What can any individual do to make the world a more compassionate place? Firstly, we must consider others as more important than ourselves! I think that is basic Truth.

Chanakya, a great politician of India, held views which were quite similar to the Teaching of the Buddha, but in one area their views are quite opposite. Chanakya says: "For the sake of the nation you should sacrifice the village, but for the sake of Self, you should not hesitate to sacrifice the nation." This is Chanakya's view. But the Buddha says: "For the sake of any other, even the enemy, your self should be sacrificed."

DR: So it is the sacrifice of self, the regarding of others as more important than myself, that is the real first and last step in making the world a more compassionate place?

RINPOCHE: That is the root of the basic philosophy, and then what I talk about these days is the necessity to dissociate ourselves from structural violence even though this is a very difficult position to uphold.

If you cannot oppose or stop this kind of violence, then stepping out is necessary. For example, America was waging war on Iraq and we were silent here. We did not do anything to overtly oppose it, but I think it is our responsibility at least to mentally oppose it, and vocally also when necessary. We should not act as though we appreciate it as something justifiable. Remaining silent is also a kind of acceptance.

So wherever evil is present we must have the courage to dissociate ourselves from it and also compassionately to oppose it: that is the responsibility of the wise.

CULTURE

DR: The evolution of culture is centered in the human ability to manipulate the environment and to interpret it mentally—thus culture subsumes social organization, science, technology, and art. It also includes religious systems and rites, and the general ethos and moral strictures found within a given society.

To what extent do we need to conform to and maintain, and on the other hand, to escape and transcend our evolved cultures in order to live in accordance with Truth? Or is Truth always relative and subjective?

Intercultural influences on cultural evolution are a fact and are inevitable. Should our tendency to want to preserve our own culture be exclusive of or open to outside cultural influences? And to what extent should we be open?

We are taught that we should respect other cultures—but are all cultures equally worthy of respect, considering the diversity, for instance, in the area of morality, in the various cultural evolutionary paths, both in retrospect and in prognosis? What makes a given culture worthy or unworthy of respect and how can an unrespectable culture be brought to respectability along evolutionary lines?

RINPOCHE: I think that the definition of culture has not yet been formulated very correctly. We talk of culture in many ways. First I have to define my understanding of culture and then I can go on with the rest of my views on it.

I do not consider that forms of perpetuated customs or habits are necessarily "culture." In my view culture means a cultivated mind: the raw mind that has been cultivated through proper practice, meditation—when the mind has become purer or more conformed to its original or true nature; that kind of cultivated and purified mind is "culture," and whatever expression comes out of that cultivated mind is in my view cultural expression.

Chanting, music, dance, and all those things, cultural expression such as painting, literature, poetry, and those many things which we call cultural expression or cultural objects can only truly come out of such purified or cultivated minds.

So it should always be a positive source; nothing which comes from a negative source can be termed a "culture." We use the word "culture" for everything: "culture of war," "culture of destruction," "culture of violence"—I don't think these are forms of culture.

Culture is an expression of, or the nature of, a calm and purified mind-state and the creativity which comes out of such a purified mind-state. This kind of culture must be shared with each other and the confluence of this kind of culture is good for humanity.

But any confluence of culture should not become combined with domination or influence over each other: cultures should meet but cultures should remain within their own identity or within their own nature. Intercultural influence may not be good for a given culture or for the people of that culture, but this does not apply to sharing goodness or wholesome culture with each other. If an alien culture has a goodness which can be shared with another culture without distorting the originality of the other culture, that is positive and that is necessary.

So first we should know what culture is, and secondly we should know how to converge these different cultures, and thirdly how to keep these different cultures from dominating each other, yet sharing the goodness.

Does it make any sense?

DR: It makes sense.

Appendix: The following is an extract from Samdhong Rinpoche's essay, "Contribution of Buddhism to the Culture of Peace" (Published in *Maha Bodhi*, Vol. 101, No. 1, 1993).

From the global canvas of war to the subtlest inner conflicts of a single individual, all is the outcome of one's delusion. Owing to delusion and past impressions accumulated in immeasurable time, the person's mind becomes incapable of perceiving the true nature of things. Due to this one conceives "I" as an independent inherently existent entity. Thus delusion confuses our conceptions in relation to such inherent existence of "I." That further creates the conception of others which generates division between self and others. This division is the cause for attachment and hatred being present in one's mind. Thus mind can never be free from conflict and disharmony. No amount of effort and methodology can attain freedom from the conflict and disharmony unless the basic cause of delusion which is ignorance or Avidya is eradicated. As such the Buddha did not attach much importance to social and political systems. He was convinced that no system which is based on the conception of division and inequality between self and the other can thrive to bring about sustainable peace among the sentient beings. Surely, none among the religious and non-religious beings having a rational mind would accept the defilements such as hatred and attachment to be good things. These are held to be causes of misery which should be eradicated. But the problem is that most people do not even know the right way and method of eradicating misery.

A truly cultural mind can develop through the practice of the four highest states of mind (Catura Pramana), viz. lovingkindness, compassion, sympathetic joy, and equanimity. These four highest states of mind are most significant for the attainment of peace for all the living beings of the world.

Also, Buddhism has laid emphasis on the cultivation of the mind of the Bodhisattva or a being on the Path to Buddhahood. A Bodhisattva practices various perfections (Paramitas) of generosity, morality, renunciation, forbearance, etc.

GOVERNANCE

DR: Historically governance or rule began with the natural head of the family, the extended family, and the clan. These leaders or elders were related by blood to those they ruled. Once the clans became united, the rule was passed to the tribal leader or chief (presumably the strongest and most adaptive individual in the tribe), and the position, generally speaking, seems to have been based on two qualities: the ability to make wise, adaptive, or survivalist decisions, and the ability to wage successful wars, either of defense or aggression.

Further developments led to the establishment of the aristos—the nobility and the monarch. These positions were largely based on power and were attained by power rather than by benevolence, and there were conflicts, conspiracies, and wars to maintain or usurp leadership.

Gradually, under increasing pressure of various types from "commoners," limited forms of democracy arose and were finally developed into the democratic systems we have today. But even these modern democracies, kept in check by constitutions, laws, and the franchise, have clear imperfections.

What is essentially wrong with modern democratic systems? Why do they seem to thrive on deception and double-dealing rather than on openness and honesty? And, actually, how truly democratic are they?

RINPOCHE: I have always believed in Thoreau's saying that "that government is best which governs the least." Democracy is considered to be a form of self-rule but actually self-rule (or Swaraj) has not yet been established anywhere.

Spiritually, socially, and formatively—in all these three ways—I think that Gandhi's concept of self-rule is absolutely necessary. But I don't know whether it is achievable or not. At this moment in time no-one has yet achieved it, therefore we need a government to govern ourselves and among the various patterns of government the democratic system is considered to be better than all possible alternatives.

But I still suspect that, if there were a very enlightened philosopher-king, that might be better than the democratic system—but we have no model as yet; we have not experimented with this type of government in this generation.

Democracy in a small community or in small nations works more efficiently than democracies in large nations, and it is particularly difficult for the multi-party system of democracy to function in a righteous way. It may function effectively but it does not function in a righteous way, a positive way.

The ideal would be if each individual were self-supporting and self-disciplined—not breaking the law, not causing harm to others, not causing any problems in the society—then any form of so-called government would be unnecessary. Governments are necessary because people are unruly and they need somebody to check them, to establish law and order, and to ensure that people live in an harmonious way.

Now if those objectives are not achieved then the concept of government is just one of misuse of power or controlling the people or doing things against the wishes of the people. In such a case democracy is an hypocrisy; it is not yet a system of governance.

Democracy is very difficult to achieve. I always say that the definition of a true democracy is when there is no division between the rulers and the ruled. And that is no different from the Gandhian concept of Swaraj.

DR: But we have a long way to go in order to achieve that.

RINPOCHE: The community or the society or the nations have a long way to go to achieve it, but for individuals there are so many short-cuts. They can achieve it within our time. In India there are a few model villages. They are completely independent of the leadership and they are refusing to accept any state facilities. They are small villages but they do exist. So in that way this form of self-rule can be achieved, but nobody has made real efforts towards this and most people can hardly imagine it. Everybody thinks it is rather an idle dream. But if there is a sincere effort to establish this way of life I think it can be achieved.

ECONOMIES

DR: Primitive societies were self-subsisting hunter-gatherer groups. With the development of agriculture and animal husbandry the era of surplus commodities was established, with barter being the currency for trade.

The next important step was the introduction of monetary currency. This symbol of economic value together with increased mobility, communications, and other relevant infrastructure enabled trade between different social units and eventually between nations, and set the stage for the internationalization of trade.

The final result of these developments is the modern battle for market dominance, which has resulted in the globalization of consumerism, giant corporate entities, international outsourcing of labor, and an increasingly integrated global economy.

It looks like progress on the surface, but have we not set an inescapable economic trap for ourselves? Is there an escape from the cutthroat principles of modern economics without regression back into primitive commercial practices? Is there a way of the future in which compassion can play an integral part in commercial practice?

Isn't this what the proponents of globalization are hoping to achieve by consciously evolving or engineering one standard of commercial practice and homogenous living standards for the whole world? What are the flaws in their policies?

RINPOCHE: This is a very big question. I don't know how I can respond briefly to something which needs seven days to discuss. But in a very small nutshell: what is economics? It is necessary to understand, to define what economics is and what economic value is.

Not only human beings but all sentient beings born in a biological body also have a consciousness. They have their natural needs to sustain the body and to sustain the development of mind, but nature does not provide these freely. Nature demands of you that you make an effort, that you work hard, and if you use your biological body to achieve your needs there is no need of industry, there is no need of huge machines.

Your body and your mind can very easily be sustained. All their needs and even more than what is absolutely necessary can be met, bearing in mind the special needs of the physically and mentally handicapped. Everyone's needs can be met.

But for this there are two prerequisite conditions. Firstly it is necessary to understand and differentiate need from greed. What is need and what is greed: differentiate these two. Secondly it is necessary to proceed with determination and with power to produce the need, to achieve the need, and to remain satisfied with meeting one's needs, and not to become slaves of greed.

So the true meaning of economic welfare is that you are sustained physically and given inner satisfaction and peace of mind. That is the value of our natural objectives and these can very easily be taken from nature by your own labor, and you can find satisfaction in them.

Then, of course, as I mentioned before, we need a community life. Your period of productivity is up to 60 or 70 years. Beyond that age you will not be productive and will have to depend on others. So, a small community life with people supporting each other is a good thing. This is the necessary degree of wealth and this is the yardstick by which the value of wealth should be measured.

Now so-called free trade and globalization of material things is not good for the well-being of humanity. You know, there is one statistic which is very alarming and horrifying: this one statistic is that 80% of the world's resources are being used or misused by less than 20% of the world's community, and 80% of humanity is left to live off the remaining 20% of resources.

This is one of the results of the capitalist way of so-called economic development. It has very clearly resulted in this disparity. We can't put this down to lack of enterprise or fear of work. Many people say this disparity is due to fear of enterprise. Their view is that only 20% of people are capable and enterprising enough to use 80% of the resources, and if the 80% of idiots are not able to utilize these resources they have only themselves to blame; there is nothing else preventing them from utilizing these resources.

This is the explanation of many modern economists but I cannot believe this explanation. There are many aspects and we cannot go into many things, but I can take only one example of the total problem. The modern economy is based on competition and competition means taking your own interests as greater and more important than the interests of all your competitors. You do not compete in order to lose. You always compete for your own gain and you have to force the hand of your competitors.

Therefore the economic world defined by capitalists as "free and fair competition" is a contradiction in terms. As long as there is competition it cannot be free nor can it be fair because one party has to win and the other has to lose, and the loser will never feel that he has got fair treatment.

So globalization is very dangerous for human inner spiritual growth, human intelligence, and diversity of cultures. Cultures are being completely destroyed by the process of globalization. It is a very vast subject and we cannot go into it in detail.

The homogenization of living standards does not imply providing facilities to every individual. Rather, it is a kind of law of the jungle, the so-called survival of the fittest. This is the exact practice of the present economic system.

We have spoken about genetic inheritance, but in this case we must point to things like genetic engineering in the field of agriculture. The basic potential for self-sufficiency is going to be completely destroyed by genetic engineering of seeds.

It is based on the principle of centralization, concentrating power and control into the hands of fewer and fewer people, and the vast majority of farmers will have to depend on seeds produced by a few multinational corporations. They will be forced to depend on them not only for seeds but for fertilizers, pesticides, and even for their very market.

Everyone is made more and more dependent on less people; this is exactly what is happening today. So to escape this process I think we have to find a way back to being self-supporting, self-sufficient, and self-ruling, and not depending on the market but on our own ability to sustain ourselves.

INDUSTRY AND COMMERCE

DR: In primitive societies industry began with the adding of value to raw materials through the skills of various craftspeople and other processors. For instance, value was added to grains through primitive milling processes and craftspeople manufactured various artifacts.

But in time specialization increased so that societal interdependence in the industrial, service, and commercial sense became indispensable. In this regard we may consider the indispensable role played by the traveling merchants, for instance, in previous centuries.

Once established, the interdependent system became irreversible and encouraged and advanced the development of expertise. Guilds were formed to protect the standards and interests of craftspeople and other specialists. With time the principle of self-sufficiency became not only obsolete, but seemingly impossible to sustain.

In this scenario the potential for commercial exploitation grew. The industrial revolution led to increase in mass consumerism, exploitation of labor, and greater division between rich and poor.

The next inevitable step has been increasing mechanization, which has resulted in cheaper goods of lower quality and a huge loss of employment opportunities while simultaneously increasing the profitability of mechanized industries.

Today we live in the era of mass production, exact replication of goods, and the commercial philosophy of planned obsolescence, leading to acceleration of consumerism and utilization of resources.

The disparities between so-called developed and undeveloped nations has increased because the patterns of industrialized production have not occurred concurrently across the world. How are we to address this problem? Is it a problem which lies only within the province of pragmatic solutions or are there moral dimensions as well?

RINPOCHE: I think I have touched on this point a little earlier: in my view the industrial revolution was an opening of the floodgates of evil on our whole society. Before the industrial revolution humanity was never deprived of their needs; all of them lived with their needs being provided by nature and by themselves, and it was good.

The industrialization of production simply means that much more is produced than is needed by people. For example, people need a shirt for a year or, at best, a couple of years, but industry is producing clothes and shirts in the thousands which they are actually not able to market in terms of need. As a result they are forced to devise means of selling items which are not needed because they must have their money and their profit, enormous profit, out of it.

So they have found that the bigness of human greed can very easily be exploited. Even in the beginning of the industrial revolution there was a lot of advertising and brainwashing of the people. Today, with the help of electronic and other media, you can brainwash the people very easily, and industry has amplified and increased the people's greed by all means possible in order to find a market for their unneeded goods.

And today the human mind is completely conditioned to believe that they need all the "put ups" of the world and that they cannot survive without these commodities, without consuming them. A person gets one car, but he has always been indoctrinated to think: "No, no, when you go away and your wife needs to go somewhere, one car can't be sufficient for you. Or, you and your wife should be able to work simultaneously and should not be dependent on each other, so you need two cars." So now you have two cars and when one car is broken you have another car; now the boy grows up and he also needs a car—and so on and so forth.

I was once in the house of a rich person who had more than 20 pairs of shoes. He claimed that some shoes were for the office, others for basketball, these for cricket, those for his morning work, and these for this and these others for that. So a pair of shoes is not enough for one person; he needs more than 20 pairs! This is total psychological exploitation of humanity. It works on greed and attachment.

Unless we address this problem, this human problem, directly, there cannot be any peace and there cannot be any harmonious living among the world's societies. The present system always creates division because without division it cannot exploit greed in a more thorough way. In this philosophy division and enmity are very good instruments for increasing the market.

Now I am not talking only about consumer commodities. For example, the weapons industry is increasing day by day because it is profitable. The weapons industry needs a market, and that market can only be created if there is a constant state of war or fear of war. The weapons industry would prefer never to have two nations becoming friendly with each other at the cost of losing a huge market.

If India and Pakistan, for instance, were to become friendly, many weapons industries would lose a huge market. So they come to India and say, "Pakistan has such and such weaponry which we have sold to them and you do not have any compatible weapons. If you wish, we can supply a superior kind of weapon which will put you in a position to compete with Pakistan." And then they return to Pakistan and say, "You know, we have supplied superior weapons to India; now you can't advance peacefully because you don't have any comparable weaponry." In this way they are always increasing tension and conflict: this is very horrible.

Terrorism is one of the problems of today, but terrorism is a good consumer for the weapons industry, and it is promoted and encouraged in order to sell their products. So unless and until we learn to live in accordance with our need and not our greed, and we learn to live without any competition and enmity, there will be no end to our modern crisis. That's for sure.

LAW

DR: Concurrently with the evolution of the societal aspects we have spoken about came the formulation of social rules—the laws of given societies, influenced by those factors and others yet to be discussed.

Such laws—in Western history most notably embodied in Roman Law—reflect the mixture of evolved instinct and culture, including the tendencies of fairness, ownership, retribution, and violence that make up the conventional (that is, the unspiritual or unrealized) mind of humankind. But how valid are these laws, and are there laws higher and more beneficial than those developed by our societies?

In societies considered more primitive by Western standards, the punishments for breaking the law are harsher, and along a continuum progressing towards the most developed or "enlightened" societies we see laws becoming more subtle, with the notion of punishment replaced by that of correction and rehabilitation. Is this necessarily a good development?

What influences can be brought to bear to make the law function more beneficially? Are social laws the highest that we are capable of in social ethics?

RINPOCHE: The subject of law in the world is very vast. Sometimes dharma, usually translated as the "nature of something," is also translated as "law": the dharma of nature; how nature works.

In this case the word "law" is being used in a very much narrower connotation; a regulation which is enacted by somebody, some competent person or competent body, and it becomes a law. It becomes a matter for the courts which are made up of "ordinary" people or "ordinary" humankind rather than spiritually enlightened people.

The essential laws of nature have always existed. They neither evolve nor decay. Fire consumes fuel—this is one of the laws of fire; water is a liquid and the earth is solid, and there are laws of energy and momentum, and so forth: these are fixed laws which may one day be destroyed, but cannot evolve or devolve—from time immemorial these laws have stood and will stand in the future as well.

But social laws which are enacted by a person or group of persons, these always keep changing, and in this matter I think it is very rewarding to examine the history of laws. In the last 200 or 300 years they have been subject to constant improvement through experience. Both national and international laws are always evolving.

But they do not have an absolute value and they are also not in accordance with absolute reality and Truth. For example, certain laws forbid killing of human beings but do not forbid killing of animals, and there are laws which forbid killing of people and certain species of animals, but the rest of the living creatures are not protected by law. This is just a simple example.

26

Laws are often inconsistent, the product of human decisions, but even so we have to comply with them. One inconsistency is shown in the case of capital punishment. If you kill a human being, you yourself can legitimately be killed in punishment; you can be hanged and so forth, yet other laws do not allow capital punishment.

So the evolution of laws is variable and is always evolving in accordance with current knowledge and the pleasure of the lawmakers. In ancient times the king or ruler was also the maker of law and whatever he decreed had to be obeyed by the people. Nowadays laws are made by the legislative assembly and are passed through parliament—but these laws change from time to time according to the views and needs of societies.

Therefore laws do not necessarily accord with ethics. I think that the majority of laws, if we consider them from the point of view of absolute ethics, are not compatible with ethics. For instance, the majority of national laws permit the soldier to kill as many people as possible in defense of the nation or in the case of the declaration of offensive war, and if a soldier kills hundreds of people he will get honor and awards, and it will be considered that a great thing has been done. But from an ethical viewpoint this is absolutely wrong.

So therefore I think that the law of nature which governs the universe and all living beings is unchangeable, and if we abide with that law we can consider ourselves as ethical because they are by their nature in accordance with true ethics and provide the framework for our formulation of ethics.

But the man-made laws which may be useful and necessary are nevertheless changeable and not necessarily ethical in the dharmic sense. There are laws which are ethical but there are also a number of unethical laws, and we need to discriminate between these.

Appendix: Extracts from Samdhong Rinpoche's essay, "The Social and Political Strata in Buddhist Thought" (Published in the *Tibet Journal*, Vol. 2, No. 1, 1977).

The Buddha, indeed, was the first man to have envisaged the basic concepts of social living and human relationships. His ideas were as dynamic and revolutionary as they were original. It is not surprising, therefore, that the latest theories of socialism and democracy seem to have live wires in the original thoughts of the Buddha. . . .

In the Buddhist scriptures the term "social" has a wider sense than its usual application to mere human existence. . . . The Buddha included the six worlds and the four kinds of birth, thus extending the social sphere to the aggregate of all sentient beings.

Similarly, political thinkers could only conceive of a temporary well-being or happiness, while the Buddha showed the means to achieve permanent success. He gave the world a modus operandi to abandon forever the source of misery.

Buddha aimed at the preservation and promotion of the real causes of social harmony. With this end in view he laid down principles which are well balanced and broad-based. . . . He gave much importance to the individual's rights and benefits while simultaneously encouraging him to give up his rights and benefits for the cause of the larger interests and social benefits of the state. These developed not by force but voluntarily.

This method is the only remedy to moderate social harmony and is practicable without hurting anyone. As regards individual rights, the prohibition of the ten evil deeds is mainly based upon the protection of everyone's rights in a society. In the ecclesiastical organization if a single individual in the jurisdiction of a particular Sangha did not turn up personally or surrendered his right to vote, no Sangha-Karma could be performed even if thousands of monks had assembled for that purpose. . . .

The greatest demerit of today's social and democratic systems is that the representation of people is a one-way traffic, and the ideas and the rights of the minority are always superseded by the majority.

In Mahayana Bodhisattvacarya every individual has his or her proper place and rights on a reciprocal basis. It is in this way that real social harmony is practiced in Buddhism, but these are generally ignored in the political ideologies of our times.

The social perspectives can be summed up in six Paramitas:

1. The Dana Paramita may be taken to mean the equal distribution of wealth.
2. The Shila Paramita means the harmony of social beings through practices avoiding violence.
3. The Ksanti Paramita means tolerance of violence and criticism from one's opponents.

4. The Virya Paramita means to work incessantly for social well-being.
5. The Samadhi Paramita means to purify the mind and make the mind fit to bring about social harmony.
6. The Prajna Paramita means attainment of wisdom to enable a person to become capable of understanding the rights and wrongs and to practice good for society.

The head of the state, the *Sutra of the Wheel of Law* says, must have two virtues for proper governance: caution and compassion. Caution to avoid being led by power and authority, but remembering always that power, authority, and even the state itself are transitory. . . . Compassion is to be shown to all the people of the state.

The Sutra has indications for punishment of offenders by compassion and not by anger or a spirit of retribution. It adumbrates five principles of punishment: Proper, Timely, Purposeful, Soft, and Amiable. "Proper" connotes that the sentence should be passed on the real wrongdoer. "Timely" means the time at which the judiciary is able to pass the right sentence, and also to determine that the person is capable of bearing it. "Purposeful" signifies that the "punishment" should result in real improvement in the actions of the criminal. "Soft" must be the nature of punishment. If the criminal improves by a warning, that is best. The judiciary must try to keep the punishment to the minimum level possible, which is "Amiable." Execution is strictly forbidden in this code. . . .

The sutra says that the head of state or government should always have eight considerations in mind:

1. The citizens of the state should be considered as sons and daughters.
2. Miscreants should be considered as patients.
3. Sufferers should be considered as objects of love and kindness.
4. Well-off persons should be considered with a rejoicing rather than an envious attitude.
5. The enemy should be considered from the point of view of eliminating the cause of enmity.
6. Friends should be treated in such a way as to promote their genuine interests.

7.   Wealth should be considered as a medicine of life.
8.   The self should be considered from the angle of selflessness.

PHILOSOPHY

DR: Philosophical speculation starts at the point where humans begin rationally to question the nature of phenomena and mind, and progresses towards ascribing meaning or lack of meaning to life, as the case may be, from an anthropocentric viewpoint.

In the course of its development it divides into the areas of pure philosophy (e.g. metaphysical or ontological and phenomenological investigation) and practical philosophy (investigation of social, moral, and ethical problems).

In the West, over a period of around 2500 years, we have seen philosophy develop from quasi-religious and mystical interpretations of reality, through various schools of classical philosophical thought, to the subjective and varied schools of Existentialism and to the philosophy of the absurd, where the roots of meaning, morals, and ethics can no longer be discovered. Of course this development has deeply and negatively affected our spirituality.

We have reached the stage where we are forced to admit that we cannot know completely and the possibility that we cannot know at all. This admission drives us to embrace the obvious and mainly selfish advantages of pragmatism, the more so as philosophy becomes increasingly constrained by the pure sciences and the ultimately irrational notion that reality can only be accurately interpreted by "scientism"—science itself having become a philosophy.

It is not enough to postulate or believe in a set of philosophical principles, even if these are supported by logical proofs. The real problem is whether our philosophies can be tested by the scientific method and proven true by repeated experiment. Thus our thinking about ourselves and our reality has become severely restricted.

But these scientific constraints must surely be ultimately arbitrary in themselves since science, with its focus on objectivism, cannot validly claim omniscience or even aspire to omniscience without an accurate understanding of our subjectivity.

What should be the true and valid constraints which we impose on our philosophies? And, is Truth at all discoverable?

RINPOCHE: We discussed the other day about the evolution of the universe and so forth, but we did not discuss the definition of evolution. I think to avoid miscommunication or misunderstanding I must be very clear and carefully explain what I mean by evolution and, certainly, what I mean by philosophy. So, if we do not clarify what we mean by these two terms we may miscommunicate.

Evolution is basically a Western viewpoint. They think that everything is gradually and slowly evolving into a betterment, or into more goodness. And it is a process which, along the lines of biological evolution, slowly progresses towards the optimum.

Buddhists do not deny that there is a process of evolution in certain things, but this principle of evolution cannot be applied to everything. As far as philosophy is concerned, Buddhists may not accept that philosophical tenets evolve in a gradual way towards the realization of Truth. Their viewpoint is a bit different.

The Buddhist viewpoint is that, in all areas of Buddhist philosophy, the Truth emerges complete, in its proper form, and then gradually deteriorates. It does not grow through development; it always decreases and deteriorates after the initial revelation, and then after a certain period of time it will disappear completely.

The Dharma taught by the Buddha in his lifetime was transmitted in its full form and after the passing away of the Buddha it gradually decreased and deteriorated. And now, 2500 years later, it is midway in its disappearance from the world, and in another 2500 years it will be present in name and form, but not in experience. So within 5000 years from the Buddha's lifetime it will have disappeared completely.

So in our view the Buddhist teaching is in the process of decaying, not in the process of evolving. Philosophies of Truth do not evolve; they come in their full form and are correctly understood by certain people, and then gradually comes deterioration, distortion, and decay. And then gradually it completely disappears. That's one thing: our viewpoint regarding the things of Truth.

The second thing is "philosophy"—I don't know whether "philosophy" has an equivalent connotation in Buddhism, whether it is an equivalent for the Buddhist connotation of "reduction": View, Meditation, and Conduct. These three are the "reduced" essential parts of Dharma practice.

So in this matter the Madhyamika philosophy means the exact perception of things as they truly exist, the sameness of the object and the interpretation of the object. There are so many other queries we may address—theoretical queries—but they are not part of the central philosophy. They may be regarded as a peripheral part of the philosophy, but they are not Darshana, the central teaching of Buddhism.

In the Buddhist canon when we talk about Darshana today, it is translated into English as "philosophy," but in the English language "philosophy" has its own connotations and a number of ideological theories also fall into the category of philosophy. But in Buddhist terms these are not considered philosophy.

Now when I use the word "philosophy" I am referring to the Buddhist term "Darshana" which means the "suchness" of things, and for this the various Buddhist schools have different views, but all four schools talk about the same ultimate reality of things. In this context there are four different schools of Buddhist thought: Sautantrika, Vaibashika, Vijnanavada, and Madhyamika, and all of these four schools, when they examine the nature of the essence of phenomena, their position, view, or perception differs and therefore different arguments are established, but the same ultimate reality is recognized.

When the original propounders of these schools were alive and teaching these philosophies, these teachings were at their highest and clearest levels and given in their fullest form. Then of course there was a process of development also, but that process of development was in the use of language, the expression of the teaching by subsequent teachers. The real knowledge of the thing is not subject to development; it is fully there from the time of its revelation and it might be transmitted down to a certain point in the lineage, then it begins to deteriorate. But there are a lot of good teachers of religion with their unique way of expressing and sharing the knowledge. That aspect has a process of evolving or developing; otherwise, the real philosophic tenet itself: with regard to it there is no process of evolution. It comes once in its full form and then it begins to decay. So we need to understand this different viewpoint.

Then coming to the question of the scientific examination of philosophical concepts or precepts: these two are not compatible with each other. The basic reason for this is that the modern scientific way of analysis or examination is simply a matter of repetitive experiment by the ordinary person through the ordinary mind.

Science does not understand that people can develop a much higher level of spirituality, mind can be sharpened, or mind can become more consolidated through meditation. This has never been accepted by the scientific community.

What they claim to know is that a person is a person and he or she will remain in that capacity, and the person's mind is identical with the brain. And if you have a good brain you have a sharper mind and if you have a bad brain you may be dull—but in their view the brain has its own capacity and there is no way to elevate it from the present state to a much different and much higher level.

They cannot understand that, if the mind has been trained through meditative practice, you can comprehend so many deeper things. For example, you can see things much more clearly and in a much different way. The Theosophists Annie Besant and Blavatsky did so much analysis in physics. They just developed their minds and began to study small particles, and they wrote a book about this in the early 1900s. In that book they discussed the status of atoms and sub-atomic particles, proving in what way they exist. And now quantum physicists have confirmed a number of their findings and of course these confirmations only came much later when appropriate experiments could be devised because the necessary technology was there.

So what I want to emphasize is that human mind can develop to a much higher stature and power. Instead of the use of sophisticated magnifying devices, the ordinary eye can see these very subtle particles—and also so penetrative: hundreds and thousands of miles away you can see through this naked eye. But these aspects of the possibility of refinement of the mind are completely ignored by scientific study groups. So they have accepted that, whatever limited mind we appear to have, that is its final status.

They can improve their scientific instruments, various devices through which things can be enlarged by the help of glasses, and so forth, and then they can experiment into the real surface by various methods. But apart from such experimentation they do not have the enlargement of the power of mind.

Therefore these two, science and philosophy, cannot go together. Through a scientific examination you can draw certain provisional conclusions about a material or ordinary thing, but you cannot finally decide anything because scientific knowledge always needs to correct itself by more and more experiments. Their ideas are always changing and this proves that they are not able to penetrate to the absolute nature of the thing. They arrive at findings, they presume certain conclusions by means of their experimentation and these conclusions again destroy some previous conclusions or presumptions that until then were considered valid. So the findings of science are always changing, but the philosophical schools—in the sense of the Darshana—have been given the thing by the person who has seen it in a final way.

If you investigate all the religious traditions, there are only two categories of revelation that can be established. One category holds that absolute knowledge is somewhere else and that absolute knowledge employs a certain medium or messenger, and that ultimate knowledge of the real is revealed by that messenger. This is one kind of religious tradition that has come into being.

The other kind is where a human being has been developed to the highest level so that he knows everything directly and he reveals this knowledge to people, as did the Buddha. The Buddha attained Enlightenment himself and then through his Enlightened Mind he revealed things in language which was understandable to ordinary people; and this does not mean that he was revealing his entire knowledge, but he spoke about the ultimate reality, the Absolute Truth, through a very simple language which could be comprehended by ordinary people.

Therefore his teaching sometimes seems inconsistent, but this inconsistency does not mean that he is telling the untruth; he is telling the Truth in accordance with the listener's capacity to understand. So in this way the listener is reached.

And these kinds of dharmic dispositions cannot be confirmed or certified by the scientific way of inquiry and analysis. Therefore we shall have to keep this insight as a separate way of knowing. We have to understand the limitations of the ordinary mind and of science.

RELIGION

DR: Paleo-anthropologists generally hold that the earliest human religious beliefs and practices originated in the primal human need to make sense of the natural phenomena which on the one hand sustained and on the other often threatened their survival, and to gain a measure of control, however delusory, over these phenomena through the practice of certain rituals.

This theory implies that the development of religion was based on primitive fears associated with the struggles of this life and the mystery of death and the afterlife, rather than arising from the authentic sense of an internal or mentally latent spirituality.

Concurrent with these primal religious developments we find the rise of the shaman or priest in the social unit: the chosen one who could intervene with the spirit world on behalf of the community, and this system endured over long periods of our religious history, still surviving in some cultures today.

Much later, in the course of the last 2,500 years or so, a gradual "democratization of religion" began to spread. The result of this development is that every individual has direct access to the spiritual realm and to their particular deities, saviors, or prophets.

How does one explain this development? Is it the by-product of biological, social, and cultural evolution or is it an indication of a real gradual process of spiritual enlightenment of increasing numbers of people in the world?

RINPOCHE: Here again I would say that we need to define the meaning of religion and the meaning of the Buddhist term "Dharma," or the expression of these. I would use three different terms: religion (English word), spirituality (English word—particularly pertaining to Christianity), and then the Indian word "Dharma." These different words actually have different meanings but in our day-to-day communication these three words have become almost interchangeable in a kind of synonymity: religion, spirituality, Dharma.

As far as I understand it "religion" refers to a much wider scope and "spirituality" is narrower than that, and "Dharma" is much more precise. So these three things should actually not be intermingled.

Religion may embrace traditions, rites, and social customs; so, in this case, as you mentioned in your question, religions are gradually evolved with the social and economic development of human beings. I do not disagree with that. Fire worship, sun and moon worship, and so forth, and many other nature rituals: they might be evolved out of ignorance and out of fear and the desire to escape fear; and some priests and shamans become more influential and they institute certain practices. These are possibilities which I do not dispute. It may be true that this sort of religion evolved in that way, but I can't assert this absolutely. I can only say that there is a possibility that it may be true.

But coming to the tradition of spirituality and the tradition of Dharma, these are again not an evolution. They are revelations of teachings coming from a Higher One.

Therefore I always carefully define the word "tradition." An authentic tradition must have three attributes or qualities. First, it is taught or revealed by an authentic source or, we can loosely say, by a divine source. Second, it must be transmitted by means of an unbroken lineage from person to person. And third, it must be verifiable through common sense and self-knowledge. So if these three factors are present, then it is an authentic tradition. Otherwise a long perpetuated custom need not necessarily be a tradition.

For example, in Hindu society there is the concept of untouchability and concepts of different races and colors with religious significance, and this cannot be a spiritual tradition. These are perpetuated evil social customs which divide humanity and they have nothing to do with true religious tradition or spirituality or Dharma.

And I think this kind of thing is intermingled in most of the religious and spiritual schools. We have a pure tradition combined with so many impure customs and habits, so we need to differentiate them from what is valid.

Then coming to the Dharma: the Dharma was taught by an authentic person, that is, the Buddha. We consider that there are three valid reasons for the authenticity of the Dharma, and these correspond with the three Jewels of Refuge. First, the Buddha knows the Dharma fully and is therefore qualified to teach it. He is an indispensable Teacher and will not become dispensable in the future. Second, he taught the pure Dharma which can save you from misery and set you free from bondage; and therefore the Dharma is a real religion, like medicine, a valid remedy. And third, the Sangha goes with you to help you in your practice, the Sangha being the fellowship of Buddhist practitioners. So we consider that these three objects of refuge are necessary and indispensable to achieving the highest level of spiritual attainment: complete freedom from bondage.

So this is not a philosophical path or religious path influenced by human social development like other so-called primitive religions. Dharma was taught to us by the person who actually realized it. And that same Dharma was also practiced by many other people who would become the Sangha, people who have attained the spiritual achievements and who also testify that practice of Dharma dispels defilements and ignorance. They have experienced this for themselves.

So this is not an evolution of a tradition. It may be an evolution in the life of an individual: today you don't know the Dharma, tomorrow you hear the Dharma, and the day after tomorrow you practice the Dharma, and you gradually evolve your own spiritual life in that way. That may be an evolution but Buddhism itself is not part of evolution or driven by evolution.

Buddhism comes into being in the full manner in the Buddha's lifetime and then it begins gradually to decay. And now it is halfway on the road to disappearing. So it is not evolved, but comes to us in completeness. So we shall have to differentiate in this way between evolved religion and non-evolved Dharma.

DR: Why must Buddhism decay? Why is this inevitable? Why can't the Dharma always remain with us in its complete or full form?

RINPOCHE: Here we also need to differentiate carefully. What is Buddhadharma? The Dharma is defined as the wisdom-realization and the canon. The Buddhadharma is Truth in the form of canon and of wisdom-realization, and Wisdom which has been awakened in the individual mind can never decay. The Buddhadharma is undecayable once the Arya Mark, once the Enlightened Path has grown into one's mind. It will grow up to the realization of the Buddha Nature and it will never decay.

But the duration of the Shakyamuni Dharma in the world is described as 5,000 years, but what does this mean? It means that the teaching and the continuity of the tradition and lineage will eventually disappear, and that this will be due to the mental conditioning of people.

People will become less and less qualified to receive the teaching afresh. The formal teachings will always be preserved and they are not going to decay, but the effectiveness will decay because persons qualified to receive the teachings of the Buddha Shakyamuni afresh will become fewer and fewer. Their ability to understand penetratively will decay as time passes, as socio-economic values and conditions deteriorate, and people's interest in Dharma lessens.

Therefore attaining new Enlightenment through the words of the Shakyamuni Buddha will come to an end. It is natural decay and I don't think it is possible that we will always have people qualified to receive the transmission. That comes to an end with a span of time.

Therefore we consider that in this eon there will be 1,000 Buddhas of whom four have already appeared. Some of these Buddhas' teaching remained only during the lifetime of the Teacher and soon afterwards it disappeared. And some of the Buddhas' teachings might last a year or so. But the teaching of the Buddha Shakyamuni is able to endure for 5,000 years because of the temporal conditions on this earth and because of the disposition of the people.

This is very evident to all of us and to our teachers who see that the establishment and acceptance of Dharma is continuously lessening with every generation and this, I think, is the nature of decay, and nobody can stop it.

DR: But the Truth always remains. Some Buddha will arise in the future to reteach the Truth.

RINPOCHE: That's very true. That is the Buddhist way of seeing it today. As I mentioned, there will be 1,000 Buddhas before this earth is destroyed, and the Shakyamuni Buddha is the fourth. There were three who preceded him and their Dharma has disappeared, and then the fourth Buddha has reproclaimed that Dharma. Thereafter the fifth Buddha will come into this world; that is, the Buddha Maitreya—and so forth. So—decay and remanifestation. It is like the law of nature: constructing, destroying, constructing.

MORALITY

DR: Bearing in mind the early or primitive social development of humanity we can postulate that morality arose as the result of an evolutionary pressure based on the human need to bond and cooperate in order to survive, and on its function as a mechanism for ensuring acceptance and security at both the individual and the social level.

But as the initially small social structures expanded into tribal units and nations the ties of blood and personal friendship became thinner, and although bonding imperatives remained central, new room was made for selective and advantageous bonds, giving rise to allegiances and conspiracies. The need then arose for moral rules which would prevent betrayal. Overshadowing and underpinning all these survivalist and pragmatic mores were the rules or moral laws transmitted in the religions of various social groups.

In the individual context we can argue that the more abstract and subtle, less biologically and socially driven moral imperatives, evolve together with our evolving ability to reason and to perceive and understand our own psychological pressures such as guilt, depression, and anxiety.

The morality we encounter in the modern world reflects all these aspects together with other refinements such as the code of chivalry, the notion of duty, the financial rewards of the pragmatic ethos, and so forth.

But are there deeper wellsprings of morality which remain largely unexpressed in modern individual and social conduct? And, if so, why is this the case? And, what are these wellsprings?

RINPOCHE: In Buddhist terminology we talk about virtuous and non-virtuous deeds, Kushala and Akushala Karma, and the word "morality" is not very popular in the Buddhist canon.

Nevertheless, the seed of virtuous conduct (Shila) is required for one's own development and also for the establishment of social harmony. The need for virtuous conduct extends to both poles. The development of morality cannot be based only on the premise that it is a social necessity. It is even more necessary for the proper development of the individual. That is the Buddhist viewpoint.

As I mentioned, Buddhists talk about virtuous and non-virtuous conduct or right and wrong conduct. To refrain from direct or indirect harming of others is right conduct, and to indulge in an act which directly or indirectly harms others is wrong conduct. So this is a very clear definition of right and wrong: it is violent or it is non-violent.

Firstly, it is a fact that nobody wants suffering: every sentient being looks for happiness or peace. A person of higher attainment may not be looking for pleasure or happiness, but still wants peace and tranquility. Pleasure, happiness, and peace are wanted by every sentient being, and nobody wants pain and misery.

So there is this equality of all sentient beings. This equality lies in the fact that one does not want to get hurt and seeks ways to protect oneself from being hurt. The only sure way to protect oneself from getting hurt is to refrain from hurting others. So, from a very "selfish" viewpoint, if you do not want to get hurt, then refrain from hurting others. This is a sufficient argument for non-violence at a lower level.

The second argument or reason is that you and the other are equal: therefore you have no right to hurt the other. And if you hurt the other, the other will feel miserable just as you feel miserable yourself when you are hurt. Therefore you must respect the other as a sentient being completely equal to you. This is the argument at the medium level and it is based on an inner recognition of the truth of equality of sentient beings rather than only on the "selfish" advantages of harm-lessness.

The third and higher category of response is that you must save or rescue others because you have the insight, the capability, and the responsibility. You are more enlightened than the other; you know your responsibility towards sentient beings and you know your universal responsibility as a human being. Therefore you must not only refrain from harming others, but you must also benefit them.

Therefore the basis of morality comes from these three arguments for harmlessness. Now there can be exceptions to everything, but by and large these should be the criteria for deciding what is moral and what is immoral.

And then there are many other things which are moral or immoral at the gross level or in a lesser dimension. These are dependent on social and cultural background. For instance, in Tibetan culture a particular word may not be considered harsh or impolite, but in other cultures it is regarded as impolite. So the question of politeness is related to morality, but this is not defined by certain spiritual, inner reasonings. It is defined by the cultural custom.

In Tibet, whenever we met someone we used to ask, "How old are you?," and this was considered very polite, but in the West, particularly in the case of a lady [a wry smile] . . . asking her age is considered very impolite. So this kind of morality differs from culture to culture and from custom to custom.

SPIRITUALITY

DR: Some people assert that the spiritual growth of humanity is driven by the evolutionary pressures of biological, cultural, and social development. They argue that our spiritual paths and experiences are simply the function of evolved neurological processes, social conditioning, and cultural inheritance. In neuropsychological terms our spiritual tendencies can be interpreted as the result of an increased imaginative capacity and an evolved ability to project our inner anxieties and desire for acceptance as a "spiritual goal"—that is, a projection of a "spiritual path" or "spiritual being" which can free us from these inner sufferings.

If we speak about an ontological spirituality, an Absolute Truth about reality and about ourselves which exists before the dynamics of evolutionary pressure (and which, in that case, would be the principle responsible for all aspects of our evolution), why is it so hidden from our sight? Why do we need to discover and nurture it rather than simply finding ourselves at home in it as our natural medium of being? Why does the course of our evolution in all its aspects seem actually to be in conflict with our spiritual tendencies and beliefs?

RINPOCHE: Here I would completely disagree with the formulation of your question. Spirituality is not evolved through the social and biological evolution of humankind. Spirituality is always there. Spiritual evolution or growth can be spoken about in the case of an individual's life or mind, but there is no evolution of spirituality as part of the wider processes of evolution; quite unlike the evolution of religious customs or religious rituals, spirituality did not evolve by means of biological evolution or social conditions. It has nothing to do with that.

The mind is by nature clear and there is no dirt in it or dirt in its nature; that nature of mind is completely pure and completely clear. But it has for centuries and centuries been conditioned by external defilements.

[At this point Rinpoche snatches up an official looking document from his desk and rolls it up into a tight cylinder] If I roll it up tightly for quite some time, then it becomes conditioned in this way. [The tightly rolled paper cylinder lies on the desk] Then I cannot put it straight like this. . . [Rinpoche spreads the cylinder flat on the desk, but it curls itself up again]. It will always go back. . . [Now semi-rolled up]. You have to apply pressure. . . [Continues to spread out the cylindrical document which stubbornly continues to revert to its cylindrical shape]. It will go back. This is like the conditioning of our minds.

For so many countless births and rebirths we have been completely conditioned. Therefore, in spite of the fact that the nature of mind is clear, in spite of the fact that the nature of this piece of paper is flat, it has been conditioned and that conditioning needs to be removed. [Here Rinpoche rolls the paper cylinder back on itself, in reverse] And sometimes it has to be reconditioned in the reverse way to make it straight again. So it is true that spirituality gradually evolves in the individual mind but it is not evolved in the biological world, either by biological or social evolution.

The rediscovery of the mind's original nature is considered to be the state of Enlightenment, and that state of Enlightenment is, I think, common to most of the spiritual traditions, but the methods and language differ from each other. The methods also do not differ very much, but the basic differences are in the expression and the language.

Appendix: An extract from Samdhong Rinpoche's address delivered at the 73rd Annual Meeting of the Association of Indian Universities in December 1998.

. . . The modern idea of a university is primarily functional-pluralistic. Its first and foremost function today is to impart job-orientated higher education to the students. . . . This function is also oriented toward technological advancement as well as towards the function of educating and training young people for various jobs required by the technological-industrial-political-bureaucratic establishment. . . .

In terms of its telos, a university in its true sense does not see itself and its grand unique vocation in terms of supplying high level personnel to the governments and managerial or technological manpower to the industrial and business houses. A university qua university is the home of the intellectual. It is the shrine of wisdom: it is the guardian of human intellectuality, yes, guardian of the universe. . . .

According to the traditional perspective education is the most important means for dispelling ignorance. Here ignorance means the proclivity of human mind to follow the easiest way of seeing and accepting the world at its face value and its failure to distinguish between appearance and reality. Once a person's perspective is awakened through proper education or through intellectual intuition he/she can see the fallacy underlying the world in its formal appearances. The awakening of perception enables one to know the truth.

The knowledge of the Truth leads to freedom from all bondage and limitation. To know is to be delivered. The great selfless and wise teachers at whose feet persons like myself were educated in Tibet often used to remind us that five benefits accrue from learning: knowing the truth and getting acquainted with things unknown, developing proper understanding of the things known, dispelling unwholesome or erroneous views and clearing doubts, developing right view or right perspective that enables one to see reality, cultivation of intellect leading to the illumination or liberation of mind. . . .

Under the present dispensation one of the primary functions of education, i.e. shaping good human beings, has no place in the list of priorities. . . . Is it not our sacred duty as teachers and educationists? If a radical change in the ways of thinking is brought about, right actions can flow out, both individually and collectively. Unless a wholesome social and cultural milieu is created one cannot hope to bring about any meaningful change in our education system.

SCIENCE

DR: Primitive "science" rested on the mystical interpretation of nature, including the belief that the universe and its phenomena were mysteriously controlled by a myriad spirit beings.

Later, rational and sometimes irrational theorizing was applied to our interpretation of material processes. These theories were often derived from unquestioned final authorities such as Aristotle or followed quasi-mystical routes such as in the case of the alchemical quest.

Gradually, speculative and eccentric theorizing was brought under the constraints of the scientific method, the interplay of hypothesis and repeated experiment, and the notions of predictability, falsification, and so forth.

With Isaac Newton came the age of the mathematical formulation of physics and the scientific philosophy of determinism, which in its turn was upset by Einstein's theories of relativity and the increasingly "uncertain" theories of the new physics.

Today the new physics has opened up a whole realm of uncertainties and fundamental doubts about the true nature of our perceived reality, doubts and disparities which dog the physicists' search for the Grand Unified Theory of Everything.

What can modern science learn from spirituality?

RINPOCHE: I do agree that science is an evolving discipline, driven and directed by evolution, and these evolutionary forces are very closely related with the evolution of socio-economic structures as well. And this evolutionary process is relatively young; perhaps 500 or 1000 years. And this evolution has now reached—I don't know—the highest or rather the most critical level.

People have discovered many things which the naked eye could not previously see or the ordinary mind previously understand. They have reached a critical level and that is why the uncertainty has markedly increased.

What does this mean? It means that whatever you have decided by these methods today may be proved wrong, and therefore you are uncertain at this level and you cannot escape from this field of uncertainty.

There is an ancient Indian school of philosophy which is part of Jainism and is called Shayatavada which means "perhaps": the "Philosophy of Perhaps." A thing may perhaps be square or it may be round or it may be a triangle—I can't decide. All the possibilities of definition remain. In terms of this philosophy the ordinary mind cannot reach the perfect reality: it is beyond the ordinary mind.

And I think that modern scientists are more capable than before and are developing an insight into the Absolute Reality. His Holiness the Dalai Lama has had many dialogues with leading modern scientists as a result of which many books have been published. But these "dialogues" have in fact remained a kind of monologue—they are not really dialogues between spirituality and science in the truest sense.

I think the possibility is there: scientists can learn a great deal from spirituality. Mainly they can learn that they should know the limitations of the ordinary mind. They should give up their scientific arrogance; they should give up this arrogance of science and accept that the ordinary mind cannot attain to Absolute Truth. They should accept that the ordinary human mind is limited, and if they cannot merely accept this they should resort to experiment as they do in other cases.

They should practice meditation for two or three years to improve their minds and then come back to their laboratories and discover how differently they might understand things. The possibility of the development of human mind and the impossibility of seeing the ultimate by the ordinary human mind: these two things they must learn from the spiritual tradition.

And here I remember that Acharya Vinoba Bhave always said that, while science is developing, spirituality is already fully there, and once the two meet, that will be the day when humanity will have a new spiritual revival. And perhaps that will happen.

ART

DR: Primitive art is considered to have had an exclusively religious or magical function in terms of which spirit beings or natural forces could be influenced by the creation of effigies and other artistic depictions of survivalist activities whose outcome was believed to be determined by these spirits or forces.

Such artistic depictions (such as cave paintings) were contrived in order to ensure a certain result, such as the success of a hunting expedition or a good harvest. From the point of view of the artists or shamans who created these works of art, they played a functional and determinist role in the survival of the group.

In later development art began to take on many other functions. For instance, it might function to preserve the magnificence of a given ruler for posterity, to depict gods and goddesses, to tell the tale of mythical and real historical exploits, and so forth. Yet for a long time it preserved its largely religious role, providing tangible and visible symbols for objects of worship. It also had a didactic and "reminding" function. This functional aspect of art continues to this day.

Gradually, and much later, the development of secular art began to overshadow religious art in effort and importance as well as in experimental technique, and eventually became an end in itself: art for art's sake, where the main aspect reflected is the human condition and the ideas associated with the human condition at a particular time.

Modern art, beginning with the Renaissance, where religious art was chiefly used to decorate and magnify the religious institutions which commissioned it, became increasingly and finally almost exclusively humanistic and anthropocentric.

In its modern development it became more abstract and less associated with the perpetuation of tradition and as a result became also more obscure. We all know how hard it is to fathom much of modern art, and there is a great deal of cynicism and even open ridicule directed at it.

One of the legitimate functions of art in all its genres is to reflect the human mind and its perceptions of life, its understanding of meaning, and so forth. It has been argued that modern and, more particularly, postmodern art reflects the slide of humanity into meaninglessness and absurdity. Life can have no meaning or purpose or destiny other than that which the individual decides to ascribe to it, if any. We are all free to formulate our own truth or to express our own delusion as truth.

In this progression modern art presents us with a very important warning. How can we as individuals and as societies counter this gradual decline into meaninglessness and how can the arts be helpful in this endeavor?

RINPOCHE: I don't know how to answer this question. It is a very profound question and I don't know much about art. Here again, I do understand the notion of the evolution of secular art, artists becoming more proficient and improving their use of color and so forth, which develops together with biological evolution as well as socio-economic development. So it evolved; that is for sure.

And secondly, how are we to demarcate the difference between what is religious and what is secular in art? In contemporary art we may be able to demarcate but, for instance, in the case of very old cave paintings which we have rediscovered and of whose age we have some idea through carbon dating: how can we decide what the real intentions of the artists at that time were? Anthropologists have decided that their art must have been for this or that purpose.

I still remember a conference on yoga during which somebody was speaking on the evolution of yoga in primitive times, and he brought a picture of a human being sitting cross-legged with a pair of horns on his head, and he tried to prove by this means that the practice of yoga was present during those primitive times. But I don't think this picture necessarily represented yoga practice—it may have represented something entirely different.

What I mean is that we cannot decide the mind, motivation, and purpose of the artists at that time. The art is very old and the artist is no longer here. So in this way we make the statement that primitive art is more relevant to truth than modern art. In this we need to exercise caution.

And then coming back to religious art: religious art in the Buddhist tradition is not evolved. Buddhist religious art has not undergone processes of evolution. It is completely clear. For example, the mandala, the very complicated mandala, both mandala painting and construction of the most complex kind: neither are the result of the gradual evolution of art.

These were revealed by the Enlightened One: how to make it, how to measure it, and how to color it; all this was revealed at the moment of beginning and has its own significance.

For example, the making of a Buddha's image and the measurements are prescribed in the book of art, the book of making the Buddha's image, and that book is as old as the Buddhist literature, as old as the canon. During the Buddha's own time the measurements were already decided; they were not gradually evolved or handed down at a later stage. And these measurements are perfect for every human body and essentially you cannot find any fault in these measurements or dimensions.

If the scientists today were to examine these things, the measurements and instructions for drawing the human body in exact geometric proportions, they would have to say that it is very advanced and very "evolved" art. They would have to acknowledge it, but I don't think that anyone has yet examined it. So these are not the result of artistic evolution. They existed in their present form from the time of the Buddha.

Then coming to modern art and postmodern art, I am not knowledgeable. But I don't know whether they show the manifoldness of human life or whether they try to condense this manifoldness. That also probably differs from artist to artist.

I met quite a famous modern artist a long time back and I asked him, "I do not understand anything of your art, and what is the meaning of modern art?" Walking along, we saw on the roadside a goat which was eating vegetable leaves, and he immediately told me that the intention of traditional art was to depict the goat, the leaves, and the eating—everything in totality—but that modern art only depicts the eating; neither goat nor leaves, but the action of eating is all that modern art attempts to depict.

It doesn't make any sense to me, although it may be true. I don't know: it may be an expression of "manylessness" or it may be an expression of something else. But an artist should not convey that life has no meaning.

I think that through the practice and appreciation of art a person could realize the manifoldness of life much more than others. This is my opinion although I do not claim to know. I cannot answer this question appropriately since I am not an expert in the arts.

COMPLEXITY AND ESCAPISM

DR: The result of the interplay of all these historical strands, and others besides, is the position in which we find ourselves today, a place of unprecedented and often bewildering complexity.

The Weltgeist has disappeared in favor of the specialist because knowing everything there is to know has become impossible. But how can we discern that knowledge which is important, vital, crucial—around which all other knowledge may orbit, but to which it is not essential?

How can we simplify our minds and our lives, bearing in mind that the degree of complexity with which we have to cope today places tremendous stresses on the psychology of the individual and of society? One of the results of stressful modern complexity is the surrender to apathy: we blindly follow our leaders, academics, scientists, religious teachers, and so forth, because the process of separating truth from falsehood, fact from speculation, and the essential from the incidental has become too complicated a task for ordinary people who no longer have time to spend on these questions, caught up as they are in the highly demanding economic systems of the world.

It also leads to various forms of harmful escapism, and even religion is often not much more than a means of escaping the emotional pressures and anxieties of everyday life. How can we distinguish between true spirituality and those religious practices which are simply alternative forms of escapism, forms which are perhaps less crude than escape into alcohol, drugs, and various types of distracting pleasure?

RINPOCHE: Before coming to the answer of this question, I would dwell a little on the construction of the question itself. There are two relevant quotations I would like to offer in this regard.

The first was uttered in the *Pramanavarrtika* by Dharmakirti. Speaking about the omniscience of the Buddha's mind in discussion with others, he says that omniscience may entail knowing how many creatures dwell in the vast ocean, the details of the creatures in the vast ocean; but it has nothing to do with me. This knowledge is of no use to me. But what is of use to me in the omniscient Mind of the Buddha is what I should do and not do in order to gain freedom and Enlightenment. That matters because that is the knowledge which brought him to Enlightenment. And it is relevant to me and it is useful to me. There are many other things I may know, but I have nothing to do with them. They are of no use to me.

So, all the complexities of knowledge and the details of knowledge which, although manifold, are of no use to an individual's life or to the improvement of an individual, or to the evolution or development of an individual: we should just leave them aside and go on without them.

And the second quotation which I remembered is that the human lifespan is so short and the subjects of knowledge are so vast, and we also do not know how long our own lives may be. Therefore we shall have to choose the subjects of knowledge or the subjects of study very carefully, just as a certain mythical bird chooses only the milk which is found in the waters of the ocean!

So those statistics and details and complexities of information which surround us need not be a burden or a disturbance to any individual. You can choose which information to take in and which to leave aside. For instance, your mind can leave all viewing of television and should not be disturbed by that loss.

DR: Of course when it comes to information there are many things we can leave aside, but there are other complexities which we can't seem to escape: we must have a bank account, we must have a telephone, we must have electricity, we must have a motorcar, and we are compelled to play our part in the larger economy. And we have this overburdening amount of structural complexity which imposes itself on our lives, and from which we cannot break free in any way. Is there a radical way of dealing with these complexities?

RINPOCHE: I'm coming to that. Your question is about escaping the imperatives of complexity, and I'm coming to that. I'm just commenting on the background of your question. You have enumerated so many "musts" and I would question how they have become "musts."

I have two telephones at this moment. It's OK. And there are times when I have no telephone around me. I feel I have less complications at that time. And after some time all the telephones will go out of my life and I will still enjoy myself—much more, in fact, than when I was surrounded by telephones.

A bank account, a telephone, a municipal permit: all these are perhaps "musts" for so many people, but these things are not very complex and difficult. You can open a bank account and have a plastic card and go around and purchase things, and put your life and deeds under the system of credit—and this is a new economic system which people seem happy to adopt.

But if you are not happy with it you can give it up. Electricity, computer, email: they were not existent in ancient times and the ancient people lived the fullest life and did better things than people are doing today. So the lack of these commodities were not a handicap. So I don't think any of these things are a "must." "Must" in this case is a conditioning of mind: you cannot live without these things because of conditioning. If you can remove that conditioning, then none of these things constitute a "must."

As I mentioned earlier, there are a few "musts." The biological body needs water and food, clothing and shelter. These are the basic needs. The body's need for water does not produce other related "musts." It does not make beer a "must," it does not make alcohol a "must," it does not make wine a "must"—none of these are "musts." Water is the only "must" in this category, so ordinary water can fulfill your need. And this applies to all "musts." It is a question of physical need as opposed to conditioning.

For the purposes of this discussion we can coin the expression: "Temporary acceptance of things that can ultimately be rejected." All the modern facilities we can accept selectively, given the mind that we can reject then ultimately. We can accept a telephone; it is quite innocent. Email and air-travel we can accept, and there are many other things which are not "musts" but which we can accept for the sake of convenience of function or work. But we must not be ultimately dependent on them. If there is a telephone it is OK, but if there is no telephone I must not feel myself handicapped. I should be able to lead a full life without a telephone and without a bank account.

I have lived in India for 44 years now, and for the first ten years I had no bank account. And then I had a post-office account after 10 years, and I think I have had a bank account for some time during the last 20 years, and it makes no difference to my life. When I had a bank account it was no better for my life; when I did not have a bank account it was no worse for my life. Our perceived need of these things is all a matter of mental conditioning.

Then coming to the question of escape from the tension and anxiety which arise from all these complexities; the spiritual practice is certainly not for the purpose of escaping these. I can say this with reasoning and logic.

If you use spiritual practice as a means of escape from modern complexities you are definitely not practicing spirituality. Fooling yourself, thinking that it is a good escape from the complexities and miseries of the burden of tension; these are not authentic motivations for spiritual practice. That inner inspiration must be authentically for Enlightenment and Freedom, freedom from the bondage of ignorance, attachment, and aversion. And true spirituality requires this intention because that is the nature of spirituality, even though it may not be seen that way in modern times.

If taking a sleeping-pill, drinking alcohol, and going to a meditation center are all equally motivated by the desire to escape complexity or the pressures of modern life, I would recommend choosing alcohol or sleeping-pills rather than meditation. The first two options are without any hypocrisy, but practicing meditation as escape has the dimensions of hypocrisy and deluding oneself.

So meditation must be for the evolution and improvement of one's mind, and for its purification. For that one must have a conducive inclination and intention, otherwise the motivation is wrong and then everything will be wrong. There can be no spiritual practice which is motivated by the desire to escape from complexity.

Appendix: Extracts from Samdhong Rinpoche's "The Basic Crisis and the Remedy" (Published in *Indian Horizons*, Vol. 43, No. 3, 1994).

. . . Let me assert that the external crisis by which we are so much aggrieved is not beyond remedy. If the world at large takes seriously its common . . . responsibility, and is ready to renounce its selfish personal, national, and regional interests, the entire . . . system can be easily managed.

But I perceive today a greater inner crisis. It is basically the crisis of human mind. I would say modern civilization suffers from unmanaged conflicts of the mind, such as the fear of ecological disaster. But it is not prepared to give up its rampant avarice for development. The unwillingness to forsake or limit the industrial and economic outgrowths which are hazardous . . . leads to further accentuating the crisis. . . .

Human thought has attached much pretentious value to wealth and money, especially in the modern age in the name of economic development, so that it has irrationally conditioned human beings towards a "value premise" directed to unceasing accumulation of wealth. The craving for wealth has manifested itself in multidimensional forms of exploitation of ordinary people. . . .

In fact we have never tried to identify correctly the crisis of our time. We presume it to be an external affair, and blame others; and holding them alone responsible for what is happening, we also try to correct them in a superficial manner. . . . The present socio-political system does not allow a person or society to correctly understand and identify the crisis.

A crisis that is harmful to one group is considered to be beneficial to another group, or groups. Therefore the common will of all the people cannot be taken into consideration for managing the crisis. A nation transmits its own crisis to another, or a person transmits his crisis to his opponent. Thus a crisis continues, is preserved and protected by someone to harm or control others. This phenomenon is found in the case of individuals and societies. The discrimination between the "self" and the "other," "friend" and "enemy," "ours" and "theirs" perpetuates the unceasing sequence of crisis. Unless the basis of these discriminations is eliminated, we cannot expect to solve any crisis for all time.

. . . The Truth of Selflessness . . . emerges as the real remedy for all the crises of our time. . . . It may be said that this kind of remedy is unpragmatic and idealistic, which might be attainable by an individual but not by the society as a whole. But in my view without an effort and experiment we cannot judge a thing to be pragmatic or not.

The right to live and survive equally for all sentient beings without distinction could be realized by the successful universal practice of the following ethics:

1. The interests of all sentient beings must be considered more important than that of a particular entity, race, or group of sentient beings; likewise, the interests of the global, regional, and national communities should be kept in such order of significance as in the sequence given above. The lesser interest must be sacrificed for the larger interests.

2. Every individual must know their own genuine needs for living a rational and reasonable life through the practice of "Right Livelihood," and all must sacrifice the artificial needs which are superimposed by commercial enterprises.

3. These actions must be genuinely taken out of love and compassion for all sentient beings, based on the "Right View" and must not be taken from any form of selfishness based on false views.

CIVILIZATION AND DECLINE

DR: The net result of all the factors we have discussed is what we call modern civilization. But has the human mind become essentially more civilized? Perhaps we have become more acute, more inventive, more productive, more creative, perhaps more worldly-wise and conscious of the compromises which seem necessary to increase social justice—but can any of these qualities be said to have made us into more spiritual beings?

What is there to prevent a new decline into darkness, a new barbarism qualified by the irresponsible use of advanced technology and its huge potential to cause cataclysmic destruction?

In other words, what is lacking from our "evolved" civilization? After all, we still practice all the ancient vices: we have criminality, we practice violence and go to war, we deceive and exploit our fellow human beings, and so forth. What steps do we need to take to move beyond these ignorant practices which are so prevalent in spite of the great increase in human knowledge and insight?

RINPOCHE: I had better not answer this question because my answer will be very discouraging. But since the question has been raised, I will have to answer it.

I am a very strong follower of Mahatma Gandhi, even though there is the essential difference in that Gandhi believed in a Creator whereas, as a Buddhist, I do not. So in this regard there is no common ground.

But Gandhi's critical ideas and critical advice were very solid and very valid and based on indisputable reasoning and logic. Therefore I appreciate his thought very much. And he said unambiguously and categorically that this so-called modern civilization is evil.

I may agree that humanity has acquired more information and more knowledge, but humanity has not acquired more insight. In fact, insight has very much decreased. And what we have achieved is the amplification and enlargement of our vices.

Man landing on the moon may have lost some weight due to gravitational factors, but he lost none of his greed, envy, ignorance, and hatred. He brought all these back home with him to earth. And after returning from the moon the person who came back was evidently the same person, as good or as bad as before. No mental development has been achieved by these kinds of technological feats.

And in ancient times wars were fought for increase of power or for defense; enlargement of power and defense of power are usually the causes of war, and sometimes wars are fought for revenge. But in ancient times people had to fight face to face and you needed a lot of strength—and at most you could kill 1, 2, 3, 4 or 10 persons. So it was in those proportions, and generally people did not look for war. Wars were generally fought when unavoidable.

Today war has become trade and an economic entity. Wars are no longer fought on the battlefield but by people sitting behind a remote control—and by pushing a button you can kill hundreds of thousands of people. We have the recent memory of Hiroshima and Nagasaki, a terrible event that was not necessary but which was done just for the sake of experiment. Before August the Japanese had stated their willingness to surrender but the process of surrender was intentionally delayed by the Americans and their allies in order to experiment with the atomic bomb. Part of the earth and its inhabitants were completely destroyed but none of the killers had to expose themselves to danger.

And now warfare has become a necessary part of the marketing of weaponry, but the war is always kept far from the land of production. And now war and fear of war are always kept alive in order to enlarge the weapons market. It has become part of the world economy, a source of profit based on the philosophy that the death of human beings is more profitable than other productive economic ventures.

A bullet is used for killing a person and if one bullet kills one person another bullet needs to be produced, and even if it misses the other person, another bullet needs to be produced anyway. This is a terrible aspect of so-called modern civilization.

And another very good example that we can talk about is medical science. Medical science is very useful for humanity, but it can only be accessed by the rich. It is of no use to the poor who cannot afford it. And the doctors need more and more patients. If everyone is healthy the doctor cannot make a living. Therefore they need to encourage unhealthy lifestyles if their business is to continue to be profitable.

So these are only two aspects of modern civilization which I have touched upon, and civilization is so vast! I would recommend that you read Gandhi's work on Swaraj (1909), which sheds light on the evils and categorically denies the "goodness" of modern civilization.

It is on these grounds that, whenever I introduce myself, I always say that I am a savage and proud of it, and fortunately I am not influenced by modern or postmodern or even ultra-modern civilization. I still live in the civilization of seventh century Tibet and perhaps due to that I am less harmful to others than the average modern civilized person.

So I can say without hesitation that humanity has significantly enlarged its knowledge and know-how, but has failed to acquire a corresponding degree of wisdom. There has been no increase in the wisdom of insight or insight-wisdom. And we should not hesitate to announce this reality to the world.

THE FUTURE IN PROSPECT

DR: In speaking about the future of human development we have to distinguish between two possibilities: those over which humanity has no control, and those which can be influenced by our own knowledge and technology.

Considering what has been discussed so far, what can we say about the negative and positive prospects and what can we do to ensure more positive outcomes? Can all this be simplified into a few basic rules or views?

RINPOCHE: If we are believed to be the mere product of evolution as propounded by modern scientific theories and many modern schools of philosophy as well—still I would say that evolution is not completely independent. It is being controlled or influenced by many forces external to itself: for instance, cultural environment and, now, technology.

Technology can to a great extent control or alter the forces of evolution and drive them in various directions. We now have abundant evidence that genetic engineering and such techniques as cloning—the cloning of human beings is not far away—can affect, alter, or control our biological evolution. So there are these possibilities for modern technology.

But evolution also depends greatly on the transformation and "change of mind"—it is a fact that change of mind (maybe on the side of betterment, or maybe on the side of deterioration, decay) has much relation to and much control over the change of the material reality; the evolution or decay of the material reality. Matter is much affected and sometimes controlled by the mindset. So this also needs to be understood.

And it should be understood as true, not as imaginary. The person who is able to overcome and to regulate their own being, the forces of the working of the immanence within their own body: such a person is able to control or regulate the elements outside of their physical person, and this is also quite evident to us.

So, bearing in mind these realities, we cannot make the statement that evolution is outside our control or is completely independent or random. Humanity can influence its course.

Yes, humanity cannot do anything about certain conditions. As I mentioned before, humanity cannot eliminate death or any of the qualities that are permanent or eternal. This is of course not possible.

If the time should come when humanity may overcome physical death and decay and make human life permanent, then of course we would have to revise the truth concerning these things, and no further arguments will be necessary. Until that happens, death will remain beyond our control.

Today people claim that they can delay death; they can keep the human organ alive for a couple of hours, weeks, or months by the use of certain medical techniques. They might keep it alive for years by these means, but I do not consider this a delay of death. It is just an artificial sustaining of the body without any essence, without any consciousness in the deeper sense. That cannot be interpreted as a delay of death.

Of course, untimely death can be avoided. It can certainly be more easily avoided by medical techniques. But the real time of death can in no way be avoided, not by all the medical sciences, neurosciences, and other biological sciences. They can neither deny the inevitability of death or postpone the real time of death. This is a clear fact. If it can be proved otherwise, then our entire Truth will be quite different. In the meantime we have to live carefully, mindful of decay and death.

So, if I have understood your question correctly, then I would answer that the evolution of an individual and that individual's world can be very much regulated and controlled by the mindset of that individual. By the development of one's mind, by dispelling the defilements of one's mind, and by purifying of mind there can be a very positive evolution of that mind and its environment.

And then the question how this principle can be applied to a community or nation or whatever group—how it can be enlarged and extended: I don't think there is any one way which is applicable to all human beings or to all living beings. So far it has not been possible to discover one way which applies to all or one method which all can understand and accept.

But positive evolution can be extended as much as possible in spite of the differing natures of individual human and other beings, their different dispositions, backgrounds, conditioning, and inclinations. Because of these differences we cannot accommodate a collective Karma to make everyone uniform. Diversity is a law of nature, and therefore diversity will always be there.

As long as individual ignorance and defilements are present there are bound to be differences, conflict, and disharmony. But what we can do is find ways to reduce these to a minimum and means to enlarge the positive way as much as possible. Since it is possible to achieve this, we should pursue these possibilities.

PART II:

THE MODERN INDIVIDUAL

INTRODUCTION

The modern individual is not an abstract unit in the total society. You and I and the other are the modern individual. This being the case, we should test every theory and notion about the modern individual against our own subjective experience to find out whether they are authenticated in our own minds and in our daily lives. That degree of awareness is our first line of defense against becoming what we are told we are but actually are not. Distorting the truth of our being to make it square with the ideas of psychological, religious, and social theorists is the chief cause of our alienation from our true nature, and of our shallowness. Abandoning what we authentically know about ourselves in order to conform to the demands of our society drags both ourselves and our societies down to the level of something functional rather than something alive.

Fundamentally there are only two ways of considering the individual. We have to look inwards to discover what we are within ourselves. We have to look outwards to find out how we are related to our environment and to other living beings in that environment. Searching carefully in both directions we again need to authenticate or differentiate theory from truth.

The Western perception of individuality or personhood or self has undergone many revisions. All of these revisions are based on a fundamental misconception about self, in that we have never doubted that our personhood is essentially identical with our immediate experience of ourselves. That is, we have seldom if ever questioned the conclusion that I really am what I seem to be. This, with all its turmoil, negativity, hope, and fear, with its capacity for love and hate, desire and indifference—all of this is "I." Even in our spirituality we tend to entertain the notion that this same "I," much cleansed and exalted, will live on forever in Paradise or, much debased, will suffer eternally in Hell.

Taking as their starting point this belief in an "I" which really exists the way it appears to exist, the pseudo-science of psychology has led us into a labyrinth of theoretical schools from the Freudian to the Behaviorist and to the ultra-behaviorism of B.F. Skinner. All of these miss the mark and ultimately fail in their therapeutic aims because their foundational view of self is not valid. They all attempt to analyze and heal what they conceive of as an entity or a process, but which is actually only a mental projection or construct. They are a bit like the Ghostbusters who come in to rid your house of the spooks which are causing your electrical appliances to pack up.

Only when we begin to understand the self as a mental construct are we able to correct it, because we are then able to objectify it, to take distance from it, to examine it.

As long as we continue to conceive of self as an entity, as "I am this," we remain powerless to bring about permanent change or healing because "I am this." If I am this I must always remain this because this is what I ultimately am. I can tweak it a little this way and that and I can present a persona to the world around me, but in the final analysis "I am this."

But somehow being "this" is not enough for me. It is an unsatisfying "thisness" which often causes misery to itself and others. In merely experiencing itself it does not know itself. So we begin the quest to find out what "this" is or we busy ourselves with every kind of distraction to avoid the nagging question. Or we accept the theories that have been neatly worked out for us by greater minds than our own. Self-help books, books on the subject of "I" and how to develop "I" to its maximum potential abound. Every year there is a new best seller about how to optimize "I," a new theory of "I," and a new hope for "I." Again and again people fall for the revised, more optimistic interpretation of "I" and its supposed potential.

Even more puzzling is how "I" has managed to survive the largely Christian spirituality of the West with its recurrent admonitions to deny the self, to overcome the self, to put the self to death. Somehow this urgent truth has come to be interpreted as an overcoming of all the bad aspects of "I" while striving to increase the goodness of "I"—or it has been taken to mean the spiritual aspect or power operating within the "I." Very rarely is the teaching understood and practiced in its true sense: the replacement of "I" by the spiritual power or wisdom.

One way or another the "I" continues to flourish and the result is increasing selfishness, self-centeredness, and inevitable superficiality—because this mental construct which I mistakenly identify as my self-entity is capable of only the shallowest modes of self-awareness, those modes which reveal themselves in grasping and self-defense in thought, speech, and conduct. Its motives are similar to those of the parasite: to feed off that which is truly alive in order to sustain a semblance of life. And we pay for all this in suffering.

The Buddhist view of "I" can help to remedy the delusion. In Buddhism the analysis of "I" is subtle and complex, as subtle and complex as it needs to be in order to unmask the delusory trickiness of this dangerous mental construct. It is not easy to fathom the trick, but it can be done with sufficient effort and determination. And it is a liberating exercise for those whose struggles with "I" have resulted in self-sickness.

The first step is to negate through close analysis the possibility that "I," this personality, can be said in any way to exist inherently, from its own side, as an entity. The analysis does not negate the relative existence of "I," but only its ultimate "entity-ness." The "I" is understood to arise on the basis of certain causes and conditions, and one of the strongest arguments for its non-inherent existence is the fact that it depends for its apparent existence on these causes and conditions. For how can anything which depends for its existence on other factors be said to possess the quality of inherent existence?

It is like one of those "trompe l'œil" three-dimensional pictures which are made up of dots, squiggles, and shades. At first one sees on the paper only the dots, squiggles, and shades, quite abstract or meaningless or formless in themselves. It is only once one has conditioned the eyes to focus on them in a certain way that the picture in all its three-dimensional glory suddenly appears. When the eyes return to normal or valid focus the picture disappears and only the dots, squiggles, and shades remain. We can't negate that a three-dimensional picture can arise from them and that this picture "exists" for as long as we focus on the dots, squiggles, and shades in a certain way. But the three-dimensional picture does not inherently exist. It only exists for as long as we impute its existence on the basis of the way we have conditioned our focus. It arises in dependence on the dots, squiggles, and shades, and on the way we condition ourselves to interpret and perceive them. But where is the three-dimensional picture in ultimate reality or in terms of its own inherent existence? It is nowhere to be found.

This, in comparison with the highly developed Buddhist analysis of Anatman, or not-self, is an extremely simplistic analogy. The view of self will be discussed at greater length in the section on Buddhism.

What is important here is to gain some idea of how profoundly conditioned our unliberated view of "I" is.

Of course the individual does not only have a mental component, however conditioned. We have our bodies, our means of relating to the material world and to others, and in many ways a determining factor in shaping our ordinary self-view.

Looking inwards, our bodies, while functioning to make us present in the world, have needs and are infused with inherited drives and instincts. In these areas we again have to distinguish between the essential and the non-essential; those needs, drives, and instincts which are authentic and those which are the products of our conditioning. We also need to distinguish between those which are wholesome, leading us to inner contentment and peace, and those which are unwholesome, resulting in suffering for ourselves and others.

In considering our bodies, the instruments of thought, speech, and conduct in this world, it is crucial to begin to grasp what an influential role the mind plays in relation to the body. In correctly understanding the interplay between mind and body, we are enabled to exert much more control over the negative patterns of thought, speech, and conduct that bring misery to our collective society.

It is only when we are able to think, act, and speak in conformity with the wisdom of selflessness and compassion that we become empowered to transform ourselves, our environment, and, by extension, our global social order. These improvements will only prove genuine and durable through the transformation of the individual. The increasing complexity of national and international legislation and the proliferation of new social theories have only managed to bring us to the place in which we find ourselves as individuals and as societies right now. But is it a good place to be? As the Dalai Lama has said: It is a time when there is much in the window but nothing in the room.

Looking outwards into the environment and into the society of which we are a part, individuals are forced to consider their needs, rights, and responsibilities for others. In today's environment and the society which inhabits it these factors no longer present a question of maintaining a balance, but the predicament of how to address a dire and critical imbalance.

Our invalid overestimation of self has led us into ever more ferocious competition, not only with others, but with the natural environment itself. And in this struggle the self-preserving and self-centered

"I" is prevailing at an increasingly alarming cost. It is "dog eat dog" in the battle for survival and, so far as the environment goes, it is "after me the flood."

While we endlessly debate the issues of social justice and environmental and ecological destruction, our conduct and essential attitude remain unchanged. We claim to be more socially and environmentally aware but this increased awareness has not changed the patterns of exploitation and violence that are the chief hallmarks of the new millennium.

At the very least we need to find ways to become less harmful.

The Dialogues

DR: Our history has culminated in the conception and life-view of modern personal individualism and many evolutionists, anthropologists, and psychologists would argue that this development, in addition to being inevitable, has been humankind's most beneficial mental adaptation. With a strong sense of our own individualism we are able much more efficiently and determinedly to exercise our volition and energies to our best advantage and to the best advantage of the human race. More tribal or group-oriented peoples are seen as relatively undeveloped and it is assumed that their further development depends on the cultivation of a stronger sense of individualism.

In the West the idea of the personal individual has become paramount in the social order, and it has taken a relatively short period of history (perhaps 800 years or so) to develop from the "primitive" group-mentality through various societal revolutions and humanist shifts in thinking to the point where individual rights and the individualistic life-philosophy are the dominant elements in our self-view and in all our thinking about society. One might call individualism one of the foundations of our social structures.

Psychological theories have played a large role over the last century in the formulation of ideas about the structures and processes, as well as the pathological aspects, of the individual psyche. We have traveled from the sexual instinct-based theories of Freud to the almost mystical psychological archetypes of Jung, to more sophisticated "scientific" theories of self and selfhood.

With ideas ranging from the ego-superego-id triad, through the vast concept of the collective unconscious, and to the objectivist views of the behaviorists, we have now arrived at the attempt to explain the individual in purely neurophysiological terms.

Still, we seem to be a long way from any sort of emerging consensus among neuroscientists, psychological theorists, religious teachers, and ordinary people about the final structure of the individual mind. Nevertheless, we cling to the freedom we believe to be associated with individualism and we are forced to admit that this growing sense of selfhood seems to have brought much benefit and led to more just and compassionate societies in the West.

How can we explain this paradox? After all, Christianity teaches the denial of self rather than self-assertion, and the sacrifice of self for the sake of love and truth. Essentially, Buddhism teaches the same principles in its insistence on Anatman or not-self.

Yet if we look back in history to a time when the West was highly religious and dominated by religious ideals, we find a very cruel and intolerant society. Indeed, it almost appears as if selflessness was imposed on the masses by the over-inflated egos of the religious leaders of the time in order to make their power more absolute.

It seems clear from this and other historical lessons that a highly developed sense of individualism is necessary to create the sort of social tensions that will result in just and relatively compassionate societies.

How do we reconcile this with the notion of selflessness required by religious practice and true spirituality? How should we view ourselves in order to be optimally happy and also beneficial to others? And at the same time to ensure that the non-spiritual power-hungry egotists are not simply allowed to take dominance over our societies? Where does our duty lie?

For instance, can we be said to be acting correctly if, based on selfless spirituality, we withdraw ourselves from the struggle to keep our societies just and compassionate? What is the right balance between the view of self as not-self (or the Christian teaching of self-denial and self-sacrifice), and active participation as individuals in an individualistic world? What is the right view of self in the social vision of Satyagraha (non-violent Truth-Insistence)?

RINPOCHE: Indeed this is a very long and complex question. I don't think I can easily and appropriately answer all the questions embedded in this thesis. We need more dialogue, more information, in order to make all these things clear. But I will try to mention something which might be used as basic material for formulating a complete answer to these questions. And we should go step by step.

Firstly I would emphasize that the Buddhist theory of selflessness does not mean the complete negation of self in the negative sense. The negation of self must be understood as the negation of self as we ordinarily conceive it or project it to be. And we negate that conceptualized self in order to establish the real nature of self.

In the process of interdependent arising (see section on Buddhism) the "self" appears, and we must understand self in that way. That is the Buddhist view. Therefore it should not be considered as contradicting the possibility of self-esteem and self-confidence with the simultaneous awareness of selflessness. So these two, the importance of self-esteem and the importance of self-confidence, can go very well and very comfortably with the Buddhist view of selflessness.

On the contrary, when you do not negate the concept of self (as it is viewed by the ordinary, distracted mind) by the understanding of interdependent arising, then there cannot be a positive self-esteem nor a positive self-confidence because the person does not truly recognize what "self" is. One is ignorant of the true nature of self, therefore one's confidence cannot be real, since it is based on an unreal construction of "self."

If we look more closely at the Indian tradition we find different schools of thought saying the same things in different language. The Vedic schools say that you cannot attain Enlightenment without recognizing the Atman (self) and the Buddhist schools say that you cannot attain Enlightenment without recognizing the Anatman (not-self).

Both are actually agreeing that the unenlightened person cannot see the self for what it truly is. To use a common metaphor: I can say that a glass is half-filled or that it is half-empty. Apparently these would be opposing statements, but actually I am saying the same thing.

Words are not of prime importance. The meaning is what is important. So this is one aspect that should be investigated in relation to individuality.

Then, coming to the importance of the individual as being a source of actions having a good result. Now in this regard the Buddhists speak about the other as being more important than the self. For the sake of others we should be prepared to practice self-sacrifice. I think most, if not all, of the Buddhist schools agree on this point.

How to take responsibility for others in practice might be a contentious point, but "the other is more important than the self" is common throughout Buddhism. And there are different ways of demonstrating that this is a truth.

One of the logical arguments for this point of view is that others are many but self is singular: quantitatively others are clearly greater than myself. Then, when we come to the meeting of one self and another, myself and he or she, there is no question of quantitative difference: it is one person interacting with one person. Then here the logic is that you should sacrifice or put yourself in the second place in relation to the other because you can never be sure that, by putting yourself first, you are doing good either for yourself or for the other; whereas, by restraining yourself for the sake of the other, you can be certain that you are doing good both for yourself and for the other.

Doing good to the other also means that you are doing good to yourself, just as, if you harm the other you are necessarily harming yourself. So this is the fundamental and simple rationality behind the view.

It does not mean that you should lose your self-esteem or self-confidence. In order to refrain from harming the other you actually need much more self-esteem and self-confidence. If you are influenced by fear or doubt you cannot sacrifice yourself. You become nervous and agitated and don't know what to do under very compelling or stressful circumstances.

But if you know yourself, have self-esteem and self-confidence and faith in yourself, only then can you sacrifice your own interests for others and refrain from harming others in critical circumstances.

When things are calm and leisurely you can sacrifice your own interests quite easily, but when fear enters and you have no self-confidence, you cannot respond properly—and those are the occasions when it is most important that you respond properly. Therefore you need the highest level of self-confidence and self-awareness for giving up your own interests when it really matters. So this is entirely different to a selflessness which implies no self-confidence.

Then the third aspect which I would like to discuss is the importance of the individual for making a good society by combining in himself or herself the truths of modern socio-political and scientific theory and ancient wisdom.

Ancient wisdom maintains that we should try to build a good society and modern political theory also aims at an ideal society, whether or not it is actually achievable. Even Communism, for example, speaks of an ideal egalitarian society where there is no governmental control—all the people work according to their capacity and are served according to their needs. Capitalism also seeks this kind of eventual ideal.

But I can summarize the essence of the problem in two concepts. Modern political theory speaks about human rights or individual rights, but ancient wisdom speaks about individual responsibility. So each is considering the issue from a different viewpoint.

And Buddhism, and for that matter most of the spiritual traditions, will emphasize individual responsibility as the key element to establishing a cohesive and peaceful society. If each individual fulfilled their responsibility correctly their would be no cause for social conflict or social injustice.

We transgress our own limitations and thereby violate the others' rights. We tend to think of our own rights rather than our responsibilities, and then, in defense of our own rights without considering the rights of others, we transgress our limits. This is the cause of conflicts, quarrels, and division.

So, if you are aware that you have an individual responsibility towards yourself as well as an individual responsibility towards the universe, then the correct balance is struck. The Dalai Lama always speaks about universal responsibility and, indeed, the individual does have a universal responsibility. An awareness of this responsibility is absolutely necessary and important, whether it is in the case of two people or many or that of a group or a nation, since all are part of the universe.

So the individual's importance lies more in their responsibilities than in their rights. Buddhism and other spiritual teachings will never say that you can negate the individual, but they would certainly say that individual interests should be sacrificed for the many or for the society. But that does not mean that the individual is negligible and of no importance.

The individual must become developed to the state where he or she is fully aware of his or her responsibility, and mindful of carrying out those responsibilities faithfully. This is the basic condition for a just and peaceful community.

Appendix: Extracts from an address given at the World Congress of the Theosophical Society: "An Individual's Universal Responsibility" (Published in *The Theosophist*, Vol. 122, No. 8, 2001).

. . . According to Buddhist tradition, the universe manifests through the collective as well as individual karmic force of all its sentient beings. Favorable karmic forces generate forms that are in tune with the life process, and the living universe creates a non-living universe in tune with it. This positive karmic force has the power to convert forms that are not in tune with the universe into those which are in such harmony.

During the emergence, growth, and mature life of an individual planet there is cohesion between its living forms and its own nature. This is called the Golden Age or Satya Yuga. But after a specific period of time this positive karmic force gradually recedes and a negative and non-cohesive karmic force gains strength, which creates conflict and contradiction between living and non-living beings, and causes those beings and the planet itself to be out of tune with the universe, pushing it towards deterioration and total annihilation. This is called Kali Yuga or the Age of Decay.

Today this small planet earth is suffering from a lack of cohesiveness resulting in conflicts, and its sentient beings are subject to untold miseries and fear. This is basically due to the collective black karmic force of living beings, which is not very easy to improve or correct. However, we cannot wait for the transformation of the collective karmic force of society as a whole to solve the problems we are experiencing in our day-to-day lives. Therefore we must be more attentive to an individual approach rather than a collective one, in order to regenerate ourselves and the world at large.

. . . Today each one of us, individually, must step out of the current of modern civilization and fulfill his or her universal responsibility. In this way each individual can attune himself or herself with the universe, and also put the universe in tune with themselves.

. . . Some practical suggestions arise from the Noble Eightfold Path of the Buddha. This path is not only for spiritual upliftment, but also for living in a righteous manner, creating a cohesive and non-violent society, thereby promoting spirituality. The first step is to have a right view and clear perception of today's materialistic and selfish society with all its demerits, and also a vision of how to dissociate oneself from it.

After obtaining such a view, the second step should be right determination. One should start a non-violent, non-consumerist, and self-controlled way of life, accepting and enduring all the hardships and inconveniences, including physical pain, which may occur on the way or may be inflicted on one by negative forces.

The third step would be to speak about it without fear. The first two steps pertain to the individual. To share it with fellow living beings means to communicate one's view and determination through right speech. If one does not speak about the ills of our violent society, one might as well be considered to be a party to it.

The fourth step would be to consolidate and stabilize effort. Laziness and carelessness should not be allowed to deter the effort to live rightly, particularly in the present day. Right living requires great effort. Otherwise, one may easily be carried away by evil forces.

The fifth and most important step is right livelihood. That is the basic action of "stepping out" as well as the actual fulfillment, individually, of universal responsibility. It is most difficult today to pursue right and untainted livelihood. . . .

The sixth step is to inculcate right mindfulness. In today's world violence and dishonesty are the norm. Without right mindfulness one may fall into the materialist pit without realizing it.

The seventh and eighth steps, namely, right concentration and right action are also consistently required for a non-violent way of living.

Krishnamurti sums up the entirety of religious teaching, and I would like to share it with you:

Religion is something that includes everything. It is not exclusive.
A religious mind has no nationality, it is not provincial, it does not belong to a particular organized group. It is not the result of 2,000 years of propaganda. It has no dogma or belief. It is a mind that moves from fact to fact. It is a mind that understands the total

quality of thought, not only the obvious, superficial thought, the educated thought, but also the uneducated thought, the deep down unconscious thought, and motives; and a mind that inquires into the totality of something when it realizes, through that inquiry, what is false and denies it because it is false. Then the totality of denial brings about a new quality in the mind, which is religious, which is revolutionary.

The sentence, "It is a mind that moves from fact to fact" is very important. We repeat the motto: "There is no religion higher than Truth," but in actual life we are trapped in one or another religion. The denial of falsehood and the realization of truth, of the fact, which brings about a revolution, a transformation, *that* is actually a religious mind, and we must try to cultivate such a mind for the benefit of all sentient beings.

PART III:

HUMANKIND IN SAMSARA, ON EARTH, AND IN THE UNIVERSE

INTRODUCTION

In concluding our dialogues on contemporary social issues I wanted Rinpoche to comment on some of the most pertinent collective ills that hold us back from achieving a present world order which might be more conformed to the truest yearnings of the whole of humanity: the yearning for peace and collective harmony.

The universe is our wider abode and the earth is our homestead in it. The central paradox of our condition is that we have made our home, on the whole, a place of profound ignorance and suffering. As if it were not tragic enough that we have made our home in Samsara, we are actually acting to increase our delusion and pain.

In our world there is perhaps much superficial laughter, but there is little deep joy. There is an abundance of marvelous intellect but a dearth of wisdom. There is a plethora of cohesive legislation but an alarming shortage of authentic virtue. And even as we mouth the doctrine of peace, we embark on endless wars and acts of exploitation. It is not only that the blatant hypocrite has the upper hand in every institution of real power. The deeper problem is the unconscious hypocrisy we all practice in going about our daily lives, the hypocrisy implicit in our complacent acceptance of our failure to live up to our collective potential.

At the heart of this complacency is the terrible illusion or dark joke that we believe ourselves to be going up while we are actually sliding rapidly down to our own destruction. It is an illusionist's trick brought on by the proliferation of technology and socio-political spin. In every area of our lives, from our spirituality to our economic mindset, huge effort is made to marginalize alternative views in favor of increasing homogeneity or "globalization." It is no longer only nations, but the minds of nations, that are being colonized, and violence and threat of violence play a major role in the ongoing colonization.

As we increasingly sacrifice our honesty at the altar of expediency or prosperity, our inner darkness deepens. As we grow darker, more ignorant, less mindful, our power to discern and to act transformatively diminish. We are only "pawns in the game." We say it lightly, but if we dwelt on it with the gravity it deserves, this saying would reveal to us that it is rapidly becoming the horrifying reality of which it makes so light. It would make us look to the future with trembling.

In this section I spoke to Rinpoche on the following topics:

The Gap between Governments and the Governed
The Law as Moral Sufficiency
Destruction of the Environment
International Influence and Expansionism
Power
Violence and War
America and the Superpower Principle
Toothless International Law
The Ideal
A View on This Millennium

The Dialogues

THE GAP BETWEEN GOVERNMENTS AND THE GOVERNED

DR: In spite of all the developmental and historical changes we have undergone, it would be fair to say that the substructures of our societies have remained constant, and are composed of the nuclear and extended family, the ethnic component, and the subsuming nation (especially in multiethnic or multicultural societies).

Although there are many forms of governance in the world, there is in every case a gap, and in some cases a chasm, between the policies and actions of the leadership and the orientation of the people.

The West is firmly founded in democratic principles—the heritage of Graeco-Roman institutions—which allow freedom within the constraints of a constitution and an agreed legal framework to all the subgroups within Western nations.

But how democratic are we really? To what extent is the populace actually influencing and directing the policies and practices of our democracies? While it is true that the electorate determines which party will rule, it is by no means clear that the democratically elected party always acts with the consent of the electorate.

Our leaders are often duplicitous and prevaricating, and these vices are often viewed as a necessary part of politics and of the practice of effective pragmatism. Is complete truthfulness a practical or feasible ideal for the political functioning of modern societies, and is it always wise for our politicians and leaders to act with openness?

What sort of shifts in our social thinking are necessary to bring our societies more in line with the ideal of Satyagraha or Truth-Insistence? Is it not just rather a naïve dream?

RINPOCHE: If we wish to improve the world we must conduct ourselves with complete openness and honesty, and this applies especially to politicians. Without these qualities you cannot achieve a non-violent and truly egalitarian society or world.

Inequality and "might is right"—the law of the jungle—is prevailing in this modern world much more than in the so-called primitive world, in primitive societies, in primitive times. In primitive societies might or power was limited and limited power was exercised in a limited sphere.

Today the power of the economy, the power of violence, the power of greed, have increased hundreds of thousandfold in comparison with primitive ages. So there has been no improvement in the human mindset; it is still the same. Whoever has the power has the concomitant desire to influence or overpower the other, to dominate or eliminate weaker others. This is ongoing.

So unless there is a truthfulness, an openness, an honesty, there can be no good politics whatsoever. For instance, if the Tibetan community and leadership could become completely transparent and completely honest towards the People's Republic of China, I think we would increase our standing and would have a much better negotiation and dialogue. But we are not able to do that, so we weaken ourselves.

Secondly, democracy for the most part is not real democracy. It is mostly hypocrisy. Democracy ordinarily assumes that, while the minority may have their say, the decisions are made by the majority according to the wisdom of the majority. But this is not what is actually happening today. In fact the will of a small minority leads the majority through domination over the will of the majority and by simply ignoring the majority.

This became very clear in 2003 when public opinion, strongly expressed through demonstrations, writings, speeches, and community actions against the war on Iraq, was simply ignored. None of the leaders was prepared even to listen to the public voice. The public voice was deemed so weak and ineffectual that no leader had need to pay attention to it.

I pondered the reasons for this very deeply and I found out that the public voice was itself in this case not very transparent and not very honest. It had other limitations too and therefore was not able to prevail over the few pro-war leaders.

I asked one of my American friends about these things and he told me that there had been a huge demonstration in California—hundreds of thousands of people on the streets—against the invasion of Iraq. And he was happy at this unprecedented turnout of people.

So I asked him why such strength of public opinion could not prevail over George W. Bush and the leadership. He pondered for a while and then he answered, "They were too weak. I left the demonstration myself after the mass of anti-war demonstrators physically mishandled a small group or pro-war lobbyists standing on a corner."

So it is evident that an element of anger and hatred was present among the anti-war demonstrators. They did not have a compassionate mind towards George W. Bush; so the level of their compassion was high in the street, but not deep in the heart. It was a violent voice as well, and therefore it was ineffective.

So only transparent, honest, and compassionate politics are good and are effective. I do not consider my position on this to be utopian. It is achievable if we work hard and prepare and educate people in the principles of non-violence and honesty. If this were achieved the world would be a much, much better place to live in.

THE LAW AS MORAL SUFFICIENCY

DR: In democratic societies moral ideas and norms are always shifting. Moral attitudes and practices which were completely unacceptable (and often illegal) a few decades ago, are today accepted and even encouraged.

Where is our absolute point of reference in this regard? Other than the stipulations of our legislation, can we even speak of a social morality? Is it not rather a question for each individual member of society to answer for themselves?

After all, there is so much confusion in the realm of social morality. We are given many differing and even opposing points of view by our leaders, our intellectuals, our artists, our philosophers, and even our moral and religious teachers. How can we best define a realistic and universally acceptable social morality? Is it something that is present in our minds as part of our essential nature, or do we have to learn it by being taught its benefits?

It could be said, especially in the modern world, that the concept of law is the safeguard of the collective morality of a society and the preserver of justice and peace within a society. It is the best way that we have been able to find to maintain stability and minimize conflict in our states and nations.

But the concept of law is necessarily based on the shifting sands of conditionality and relativity. It relies on hugely technical premises and, although it is the best form of social order that we have been able to devise, it is far from being aligned with the truth about ourselves as spiritual beings.

Are there ways in which the concept of law can be made to speak to us as individuals and as societies in a more living, more essential, less formalized way? Are there not spiritual laws which transcend our human or samsaric concept of law? The point is perhaps well illustrated by the words of Jesus Christ, Who taught His followers that it is not sufficient to observe the law if people wish to attain to righteousness. By this He was of course referring to the religious law of His time, but this law can be related to our secular concept of law with its roots in morality and the notions of justice, equity, and mercy.

Although statutory and common law differ from society to society, there are certain basic legal ideas common to all of humanity, such as the illegitimacy of murder, rape, theft, and so forth. We could say that the law proceeds from the common mind of people and that the differences lie chiefly in the areas of how the laws are administered, the punishment of offenders, and certain other cultural emphases.

The effective functioning of the law is directly proportionate to the successful cohesion and functionality of societies, and where law breaks down for one reason or another we find those societies descending into anarchy and self-destruction.

This is a strong argument for the postulate that people are essentially lawless and immoral; that they need to have an overarching set of laws in order to keep them upright, especially as a social unit. From earliest times there have been laws which protect the integrity and survivalist functioning of societies. But what does this tell us about ourselves? Does it not indicate that there is no effective compass in our own nature by which we can navigate the moral oceans of our social systems?

Put baldly, are we able to achieve anything better than our modern societies, given the fact that we seem unable to survive without a written code of ethics which, besides being formulated for us, must also be enforceable through various punishments? Are we able to rise above our laws towards greater righteousness and, if so, by what means?

We may ask whether a state run on the principles of Satyagraha would need the control of enforceable laws, perhaps even more so than our flawed modern democracies, given the tendency of people to abuse the freedom offered to them by compassionate and truthful leadership?

RINPOCHE: Generally laws and codes of conduct are good because they train the mind in the basic and simple do's and don'ts. By these means even a completely unmindful person can learn to conduct himself or herself properly, in accordance with these guidelines. These simple moral and legal guidelines are helpful for ordinary people to behave properly in their group.

Now coming to enforcement: this is a very diverse concept influenced by many individual and differing opinions. Regarding punishment and reward as methods of enforcement, neither of these ever truly transforms the consciousness in the right way.

As much as detention or imprisonment may be justifiable for criminal and violent people, who, if they are not segregated from the community, will cause increase of violence and law-breaking in that community, there can be no justification for a sort of compensatory judicial violence such as mental or physical torture or abuse.

For example, to commit murder is a terrible thing, but it is also true that the murdered person cannot be brought back to life by executing the murderer. If you could revive the murdered person by killing the killer, then I think such a punishment could to some extent be justified. But since the murdered person cannot be revived, killing the killer cannot be justified by any logic.

And if we try to justify it as an exemplary preventative measure, assuming that executing the murderer would instill fear in potential murderers and so prevent them from killing—if that is so, it has never been achieved. The punishment of killing the killer has existed since time immemorial in this world and still we have not managed to eradicate murder.

So therefore I think, if we believe in rebirth, that the killer would be reborn as a killer because he has not yet transformed the mindset which compelled him to kill another person. He will be reborn into this mindset even though he has undergone the punishment of the death sentence.

So basically we have to attack the source of the problem: Why does one person kill another? Why does one person steal another's possessions? Because of hatred and because of greed; and unless you remove the hatred from the mind of the killer or the greed from the thief you will not be able to put an end to killing and stealing. This is simple logic which everyone can understand.

So in this way punishment and reward are not good methods for improving human conduct or the mindset of conditioned people. On the contrary, education and compassion for these people is necessary if you really care more about the restoration of healthy-mindedness and morality.

ENVIRONMENTAL DESTRUCTION

DR: One of the by-products of increased and intensified consumerism is the continuous degradation of the environment, and today it is no longer a question of the depletion of our earthly resources but also of damage being done to the planet in a universal context; for instance, in the destruction of the ozone layer, the increased greenhouse effect, and so forth.

We are putting ourselves, and all other beings which inhabit the earth, in danger of complete annihilation. How can we cure ourselves of our blindness with regard to these issues?

We delude ourselves with the hope that technology will eventually be in a position to restore the damage we are doing by giving money greater importance in our societies than the preservation of our planet. And, even though we are more conscious of and informed about these matters, the destruction continues unabated. Is this simply inevitable, or is there a wisdom that can bring us to reassess our priorities?

Perhaps our greatest problem is our failure to recognize the interdependence of all beings and all phenomena in our world. This is one of the results of the strengthened view of self, that we put ourselves, our societies, and our species in the center of all our thinking and planning—albeit in an ignorant and self-defeating manner. We act as though the human race is the only species entitled to benefit from the riches which our ecology has put at our disposal.

How can we employ our reason as well as our spirituality to gain a clearer perspective with regard to our true position within the total scope of the ecology of our planet and our mental realm?

RINPOCHE: The tendency of self-destruction and the tendency of suicide is, I think, inbuilt in postmodern civilization. And it is part of the ultra-modern or postmodern way of thinking. It is not due to ignorance about the consequences of harming the environment or harming oneself.

To use an old metaphor: it is obvious that, if you are on the water, you should not make a hole in your boat. If a child makes a hole in the boat we can ascribe that to ignorance, to innocence, and we can easily forgive it. But if a grown person who knows that if he makes a hole in the boat, the boat will sink, it is another matter. And we are behaving like that, intentionally making so many holes in our boat. The man making holes in his boat is the same as those people who cause environmental damage day in and day out.

The mindset of such people is beyond my comprehension. What is madness? Madness is the inability to discriminate between what is harmful and what is not. And I think that, in this regard, modern people have gone insane.

For instance, the terrorists or so-called suicide squads: they commit suicide by bombing and killing numbers of other people— their bombs strapped to their own bodies! And I have been watching this for the last two or three years increasing day by day; and you find so many people who are ready to give up their own lives in order to kill other people. And they also know that these acts will not advance their cause or achieve their ends. Yet in spite of this they continue to do these things.

So this madness of suicide has become a common phenomenon among the majority of people, and this question I do not know how to answer. Either there is a remedy for improving the human mindset or else there is no remedy and it is time for our world to be destroyed— its time has come: the need to destroy the world due to our collective karmic force. Nobody is able to make a pronouncement on this.

It is very evident that in this case even knowledge is of no use for self-improvement. That is proved clearly. I remember the statement by a former President of the United States, who clearly said that while the environment is very important, the American lifestyle cannot be compromised. And if their lifestyle cannot be compromised, then environmental destruction is inevitable. So this dichotomy and this tendency to self-destruction—I don't know how it came into the mindset of humanity.

A few years back I was talking to a person from America and I asked him whether he was aware that the planet would be completely destroyed if we do not become more environmentally aware, and he replied (and I think that his answer represents the mindset of the majority of people in modern society)—he said: "Yes, I know it is very dangerous but I am confident that there will not be any disaster during my lifetime. I can sustain myself and, after that, who cares. . . ?"

This is [laughs in amazement] the common attitude! And this was several years ago. Now at this moment I don't know whether anybody can still say, "During my lifetime nothing will happen," if we continue to destroy the environment on the present scale. A disaster might well occur, even during our lifetime.

So it is a crucial time for all sensible people who are peace-loving and care for all living beings on this small planet, to come together and try to educate the rest, and at the same time to try to do something to preserve the environment, each individual doing what he or she can.

For example, there is a movement in India which encourages people to plant one tree every year. By implementing such small initiatives we can improve the environment to a certain degree. And this is only one example. If one individual can somehow reduce the damage to the environment, reduce pollution for instance—in these ways an individual can contribute significantly. Each individual can contribute and should think about what he or she can do. And some individuals can do a great deal. Otherwise there is no hope.

One final thing I want to add here is that the outer environment is prevented from preservation due to the degradation of our inner environment. Unless we are able to improve our inner environment our efforts will not be very fruitful. Therefore each individual should try to improve their inner environment and at the same time to act to preserve or improve the outer environment. Both should go hand in hand, otherwise we are only improving our outer environment, and this will carry us only so far.

Appendix: Extracts from an interview with Kalpana Sharma: "I Have Lost Faith in Modern Science" (Published in *The Hindu*, Aug. 15, 1999).

I have realized that there are several shortcomings in science. Science has taken nature as a challenge. It regards it as the enemy. It assumes that man can overpower and use nature as he likes. This, I believe, is the root cause of environmental degradation and ecological imbalance.

Scientists think we can use nature as we like, and if natural resources are exhausted, we can find something else or they can be substituted. This is a wrong notion. Modern scientific enquiry is based on limited consciousness. People have not realized that the brain is after all a physical thing. Yet they treat the brain as the mind, as consciousness. They do not realize its limitations, its shortcomings, its conditioning. With this conditioned mind they have tried to search for the unlimited. But this has been an external inquiry, not an internal one. People take for granted that their consciousness, and the instrument with which they see, that is the eye, is perfectly alright. But this is only a partial reality, not the whole of it. It is a big illusion.

Without seeing the full reality, and even though people acknowledge that science is always changing, yet they assert that what they say is right. But look at modern medicines. These are tested and you are told you can have them. Yet two or even 20 years later you are told that these same drugs are harmful. With such limited knowledge, taking so much for granted, they are spreading blind faith amongst people. I say that as much as religion has spread blind faith, there is as much blind faith in science.

When they are conducting research, scientists do not think that what emerges from this inquiry is common, public knowledge. Instead they say, if I discover this, it is my property. This talk about intellectual property doesn't sit well with our [Tibetan Buddhist] culture. If we find something, we share that with everyone. And knowledge is universal. This effort to individualize knowledge indicates that the research is selfish. Whatever is there is mine, it should remain in my ownership. I should have control over it. So it begins with the intention of controlling nature, and if something is found it is regarded as personal property. Now even people are being seen as a resource. Because of this attitude I have lost faith in modern science.

People say that science is neutral and that it depends on how you use it. But on one side you have unlimited development of technology, on the other you have an exploitation-free society. These two concepts do not go together. Unlimited development of technology is essentially based on competition and exploitation. As long as there is competition, it cannot lead to an exploitation-free or violence-free society.

INTERNATIONAL INFLUENCE AND EXPANSIONISM

DR: The global game of regional and extra-regional influence and expansionism is as old as civilization itself. History abounds with examples of conquest and imperialism, and the most exemplary instance of such policies in the West is the Roman Empire and the ideal of the Pax Romana in terms of which expansionism and occupation are justified by the claim that the superpower is bringing the benefits of civilization to the territories which they invade and dominate.

This is an ongoing pattern in Western and in global history, the most recent example being the European colonialism of the previous five centuries. Today we see this tendency modernized in the policies of big nations, where the tendency to expansionism is practiced by means of the manipulation of economies.

However, this mainly economic approach does not rule out resort to covert aggression and open warfare. There are obvious parallels between the ancient Pax Romana and the modern Pax Americana, with the European Union standing by as a rather helpless onlooker.

Pragmatists might argue that there is no alternative to expansionism and neo-imperialism if the world is to be brought to a state of international peace and cooperation. Our history seems proof of this argument.

But is this view valid? Are there alternatives to the principles of expansionism and domination, even when such conquest is disguised or interpreted as a beneficial invasion?

RINPOCHE: This is a very complex and complicated question. Everyone interprets these things in a different way. No invader or expansionist accepts that they have done something wrong. On the contrary, they always try to justify their actions.

More particularly, imperialistic people always think that it is their legitimate duty towards the people whom they are invading or over whom they are expanding their dominance or whose countries they are occupying. They like to claim that, without their rule or occupation, the invaded people cannot enjoy their own rights, they cannot develop themselves, they cannot civilize themselves.

And in this regard I think that the indoctrination is so powerful that many well-educated people genuinely believe in it and do not doubt the intentions or actions of their imperialist leaders. They really feel that it is their legitimate duty to democratize or civilize the world.

When Tibet was invaded in 1904—exactly 100 years ago—by the British army, they had their own arguments as to how they were compelled and how they were left no other alternative but to take that military action. You will find chapter after chapter to justify their action. And people who do not know the truth, if they read these justifications, would be convinced that it had to be done for the good of the Tibetan people and for the good of British India.

And then of course Tibet was invaded in 1959 by Communist China. They had even more justificatory arguments: The Tibetan people were living completely in a dark age and needed to be liberated, that there was a great deal of torture, and the rights of the people were taken away by a few feudal landlords and feudal dictators. So it was their duty to sacrifice their lives in order to liberate the people of Tibet. And the Tibetan people are now considered to have been liberated. But even at that time many people in the communist army and Communist Party genuinely believed that they were liberating the Tibetan people.

This kind of political indoctrination, ideology, and brainwashing is very powerful. Maybe the top leaders know that they are serving their own ends, but very many ordinary people who are so powerfully indoctrinated just suspend their own wisdom to embrace a blind faith in the leadership and ideology.

I think that after some time of competition in political domination in the seventeenth, eighteenth, and nineteenth centuries, and particularly after the First and Second World Wars, the expansionists and the imperialists changed their methods somewhat. Perhaps it became necessary because some of the colonized nations became politically aware and regained their independence. But the expansionists found a new method to continue exercising their imperialist tendencies; that is, by so-called economic imperialism.

There are some small differences between political and economic imperialism, but economic imperialism is much more dangerous. If you are politically invaded and occupied by some other power you have certain legal, political, and social options to get rid of them and regain your own political power.

When you are overpowered by some other political power or military might, every individual of the occupied nation resents the invader or occupier. They do not accept them. And, secondly, they can consolidate themselves militarily or politically to regain independence as many occupied or colonized countries did in the last century. Dozens of countries became politically free from British or other domination.

Now economic domination is different. Firstly, it is actually much welcomed by those being "invaded." In the past India was also economically dominated at first and only later politically. The East Indian Company of merchants had, so to speak, purchased India, and this was inevitably followed by political domination. Today invasive economic domination is everywhere welcomed and accepted, and now it seems that there is no way to get rid of it.

If the so-called globalization process continues in this way, without any interruption, after another 50 or 100 years all possibility of regaining economic independence from this domination will be lost.

Resources are being completely manipulated and are in the hands of a very few people. The rest of the world is of course dependent on these resources controlled by the few. They either have to accept this or remain without food and other basic necessities. This is the situation that is being created.

In particular, the control over food production is very amazing and alarming. Genetic engineering in agriculture, genetically modified seed and chemical fertilization systems, are creating increasing dependence. If the whole population of the world were to come under this domination, then you either starve or are forced to depend on these seed-sellers and the few instances which control the chemical fertilization industry—and so on. And this principle can be seen developing not only in the food industry, but in every sphere.

Education is being controlled. Transfer of all kinds of necessary commodities is being controlled. So there's no end to it—I need not go into greater detail.

So I am quite clearly convinced that the only remedy for this situation is to give up or renounce dependence on outside production and to become self-sufficient and localized with regard to communal needs. Localization is of crucial importance against growing globalization. And we shall have to equip ourselves as individuals and as communities, however small they may be.

We must have a piece of land to cultivate food for ourselves and we must have some animals to support us, and we must produce our own clothes. Food, shelter, and clothing: these three basic needs; we will have to become independent with regard to them. We will have to consider how to protect these from globalization, to sustain at least this level of independence from domination.

This is the only reason I insistently try to persuade the Tibetan refugees living in India to promote their own organic agriculture in order to get rid of the dependence on seed, fertilizer, pesticides, and outside marketing. We must have our own seed banks, our own compost fertilizer, and so forth, in order to become self-sufficient with regard to food. So this is one small way of localizing things as far as possible.

Then with regard to healthcare systems: the traditional and non-chemical medicines must be preserved and promoted. This is very necessary. If we become self-sufficient and self-supporting in these areas, then we don't mind being dependent on outside instances for lesser needs such as communications or travel. We can accept a small degree of dependence temporarily, but ultimately even that kind of dependence should be avoided. By these ways we can resist domination.

And economic domination needs to be resisted because, if it is not resisted, there will be either a catastrophe to bring an end to this entire planet or, if it is not destroyed, there would be a complete dehumanization of humanity.

And once humanity is dehumanized by this culture of consumerism, then it makes no difference whether humanity continues to exist or not. Therefore we shall have to resist this kind of domination in order to save humanity, to preserve the humanness of humanity.

POWER

DR: The stability of the world order is said to be founded on balance of power, and such power—economic, military, and technological—is supposed to be used for the preservation, growth, and defense of nations.

However, we are again increasingly witnessing the use of power in policies of offence rather than defense and the world is once again in the opening phases of the political doctrine of imperialism, with large national powers vying for spheres of influence and control.

In such a world, what can powerless peoples do to defend themselves? Is it inevitable that all nations need constantly to be increasing their own power in order to survive and stave off the possibility of invasion, whether economic or military? Such a cycle can only lead to increased aggression and conflict. How can this be remedied?

RINPOCHE: This question includes so many other questions with which we have to deal separately.

First of all, power is evil; we have to understand that. No power can be positive, no power can be good. This is a certainty. I am not talking about the power of wisdom or the power of the Buddha Nature—these are not necessarily a form of power; they are an energy.

But all worldly political or economic power is necessarily evil. And so much of it is an illusion, an indoctrination of people by people with vested interests. Number one: there is no need to build up power. The need to build up power for communities, nations, or countries is a great delusion, a great deceit. There's no need of power.

And once power has been developed it can never be balanced. Power is not a commodity which can be weighed, equalized, and balanced. Nobody would accept a balancing of power.

In the past Russia and America were trying to compete and people thought that there could be a balance of power; should Russia become equal to America, then there would be a balance of power. But if Russia were to have become equal in power to America, then in fact America would immediately act to move one step ahead. They would never have been content to remain in static balance. Either America or Russia must be ahead. So, if a balance of power were ever achieved, it might last a day or two.

Now Russia has lost her power and world power has become a sort of monopolar dynamic with complete absence of balance. Now China and other groups of countries, jointly or separately, are trying to balance it. But I don't think it will ever be balanced.

It will always remain in competition and this competition happens at the cost of countless anonymous human lives. A large section of humanity will be deprived of food, shelter, clothing, and medicines because the resources for these are needed and are being consumed for increasing and intensifying power, and to build up that power for balance or imbalance, whatever the case may be.

Then there is also illusion for the smaller nations. There are many smaller nations for whom there is no logical necessity for maintaining a military force, yet they spend a large portion of their resources for weaponry and military purposes. We can see this in Bhutan and in Nepal for instance.

They are both absolutely small countries and are surrounded by incomparably huge nations in terms both of population and military power. Bhutan and Nepal are both between India and China. And if there were to be a military danger from either India or China, they would not be able to defend themselves even if their entire populations took up arms. There is absolutely no way they could defend themselves militarily in either case. Still they maintain a military force in the name of defense—but how will they defend? And they spend a lot on their military.

In the case of Nepal right now, three-quarters of the country is ruled by Maoists and only one quarter—just the capital—is ruled by the monarchy or so-called legitimate government. But still they spend a lot of money on their military, a military which is unable to control their own civil unrest. They cannot even control the militants inside their own borders. So it is very clear that spending money on the military and purchase of weapons in the case of these small nations, and others like them, is absurd.

In the past Tibet had a military—and again here is proof that this exercise is absolutely unjustifiable. There's no logic in it. But still people think they need it for the sake of the nation, for self-defense. In reality, however, they cannot defend themselves—absolutely not.

Then with regard to the bigger nations: why can they not become friendly and assure each other that there will be no military aggression or military disturbance among themselves? The whole standard of living in those countries could immediately be raised.

Take India and Pakistan, for example. India and Pakistan have fought three wars in the last 50 years, and they know that these wars can bring no final solution, no definitive victory or defeat. It will simply go on—but still they are competing. And even though the uselessness of their wars is fully understood, they are not able to give it up.

So the unjustifiable and irrational aspect of these wars and power-struggles, and their essential illegitimacy, have not prevented these people from spending a great amount of money and resources for weaponry and military force.

I think that the only instance which is thriving on war at this time is the commercial side of the weapons industry, and it is de-conscienced and has become a profitable trade. Wars can be created together with the constant fear of wars by very few people manipulating some information and the behavior of others. In that way they can consistently create distrust and fear of war among the nations. And that makes for an open market for the weapons industry.

Therefore what we should know is that power is unnecessary, balance of power is impossible, and nations cannot defend themselves by military means alone. So these three doctrines or concepts of balance of power or defense of nations or acquiring the power necessary to build and defend a nation are all misconceptions and there is no truth in them. Unless the full untruth of these notions is understood the world can never achieve peace or harmony.

VIOLENCE AND WAR

DR: The most fundamental distinction to be made in the case of war is that of offensive and defensive violence. Most people and most moral or religious systems would agree that there are instances when wars of defense are unavoidable.

In the modern world, with its complex dynamics of international interdependence and alliances, it is difficult to make a valid distinction between offensive or defensive wars. For instance, are wars fought on behalf of an ally offensive or defensive? Or, can preemptive warfare be categorized as defensive?

But even if we were able to lay down very precise guidelines, there would still be those who condemn all warfare per se. Why is it that, after thousands of years of experiencing the horrors of war, we are still unable to escape this massive resort to violence in solving international problems?

Is war an indispensable part of our total international interaction? Is there no way to transcend the apparent need to go to war, even in the case of defensive war? Is there a practicable alternative to violence in maintaining social and global order?

RINPOCHE: War and violence cannot defend anyone. That is very definite. We have to understand this reality—it is a fact. Take the simple example of two people quarrelling with each other and both of them capable of killing the other. In this case, whoever is able to attack the other more swiftly, to attack first, would kill the other, and that would constitute a "win." And either of them would argue that they killed the other in order to defend themselves: "I was not on the offensive but I was defending myself and there was no way out unless I killed him, or he would have killed me." So this might be the argument of either person, and it can be extended to groups and peoples and nations.

But in this example one human life had to be lost. It could not be defended or saved by either of the quarrelling parties. Nor did the killer defend himself from indulging in the act of killing. Neither of the parties could save both lives; one life had to go. And in this case it is more justifiable: at least one life is saved.

But in the bigger, more comprehensive wars which involve thousands of military personnel and also larger territories, in these cases also, to defend oneself by means of violence remains a matter of either winning or losing. As a matter of fact, it is all loss. There can be no winning.

When China invaded Tibet, very brave Tibetan people fought a very tough war against China's military for several years. The Tibetan guerrilla warfare continued from 1951 till around the end of the 1960s. For about 20 years there was a war of resistance. But the result was absolutely nil: loss of so many people's lives, accumulation of so much negative Karma. The only result it did have was a justification for the People's Republic of China to increase repression, to crack down on the people on the basis that there was violent resistance or violent counter-revolutionary activity, an excuse to use force. All they achieved was to provide a "justification" or excuse for the People's Republic of China to increase their violent tactics, and this at the cost of the lives of the Tibetan resistance.

I do respect their boldness and their courage and their determination and their intention to save the country and its culture. All these actions were taken in good faith and they are commendable. In spite of that, however, they were actually not able to defend anything. They lost.

And even supposing that the Tibetan resistance movement had been able to keep the Chinese forces away for quite some time, or even if, due to their resistance, we had not lost our freedom or independence for a long time, that would still only have been a postponement of the inevitable outcome. The hatred and greed in the mind of China would never have been eliminated by our violent defense. Through violent defense you may be able to defend yourself or your country for a temporary period of time, but you will continue to live in fear because you can never defend yourself permanently or completely by violent means.

Pakistan and India are a very clear example of this. Pakistan is feverishly building up its defenses, even though its people are dying of deprivation. The Pakistani people raised a slogan which is very funny, and they said, "No matter if we have to eat grass, we shall build an atomic bomb." [Laughs dumbfounded] We shall eat grass! We'll live on grass! But we must build the atomic bomb. . .

So they think they are defending themselves and they are actually not able to defend themselves, and every day and every night they pass under fear and suspicion: When will India attack? When will somebody attack?

Real defense should mean that one can live without fear and feel secure, and that kind of security can never be built up by military force or achieved by counter-violence. Although it may not be acceptable to any so-called nations, true defense lies in the ability to completely surrender. Gandhi maintained that when you are attacked, you should just surrender, just refuse to react violently.

That is similar to certain tactics used in wrestling or karate; in some martial arts you are required to simply withdraw from a force coming from one side so that the attacker loses his balance. This is only a metaphor. Violence cannot continue for a very long time if there is no counter-violence. The violent agent will become ashamed and unable to continue to act out violence.

Violence can only be prolonged by counter-violence, whether offensive or defensive. That provides ongoing cause for violence as well as justifications and excuses for continuation of violence. That is quite clear.

Once one side refuses to indulge in violence, no matter whether it is repelled or killed, if it refuses to resort to violence, that is, I think, the real defense of inner strength, the real defense of inner human values. Inner humanness can only be defended by refusing to indulge in violence on account of violence or fear of violence. That is the only way to defend oneself completely.

AMERICA AND THE SUPERPOWER PRINCIPLE

DR: The beginning of this millennium is marked by heavy, unrestrained influence and aggression on the part of the world's only remaining superpower, the U.S.A. It is as though the initial weave of global socio-political policies for this millennium is marred by a fundamental defect that will carry through the entire tapestry. This defect is the ideal of a new world order imposed on the globe by America.

On the one hand, we can admire the Americans for their very strong support of freedom and democracy, and this includes their support of Tibet. On the other hand, their support of these ideals is always laden with self-interest, hypocrisy, and violent unilateral action.

Clearly America will continue to play a huge role in world affairs in the future, in the same way that the Romans did in ancient times. In other words, America is in the business of putting together a modern form of empire.

The superpower game is dangerous and shifting. It can lead to wars the like of which we have never yet known. How can the Americans and other aspiring superpowers be brought to see the self-defeating dynamic at the heart of their ambitions? Is it realistic to think that they might abandon the superpower aspiration?

RINPOCHE: As we discussed earlier, I always consider that all so-called power in this modern world is an evil in itself. And, of course, when that power becomes a superpower it becomes a super-evil, and it must be opposed.

If the world wants to live in a peaceful and harmonious way, then the concepts of power and superpower must be absent. As long as the concepts of power and superpower and balancing of power or competition for power continue to exist, they will remain the real causes and also the effects of imbalance, disharmony, and violence. Competition is always a violence. There cannot be a non-violent competition.

Therefore none of the nations should try to become more powerful than others or aspire to become superpowers—that is for sure. And at the same time it is also a law of nature that no single nation can remain powerful or remain a superpower. The nations may remain as big or small as they are; that may not change very rapidly, at least in terms of geographical area and relative size of the population—these may remain constant for a long time. But economic and political power in the international scenario, international energies: these will always keep changing.

At this moment it appears that the U.S.A. might remain the only superpower in the world. I think this is just an illusion held by many people, particularly by the leaders of the U.S.A. Today they might be the only superpower, but they also might be only at the beginning of their decline. It will always change.

Arrogance and pride are the quickest causes of the downfall of any institution or any individual. It is the biggest obstacle to spiritual development, the kind of attitude which assumes: "I am the only power and I do not care for anything." This kind of arrogant attitude is knowingly and unknowingly sitting in the minds of the leadership of the powerful nations. And, therefore, they do not hesitate to ignore public opinion and they do not hesitate to violate international norms and laws, and they also do not hesitate to ignore the resolutions or decisions of the U.N.O., or to stop them by veto.

So this is the biggest weakness for a nation, and it will bring down any nation, including superpowers. And the principle of change will always be there. Once there is a superpower, many nations commit themselves to competing with it, which may result in another superpower or the destruction of the present superpower and its replacement by another superpower.

At this moment the leadership of China is already thinking that China must become equal with America, that America should not be allowed to remain the only superpower. Even if China does not become the only superpower, they feel that they must balance the American power. This kind of intention and determination on the part of China is clear. They are always talking about it in their media.

In this process the tendency is sometimes to join with the weaker ones and oppose the arrogant strong one. This is an unenlightened tendency, and at this time many small nations might join with those nations strong enough to challenge the hitherto unchallenged superpower. And perhaps in the international scenario it is already beginning to happen.

Yes, I do agree that it was unfortunate that the beginning of the new millennium was marked by the expression or assertion of unchallenged superpower authority, and as a result it may lead the whole millennium in the wrong direction.

This does not have to be the case, however. It was unfortunate that it happened, but there is always the chance to change it, remedy it, and alter course, if right thinking people wish to alter it. Then there is a possibility to make a new start.

As I mentioned before, today the number of people who support peaceful co-existence is increasing, and the realization that peace can only be maintained by peaceful means is also growing. The concept of peace-keeping by force and the concept that peace can be enforced by a superpower which would be the keeper of the peace in the world— these concepts are now disappearing. People are beginning to realize that there is no truth in them. That peace cannot be kept by violence or by force, and that peace must be maintained by peaceful means: the realization is growing among ordinary people that this principle is an inescapable law of nature. And because of this growing realization, the concept of superpower will not find support among the majority of enlightened, realized human beings.

Yes, I do agree that America supports the Tibetan cause, but that support is also, I think, not a complete one. The good intentions of their support need to be brought to a completeness. We have had so many different experiences dealing with American support over the last 48 years.

Some of our experiences appear to suggest that their support is not necessarily based on moral and ethical norms. So we need more support from people who support the Tibetan cause without any political motivation, who only support it because it is a truthful and just cause: to support the Tibetan cause for the sake of truth and justice. This is the real support that we need. Support as part of a wider political strategy can always change as the strategy changes. So we can't rely on it.

But another thing I would add here is that, as with any other country, America is a country where the majority of the people are good people. So we Tibetans enjoy sincere and strong support from the people of America—and that support will always remain. Their support is not politically motivated and their support is not for selfish ends. Their support is for justice and fairness, and support of the truth. Therefore it will remain.

And since America is by-and-large a democratic country—not a perfect one—but by-and-large it is democratic, with elections held every four years and so forth, and since the leadership needs to align its opinion with public opinion, the leadership will also remain supportive to satisfy their own voters, their own people.

So the support of the people is more important than governmental support. People's support comes from their hearts. So we should not blame America as a whole for its shortcomings. America has many good and wise people, and so many enlightened people who have achieved many good things in the fields of science and technology, as well as spiritual people and teachers, and so forth. And we recognize these things.

The leadership is sometimes very difficult, but a nation cannot be judged merely by its leadership. The disposition of the people and the people's culture are also very important qualities by which a nation can be assessed.

So finally, if we want to have a good future, then we shall have to give up the notions of power and superpower and we must abandon the notions that balance of power or sheer force can keep the peace: these two misconceptions must be abandoned.

TOOTHLESS INTERNATIONAL LAW

DR: Although our modern world is supposed to be regulated by an intricate body of international law we do not see much evidence that the world as a whole is inclined to conform to such legislation. Most people today would view the institutions which are supposed to uphold international law, for instance, the U.N.O., as powerless and, what is worse, selective and hypocritical in their application of international laws.

International law has not put a stop to unfair economic practices, nor to expansionism, nor to war. It is increasingly flouted by the powerful nations, including Western governments.

Does international law have a substantive role to play in re-shaping our global society into something more compassionate or do we have to find tools which reach deeper into the meaning of human existence?

RINPOCHE: As we discussed a little the other day, I feel that all man-made laws, laws which have been formally enacted by human beings, have no inbuilt mechanism for enforcing themselves. Therefore they are bound to be violated sooner or later. And so-called international laws are much weaker than national laws.

Firstly, international law has a lot of loopholes and unclarity and can be interpreted in a number of different ways, to such an extent that an international law can be violated by a given nation while that nation responds that it is not guilty of any violation or cannot be blamed for violating a particular international law.

A recent example was the attack upon Iraq by the U.S.A. and some of its allies. Now the Secretary General of the U.N.O. has clearly said that it was a violation of international law and of the U.N Charter, but nobody bothers, and they were still able to justify their illegal actions. And there's no mechanism for taking them to task or to enforce any of these so-called international laws.

The United Nations is considered to be the highest institution for enforcing international law or for protecting the weaker nations and supervising the smooth running of the Committee of Nations and guarding the sovereignty of the nations themselves. But as a matter of fact the U.N. is itself one of the most undemocratic, dictatorial institutions available in this world. Around 200 nations are considered to be its members, but decisions are carried out by only one big powerful nation, and no-one can say or do anything about that.

So how can we expect from such an institution or body of lawlessness that it protect international law or supervise or enforce international law among the nations? In this regard the international situation is absolutely hopeless.

Here again I am of the opinion that nations should be self-sufficient and self-supporting—a Swaraj, a real Swaraj in accordance with the Gandhian ideal. The only real way to peaceful co-existence of nations is firstly by not transgressing one's own laws, and then showing equal respect to other nations by not violating or interfering in their laws.

There can be an international code of conduct if possible, but if the conduct of nations and the ways of governing nations remain as they are, I think it is impossible to have effective international law. If you could have good national laws, that would be sufficient. It is impossible to maintain international law.

THE IDEAL

DR: After thousands of years of civilization, with its recurrent cycles of violence and injustice extending to the present, most people have become cynical about the possibility of establishing an ideal society. Such an ideal is considered to be in complete contrast to what human nature is capable of.

We seem to have learned nothing from our history. The only real difference today lies in the potential of our technology to bring about misery and destruction on a scale never before possible.

Still, it is worth asking what the essential qualities of the ideal society should be. And can these be achieved? What realistic steps can we take to decrease suffering and injustice in the world?

RINPOCHE: First of all I would agree that the world, with a population of unenlightened people having ignorance, hatred, attachment, and so forth, having such mental defilements, cannot hope that a perfectly non-violent and law-abiding society can be established. That is impossible. We shall have to accept the impossibility of an absolutely ideal society having no crime and no violation of any moral codes and so forth.

The highest level of human civilization should rather be considered in terms of much decreased levels of violence and crime, with the majority of people living in equality and happiness. And we can hope for and establish that kind of society.

But unless and until the entire defilement of mind is eradicated, you cannot hope for or even conceive of a society of perfect stillness. If this were possible, then why should spiritual people go away from the world and try to transcend the world and attain Nirvana, the escape from the cycle of rebirth and suffering.

Spiritual transformation always begins from the unmanageability of Samsara or worldliness, and worldliness has its own kinds of inbuilt or concomitant defects. And of course we can reduce these to their possible minimum and increase the positive aspects to the maximum, but 100% perfection in society is indeed mere utopianism: it cannot be achieved. That we have to understand. This very unachievability of utopia is the basis of spirituality, otherwise there would be no need of spirituality.

A VIEW ON THIS MILLENNIUM

DR: The first years of the new millennium have already disappointed all our hopes. The world is again hardening into an indifferent pragmatism which turns away from human suffering, from the suffering of all creatures, and from damage done to the planet, to embrace the principles of power and economic gain as being of prime importance. Peace and freedom have become mere slogans of political spin. As our social order hardens we seem to respond with a growing apathy.

In every sense, and especially in the moral sense, we have reached what might be termed the maturity of the age of compromise. All socio-political and ethical issues are tailored to reach consensus at any cost. In this process intrinsic truth, intrinsic justice, and intrinsic right and wrong are being abandoned.

Besides the question how we can improve our societies and the health of our ecology, the more realistic question may well be: How must we improve our mindset and behavior in order simply to ensure that we and our planet survive for another 1,000 years?

RINPOCHE: This is a very big question and I do not know if I am able to respond to it properly. I am not competent to respond to it. But I must confess that I am not an optimistic person with regard to these questions, and at the same time I am not certain of my judgments on this issue.

I believe very strongly in the force of collective Karma of the living beings on this earth. And this collective Karma has always been a mixture of positive and negative. Sometimes the positive Karma became more powerful and negative Karma could be postponed or overpowered, and things became better. And sometimes it has been the reverse: negative Karma becoming more powerful and hampering and affecting the power of positive Karma, and most things going wrong.

I clearly remember that from 1999 various people began to ask His Holiness the Dalai Lama to give a millennium message, and then there was also a dispute about which date was actually the beginning of the new millennium: 1st January 2000 or 1st January 2001? Many people considered that 2001 was actually the beginning of the new millennium, and other people who were in a hurry [chuckles] said, "No, no, 2000 is the beginning of the new millennium."

But His Holiness was consistently saying that it does not matter whether it begins in 2000 or 2001; the important question was whether we would change on that day. Would we leave behind all our negative emotions and mental defilements on the first day of the millennium, would our minds become purified with all the negative emotions left behind, and would we start anew, afresh, without any arrogance, hatred, vengeance, and so forth?

If that were so, we could speak of a new millennium, otherwise it would just be a matter of time continuing in the same old way. If people from the past millennium continue, without changing their lifestyle as well as their mindset, then an old or new millennium cannot by itself make this world better or worse.

Things are made better or worse by living beings, and in particular by human beings. The other living beings are quite innocent; they do not make much fuss. But things are changed a great deal due to the behavior of humanity and particularly by the modern, educated, so-called civilized humanity, mainly because we have accumulated to the umpteenth power technology which could destroy this earth several times over.

And at the same time the defiled mind, the unenlightened mind, the mind influenced by hatred and attachment, has become stronger because negative emotions have been exploited and amplified by so much external conditioning and the desire for external possessions.

So it appears to me to be a very dangerous time, more dangerous than ever before. As we discussed earlier, in ancient times people did fight, people did have hatred, but they killed each other in much smaller numbers. And they did not destroy the basic ecosystem, they did not destroy much of the environment.

Wars were won and lost and if they were lost the defeat was accepted, and if they won all accepted the victory and then things continued without much conflict. It was like this in the past because institutions and amenities were localized and aspirations were kept within the natural human capacity. There was not much technology for power and therefore people were killed in their thousands, not in their millions. Then they could more easily go on to become reconciled.

They also did not have greed much beyond their reach, and today that is not the same. Human greed has increased a million times because of the arrogance of the technology of power, the scientific technology of power. People now begin to think that they can do all sorts of impossible things through technology—"Everything is possible for me if I invent some new technology and apply it to my ambition." This kind of arrogance is growing.

As a result the scope of hatred and greed has been greatly enlarged, together with the increase of other negative emotions, their enlargement in individual minds, and their extension into society. And in this situation, generally speaking, the millennium seems to be heading for a very dark age. Our experience of the first years of this millennium may be an indication of how things will go ahead.

But at the same time there are also many visible positive signs. His Holiness has mentioned recently that in the past, if some government or nation declared a war, not a single citizen of that nation would oppose it, and if someone did oppose it they would be labeled unpatriotic. Therefore they were compelled to be supportive. This situation was prevalent during the First World War and largely during the Second World War. If someone opposed it, they could not do so openly. So that kind of social mindset was there. Once a nation was at war each one of the citizens was supposed to support that war for the sake of national defense or national pride, and nobody could speak against it for fear of being labeled unpatriotic.

That is changing, if not completely. At least we see signs of change in this. And perhaps we should thank the democratic system, however defective it may be: people can voice their inner feelings without much fear or hesitation.

In 2003, before the start of the Iraq war, all over the world—not only in England and America, but in Asia, Africa, Latin America—all over the world, in large and in small nations, the majority of people came out against it. In India not millions came out, but thousands definitely came out. And in Europe millions came out on the street, and in America and Latin America millions of people expressed their unhappiness and their opposition to that war.

It is another question whether or not they were able to stop that war. They were not able to stop it. But one positive sign is that they had the courage and they had the intention to speak out against it. And they were not labeled as unpatriotic; so that kind of bad custom is no longer visible.

So if these positive things continue to increase we will gradually be able to influence the mindset of the mischief-makers. If we are able to network and consolidate this pro-peace and anti-conflict feeling, then that kind of mindset can be consolidated and asserted in the right way. Then I think this millennium might be a good one, a millennium of peaceful co-existence.

It is possible; we should not yet say it is impossible or too late. Certain things we do consider too late, such as the condition of the environment, the damage to the ozone layer: I don't know whether modern technology can repair it. But still we can stop further damage if now, at this moment, some positive action can be taken.

And I am happy that Russia has now signed the Kyoto Protocol. Still, one can doubt whether they will definitely implement the conditions of the protocol or not, but it is a good sign that one of the big nations, at least, wants to agree to the essence of the Kyoto Protocol. And, now, only the U.S.A. is out of that agreement, but they may gradually agree to accept the Protocol and begin to change their lifestyle.

So good signs are there and danger is also definitely there; hope and threat, both are there. We are at a crossroads. We can still choose the right direction, that possibility is not completely lost. But it is a very crucial time and a very dangerous time if humanity does not choose the right path. Then destruction is inevitable; huge destruction so that this earth might be made unfit for habitation by any living beings, including human beings. This possibility is also very clearly there.

I think it was Einstein who said that he was unsure what level of destruction might be wrought by the Third World War if it ever occurs, but that definitely the Fourth World War would be fought with sticks and stones. And I think that the general view of scientists is that this danger is present.

So much compiling and upgrading of destructive weapons: poor Saddam Hussein was accused of having weapons of mass destruction [laughs] but there are hundreds of bigger Saddam Husseins in power in this world and in possession of much vaster caches of weapons of mass destruction. And up to the present they are not willing to stop experimenting and upgrading. There is no talk of destroying these weapons.

Therefore destruction can also come by accident. We have compiled so many dangerous weapons, and accidents have already happened. For instance, during the loading of weapons in New Delhi recently, 10 people were killed by an accidental explosion. So these kinds of accidents can happen to people who are simply handling explosive weaponry. And this is nothing in comparison to the much worse possibilities of nuclear accidents.

The course of the millennium is entirely up to us human beings. We need to educate and train people in an open and honest way about the dangers we are creating for the planet and all living beings on it, and we need to remind them that they can be transformed to more positive patterns of behavior and mindset. The consistent degradation of the environment is very prolonged; global warming has increased dramatically. And the consequences are severe changes in weather patterns, no snow when it should occur, no rain when it should be raining—and just in my lifetime, since 1960 when we arrived in Dharamsala, including lower Dharamsala, there were no extremes of weather; the climate was very soothing with no extremes of hot and cold as it is today. This kind of rapid change within a short period of only 40 years is very common. And of course in the 60s and 70s wherever we went we could drink water from the taps or from the wells and from the rivers, but today you have to drink bottled water.

So this much degradation in the very basic needs of people has led to scarcity of these naturally available resources. This is very alarming. So at this crossroads I think NOW is the time for either the positive or negative forces to gain the upper hand that will change the course of the future within no time.

So each individual or human being at this moment has a very heavy responsibility, an onerously important responsibility to be accountable for saving the earth, for saving all the living beings on this earth, and in order to save the cultural diversity and many good institutions—perhaps we can call it our civilization; civilization is a very tricky word—but there is so much to lose in terms of the good things we have created: art, architecture, spirituality, music, dance, monuments; so many of these things are important and abundant on the earth, and they too can be destroyed.

We have to act to save these things. And for that purpose the message of love and compassion, the message of cooperation, are absolutely essential; and spiritual leaders like His Holiness the Dalai Lama—and I am given hope by the fact that wherever His Holiness goes many people voluntarily come to hear his message. That shows two things: Number one, the essential human approach or attitude is not for violence but for peace. Because of that they are attracted by His Holiness because he gives only a simple message of non-violence and kindness, and his books are being read by the millions. So it shows that there is a basic inclination within the human mind looking for non-violence and peace, and that is only the social outcome.

And we have to consolidate that kind of human approach, human inner tendency: we have to consolidate them and give them a voice, and we have to give them a standing ground to avoid the coming destruction.

And for that matter, as His Holiness has offered a 5-Point Peace Plan for the Tibetan cause, I think that this 5-Point peace program is universally applicable. To declare this small planet as a zone of Ahimsa and demilitarize and disarm—that is, to genuinely disarm—so that all dangerous weapons could be reduced and destroyed gradually, to make this earth livable, free from dangerous military activities, make a zone of Ahimsa.

This kind of disarmament and demilitarization can be undertaken on both a large and small scale. For example, at grassroots level in India, many village people have been disarmed. They used to have guns but have been persuaded to hand them over. If disarming the village is possible, then disarming the nation is also possible. This is absolutely plausible.

And the second point of the 5-Point program is to make Tibet an environmental sanctuary; and so the whole earth can also be turned into a sanctuary for the environment, for environmental preservation and preservation of ecosystems. That will benefit not only humanity but all living beings.

Then the third is to stop human rights violations. And human rights violations are continuing in the post-millennium world—the change of millennium has not affected human rights violations in our so-called civilization. Not only in China and North Korea, or not only in Cuba; even the so-called democratic nations such as those of Europe and America: they too practice violations of human rights. So a sincere effort to improve the human rights situation, and for that we shall have to improve the human sense of duty. If everyone minds their own duty, the human rights problem will automatically go away; otherwise we are only concentrating on rights and forgetting about duty and responsibility, and then nothing can improve. So the implementation of human duty and the sense of universal responsibility, these need to be improved.

Then the fourth point His Holiness speaks about is the population transfer (of Chinese into Tibet) which is dangerous for Tibet. And in this world today there is a great population transfer and demographic change taking place in various parts. In India the villages are emptying and all the big cities become overcrowded, and day in and day out, day and night, the slums are piling up. If you go to Mumbai, the city is empty in comparison with the surrounding slums: huge unlimited slums you can see from an aircraft. So these kinds of things—where people are moving from villages to cities, from developing countries to developed countries, and from East to West and from North to South—the population transfer has been tremendously increased. And this should also be checked, and people should be free to travel as tourists or seekers or researchers, but complete transfer of habitation from one place to another brings about imbalance in the whole.

Therefore localization is important: people should remain in and improve their own areas of residence, rather than simply seeking a change of living place. So just as this question must be addressed in the context of China and Tibet, it is also applicable to the whole world. All the conflicts and disputes between human beings—of course human society cannot remain conflict-free—but these should be resolved through dialogue. Sit together, express your grievances, and then come to an understanding with each other, rather than simply abandoning your home. Accordingly the fifth point is the commencement of earnest negotiations on the future status of Tibet and of the relation between Tibetan and Chinese people.

In line with this approach we try to make a model for the world in our dealings with the huge Chinese power, the giant military machine; and that is absolutely not impossible. It is difficult but it is possible. There is no need of threatening or making wars. It is absolutely possible to settle disputes and conflicts through peaceful means. This should be understood by all people. His Holiness always says that the third millennium should be a millennium of dialogue, not war.

And if humanity is developed enough to understand good and bad, to discriminate between them, then they should opt for dialogue as the only means for resolving conflicts and disputes.

If through the efforts of all people we can work towards the establishment of such a society, then the third millennium can be a very beautiful, really evolved and developed millennium. The possibility is there; we cannot ignore it, and we should put all our effort into making it a good millennium.

A few years back a friend of mine wrote a book, and that book says that the third millennium should be a millennium of the Lord Buddha and the Mahatma Gandhi.

PART IV:

TIBET–THE MODERN WORLD'S HIDDEN TRAGEDY

INTRODUCTION

The Tibet issue is the skeleton in the world's closet, and the guilty stain in the collective unconscious of modern society. To the world's leaders and the institutions which are supposed to uphold international freedom it is a black reproach. The world community has largely written off the struggle of the Tibetan people to regain their freedom and self-determination, not because their cause is unjust, but because their struggle methodology is strictly non-violent.

Non-violent struggle is simply not newsworthy and places no pressure on politicians to act. It can safely be ignored because its response to being ignored will remain non-violent. As the only non-violent struggle in the world today we might expect it to be constantly held out in the media and in public consciousness as something unique and precious, and something that needs to be addressed with admiring determination. Instead, it is the suicide bombers and the sanctioned murder of large-scale warfare that compel our attention. Thus the Tibet question stands both as an indictment of our collective socio-political ethos and a questioning of our essential sanity.

Of course there are also pragmatic reasons for ignoring the issue. How often have we seen world leaders extricating themselves, often on ridiculous grounds, from meeting with H.H. the Dalai Lama? China is a political, military, and economic powerhouse which no world leader wants to cross. Moral cowardice plays a big role in the deafening silence over Tibet. But the deeper immorality is rooted in shallower ground: the prospect of doing business with China—the profit motive—is considered worth the sacrifice of the basic human rights of six million Tibetans.

How can such an international moral failure not have a negative impact on all of us? 1.2 million Tibetans have perished as a direct result of the Chinese invasion and subsequent oppression of their country. These conditions of oppression have endured for more than 50 years. In the meantime we revisit the horrors of the Holocaust, the injustices of Apartheid, and the violent turmoil of the Middle East. But Tibet, with its history of genocide at the hands of the Chinese regime, the theft of its territory, the plunder of its resources, and the obliteration of its deeply spiritual culture, are kept hidden from our sight. How can we refrain from ascribing this to collective moral imbecility?

THE INVASION AND OCCUPATION OF TIBET

On 1 October 1949 the People's Republic of China (PRC) was proclaimed in Peking. On 1 January 1950 the PRC promised to "liberate" Tibet. On 7 October 1950 the People's Liberation Army (PLA) invaded, halting its advance 100 km to the east of Lhasa, at what China claimed was the boundary of Central Tibet. The Tibetan Government was called on to send a delegation to Peking to negotiate Tibet's "peaceful liberation."

Although this act of aggression was brought to the United Nations General Assembly, it was decided to postpone the Tibet issue because many member states felt that a peaceful solution between Tibet and China was still possible. China's tactic of halting the PLA and calling on Tibet to negotiate was thus successful in defusing international criticism. The Tibetan Government was forced to send delegates to Beijing under threat of a continued advance of the PLA to Lhasa. Threatened with forcible conquest, the Tibetans agreed on 23 May 1951 on measures for the "peaceful liberation of Tibet," embodied in the 17-Point Agreement. As the International Commission of Jurists later recognized: "Tibet signed at pistol-point."

After the signing of the 17-Point Agreement, the PLA occupied Lhasa and Central Tibet. The Chinese Communist Party (CCP) created territorial divisions of Tibet, which contributed to the later Tibetan uprising. In 1955 Mao included the Tibetan provinces of Kham and Amdo in the "High Tide of Socialist Transformation." When the "democratic reforms" included forced public renunciation of respected Tibetan leaders and revered lamas, both areas erupted in revolt. In response, the Chinese introduced overwhelming numbers of troops.

As a means of quelling the uprising, Eastern Tibetans were collectivized during the "Great Leap Forward" of 1958. In March 1959 large numbers of Tibetans surrounded the Dalai Lama's summer residence outside Lhasa due to rumors that the Chinese were planning to kidnap him. Days of fighting ensued, and thousands of Tibetans were killed. Martial law was declared. The Dalai Lama fled to India, followed by some 80,000 Tibetans. Before crossing the border the Tibetan government repudiated the 17-Point Agreement. China immediately implemented "democratic reforms" throughout Tibet. By these reforms the CCP eliminated the Tibetan leadership and any who opposed Chinese rule. Lamas were arrested, monasteries depopulated and systematically looted. Out of 2,500 monasteries in the so-called Tibet Autonomous Region (TAR), 70 were left in 1962 and 93% of the monks forced out. In Eastern Tibet 98% of monasteries were closed.

The loss of life as a direct result of the invasion and occupation of Tibet during the period 1950-1976 has been estimated as follows: 173,221 Tibetans died in prisons and labor camps; 156,758 by execution; 342,970 by starvation; 432,705 in battles and uprisings; 92,731 by torture; and 9,002 by suicide.

TIBET AT THE UNITED NATIONS

On 9 September 1959, from exile in India, the Dalai Lama appealed Tibet's case to the United Nations. The appeal was based upon a violation of Tibetan independence, with a secondary appeal on humanitarian grounds, including dispossession of property, forced labor, mass murder, and persecution of religion.

Between 1959 and 1965 three resolutions concerning Tibet were passed by the U.N. General Assembly, the texts of which are all similar: "Gravely concerned at . . . the violation of fundamental human rights of the Tibetan people. . . . Solemnly renews its call for the cessation of practices which deprive the Tibetan people of their fundamental human rights and freedoms, including their right to self-determination."

The International Commission of Jurists (ICJ) also concluded, in regard to genocide, that evidence pointed to: a) a prima facie case of acts contrary to Article 2 (a) and (c) of the genocide convention, and, b) a prima facie case of a systematic intention by such acts and other acts to destroy in whole or in part the Tibetans as a separate nation.

THE CULTURAL REVOLUTION

In June 1966 Mao unleashed the Red Guards to destroy the "four olds" (old ideas, old culture, old tradition, old customs). The Cultural

Revolution was officially launched in Tibet on 25 August 1966, and every aspect of Tibetan culture came under attack.

Monasteries were plundered and defiled, religious texts used as inner shoe soles or toilet paper, printing blocks turned into floorboards or other objects degrading to religious sentiments. Private religious shrines were ordered to surrender all objects of value to the Chinese authorities.

"Reactionary" Tibetan customs and traditions were replaced by "socialist" Chinese styles. Tibetan songs were altered with revolutionary phrases, Tibetan dance and opera were replaced by Madame Mao's revolutionary operas. The Tibetan language was corrupted by adding a Chinese vocabulary intended to produce a "Sino-Tibetan Friendship Language."

Class struggle was fuelled by "thamzing" (struggle sessions) in which workers were set against employers, peasants against landlords, monks against abbots, students against teachers, in order to extract confessions from the accused. Then executions were carried out in groups of 18-20 people.

Communes were forcibly established by the PLA. By 1974 communes were reportedly established in 90% of Tibet's counties. From 1968-1973 Tibetans again suffered famine conditions due to communization, inept Chinese agricultural policies unsuited to Tibetan conditions, and confiscation of grain for Chinese consumption. Communization also increased Chinese control over all aspects of Tibetan life.

The period 1966-1979 represents the high point of Tibetan suffering. In this time Tibetan culture was all but eradicated and the populace repressed with horrendous brutality and loss of life.

POST-MAOIST POLICIES

In 1979 Deng Xiaoping initiated general liberalization, and the CCP decided to implement more liberal policies in Tibet. Tibetans imprisoned since 1959 were released. Exiled Tibetans, including the Dalai Lama, were invited to return to Tibet to "participate in socialist reconstruction."

Delegations from the Tibetan Government in Exile (TGIE) visited Tibet in 1979 and 1980, receiving an ecstatic welcome everywhere they went, much to the surprise of Chinese cadres who had hoped the Tibetans would express animosity against representatives of the "clique of serf-owners." The second delegation's visit to Lhasa in 1980 had to be terminated after the joyful welcome threatened to become uncontrollable.

CCP leaders realized that conditions in Tibet were not as they had been led to believe by Chinese cadres in Tibet. They convened the First Tibet Work Meeting in the spring of 1980 amid growing consternation. The meeting sent a delegation to Tibet under CCP General Secretary Hu Yaobang to ascertain the actual situation. He was shocked by what he observed, particularly the poverty of Tibetans.

On his return to Beijing, Hu proposed a radical reform program including tax relief, decollectivization of agriculture, privatization of land and property, greater autonomy, and administration by native Tibetans. Han Chinese cadres, excluding the PLA, were to be reduced by 85%, and Tibetan culture would be revived.

In the new atmosphere the TGIE sent representatives in 1982 and 1984 for talks in Beijing, but found the Chinese willing to discuss only the Dalai Lama's unconditional "return to the motherland." Tibetan proposals for greater autonomy were rejected. But the loosening of social restrictions led to a revival of Tibetan civil, cultural, and religious life. Interchange with Tibetans in exile and even tourists exposed Tibetans to new realities.

The Second Work Forum in 1984 criticized Hu Yaobang's policies for reviving Tibetan nationalism rather than alleviating discontent. His policy of reducing the number of Chinese in Tibet and allowing greater Tibetan self-government was also criticized. In 1987 he was purged from his position as CCP General Secretary.

Responding to Beijing's increasingly aggressive policies in Tibet after the sacking of Hu, the Dalai Lama chose to internationalize the issue, and seek support in the West. In September 1987 he unveiled his 5-Point Peace Plan for Tibet. The speech sparked demonstrations of support in Lhasa, which escalated into riots. Further riots occurred in December 1988 and March 1989. These confrontations left scores dead and hundreds detained.

In June 1988, in an address to the European Parliament at Strasbourg, the Dalai Lama proposed to accept the reality of Chinese sovereignty over Tibet in exchange for genuine and well-defined autonomous rights: the whole of Tibet should become a self-governing democratic entity in association with the PRC. The PRC could be responsible for Tibet's foreign policy, but Tibetans should maintain international relations through its own Foreign Affairs Bureau in the fields of religion, education, commerce, tourism, and other non-political activities. The Government of Tibet should have the right to decide on all affairs relating to Tibet and Tibetans. The whole should be founded on a basic law similar to that which was to govern Hong Kong after 1997. Tibetan autonomy was to be subject to a nationwide referendum of Tibetan people.

The PRC rejected these proposals as "independence in disguise" and as perpetuating "the idea of Tibet as a separate country." The Dalai Lama came under increasingly virulent criticism.

In July 1988, Beijing's security chief, Qiao Shi, visited Tibet and announced "merciless repression" of all forms of protest against Chinese rule. On 10 December 1988, during massive demonstrations in Lhasa, 15 demonstrators were killed and 150 seriously wounded. In March 1989 Lhasa was again in turmoil, with estimates of the death toll varying between 80 and 400 Tibetans. 3,000 were imprisoned. Martial law was declared.

Martial law was lifted in May 1990, but an Australian Human Rights Delegation that visited Tibet in 1991 observed that "it continues to exist in all but name." Amnesty International confirmed this, adding, "extensive powers of arbitrary arrest and detention without trial . . . are retained."

From February 1992, groups of 10 Chinese personnel raided Tibetan homes and arrested those found in possession of photographs of the Dalai Lama or books and tapes of his speeches. Over 200 arrests were made. This was followed again by a series of brutally crushed demonstrations and more arrests. Many of these arrests and detentions resulted in disappearances.

Towards the end of 1994 Beijing devised an array of pro-active measures to eliminate the roots of protest in Tibet. "Anti-Dalai" and "Anti-Splittist" campaigns were recommended by the Third Work Forum on Tibet, which advocated "securing the unity of our country and opposing splittism. This is a life and death struggle . . . striking relentless blows is one of the important elements of public security." This chilling directive was followed by a massive escalation of repression throughout Tibet.

Neighborhood surveillance systems were implemented, people were coerced into informing on their colleagues on pain of losing housing, employment, education, etc. Suspects were repeatedly detained for short periods and interrogated by torture. From the year 2000, suspects were subjected to interrogation and torture lasting from 4 to 24 weeks. This technique is used typically against people suspected of communicating information about Tibet to the outside world.

A report submitted by Bai Zhao, President of the "Tibet Autonomous Region" People's Court in May 1998, said that the courts had tried 6,291 people over the past five years and had found 0.73% not guilty. Detainees received sentences ranging from five years to death.

Political detainees are invariably tortured to extract confessions before the trial. In 1999 Physicians for Human Rights stated that in Tibet "the frequency of torture suggests that it is part of a widespread pattern of abuse." China's growing sensitivity to international pressure has resulted in some changes in repression strategy. Instead of death sentences, political prisoners suffer prolonged torture leading to slow, quiet deaths or permanent injury or debilitation. Almost all torture victims of this period are those who protest against ill-treatment of prisoners, show allegiance to the Dalai Lama, or express dissenting views. In May 1998 at least 10 prisoners in Lhasa were tortured to death on these grounds.

Authorities have expanded the network of prison complexes in Tibet. A new high-security detention and interrogation facility was built in Lhasa in 1997. Lhasa's Drapchi and Sangyip prison complexes were expanded in 1998. Most inmates are political prisoners. The intensification of surveillance and control mechanisms ensures that reports of abuse in Tibet rarely reach international monitoring groups.

Documented torture techniques in prisons include aerial suspension, attack by dogs, hand and foot cuffs, exposure to extreme temperatures, sexual assault, electric cattle prods, solitary confinement, urinating in the victim's mouth, forcing victims to watch torture videos, deprivation of food, water, and sleep.

THE SCOPE OF ABUSE

In 1994 the U.N. Working Group on Arbitrary Detention found that 32 Tibetan prisoners whose cases it examined were in contravention of the Universal Declaration of Human Rights.

These included:

- 10 monks from Drepung Monastery sentenced to an average of 15 years for publishing leaflets about democracy.
- eight monks from Ganden Monastery sentenced from 5-12 years for demonstrating, making posters, and calling for Tibetan independence.
- Lobsang Tsultrim, a 72 year old scholar and monk, serving six years for "failure to reform through education" and "becoming a reactionary with the hope of splitting the great motherland."
- Jampa Ngodrup, a doctor serving 13 years for "collecting lists of people detained and passing them on to others, thus . . . violating the laws of secrecy."
- Yulu Dawa Tsering, a university teacher sentenced to 14 years for speaking about independence to an Italian tourist.

The monk Palden Gyatso told the ICJ: "Paljor (the interrogator) asked, 'Why are you here again?' I replied that I had put up wall-posters in Lhasa. Paljor . . . said, 'Do you still want independence?' I stood still. . . . Paljor took out his electric baton and shoved it . . . down my throat. When I woke up, I found myself lying in a pool of vomit and urine; I had lost twenty of my teeth."

The ICJ interviewed several women torture survivors: Ngawang Choedon, a nun, was arrested during a peaceful demonstration, and she and others were taken to Gutsa detention center. "We had to go through the whole process of interrogation again. . . . I saw ropes, chains, and electrical instruments lying on the table nearby. . . . My hands were tied behind my back and the end of the rope was tied to the iron ceiling. . . . Two men pulled the rope till I was hanging in the air . . . and soon I was unconscious. . . . When I regained consciousness . . . I could not get up. . . . Someone was kicking me from the back. . . . I was hit all over my body with a thick chain. . . . One of them poked an electrical instrument inside my mouth. . . . After a while I did not feel as if my body belonged to me. . . . I was stripped naked. . . . I saw them laughing at me."

Kalsang, a 26 year old nun from Shungsep Nunnery, was imprisoned after demonstrating. "They made me undress completely . . . and started beating me with sticks. I died with shame as so many people were watching. (Other common prisoners were allowed to watch) . . . Later the beating was so unbearable that I forgot about my shame . . . The room turned upside down. . . . I was like a corpse. . . ."

Minors detained in prison are not exempt from torture. Abuse of minors has also occurred upon arrest. Three nuns from Michungri Nunnery, aged 14-15 were badly beaten for demonstrating. Six schoolchildren, aged between 13 and 17, were arrested for singing nationalist songs. They were kicked and beaten throughout the night, stripped of their clothes and beaten with wire. Sherab Ngawang—believed to have been only 12—died in April 1995 after beatings and torture in Trisam.

The U.N. Special Rapporteur on Torture has sought, without response, an invitation to visit China after "continuing to receive reports according to which the practice of torture was endemic to police stations and detention centers in Tibet."

In 1998, Lawyers for Tibet reported on the pervasive violence and discrimination practiced against Tibetan women. It described a pattern of forced abortions and sterilizations as well as discrimination against women who violate China's family planning regulations.

Several women described instances of late-term abortions: "They injected a needle where the baby's head was. The baby was born and cried. Then it started bleeding from the nose and died. . . ."

"They injected a needle in her stomach, and she gave birth. The baby . . . was put in a bowl. . . . It moved for a few minutes and then died. The baby had a hole in its head. . . ."

Tibetan children's access to healthcare also remains substandard. Prohibitive costs at Chinese hospitals and clinics often prevent access to basic medical care. Inadequate diet and poor water quality, coupled with lack of vaccinations, leads to moderate to severe malnutrition and growth stunting. A 2001 study of Tibetan children by the *New England Journal of Medicine* found that "stunting was due to malnutrition . . . and was accompanied by bone disorders, depigmented hair, skin disorders, and other diseases of malnutrition."

RELIGIOUS PERSECUTION

Soon after the invasion of Tibet, Beijing announced: "The CCP considers that its ideology and that of religion are two forces that cannot co-exist. . . . The differences between the two can be likened to those of light and darkness. . . ."

In the light of this policy, monasteries and nunneries were vandalized and plundered, precious metals and stones were looted, and religious artefacts melted down in foundries. Treasures were sent to China to be auctioned in international antique markets.

Monks were forced to shoot each other, monks and nuns were forced to copulate in public and taunted to perform miracles. Over 11,000 monks were tortured and put to death.

The liberalization policy under Hu Yaobang returned some religious freedom to Tibet. However, religious practice remained strictly state-controlled. Chinese directives laid down that: "Candidates should be at least 18 years old, should love the Communist Party, must obtain formal approval from the 'Democratic Management Committee,' must have the consent of the Public Security Bureau (PSB), and have a 'good' political background."

Political control measures became more active after September 1987, in the wake of Tibetan protest demonstrations. Members of "Work Teams" camped in monasteries and nunneries to foster "fervent patriots in every religion, who accept the leadership of the Party, firmly support the socialist path, and safeguard national unity."

The 1994 Third Work Forum in Beijing recommended the following formula to reform Tibetan Buddhism: "We must teach Buddhism to reform itself . . . to fit in with the needs of . . . stability in Tibet . . . so that it becomes appropriate to a society under socialism. . . ." These directives became the core of the "Patriotic Education Campaign." The authorities argued that monks and nuns had "become the vanguard of disturbances and the hotbed for the Dalai Lama's 'splittist' activities in Tibet." To tighten control over religious institutions "Democratic Management Committees" and "Patriotic Education Work Units" were introduced by Chen Kuiyan into all monasteries and nunneries.

These policies resulted in 165 arrests (including nine custodial deaths) in 1996 and 1997. In 1998 there were 327 arrests, and 49 in 1999. During this period 9,956 monks and nuns were expelled. In

March 1998, Deputy Party Secretary Raidi stated that 35,000 monks and nuns had been "rectified by patriotic education." "Unpatriotic" institutions were closed down, and some demolished.

Towards the end of 1998, Chinese authorities started a campaign to foster atheism in all walks of Tibetan life. On November 15, 1998, Raidi announced: "As communists we cannot . . . merely announce that we are atheists. We should make bold propaganda about Marxist atheism and insist on indoctrinating the masses . . . in the Marxist stand on religion."

In his November 8, 1997 speech to the Party Committee, Chen Kuiyan had stated: "Religious believers . . . are not able to free themselves from the shackles of their outlook. . . . They waste their precious time in futile efforts praying for . . . happiness in the next world . . . and donate money to monasteries. . . . Such negative thinking . . . prevents science and technology from spreading and impedes . . . productive forces."

TWO STATEMENTS FROM APRIL 2003

In December 1997, the ICJ reported that Ngawang Sangdrol, a young nun detained in 1991 for having demonstrated or attempted to demonstrate, "had her sentence increased by nine years because she did not stand up when an official entered the room, failed to tidy her bedding, and shouted, 'Free Tibet!'"

In October 2002 she was released and allowed to leave Tibet on the insistence of many international NGOs and other instances. She made the following statement in Washington DC in April 2003: "Ever since I set foot on the soil of the United States, I have been overwhelmed by . . . love and support. . . . My immediate concern has been my health, and doctors . . . have started my examination. I lived without freedom for over 11 years. . . . I am moved by the interest that the international community is showing in my case. I don't consider myself as anyone special. No Tibetan can stand . . . the denial of our fundamental rights. I am deeply touched to learn that many individuals, organizations, and governments have worked towards my release. I am concerned about the many more political prisoners, including my fellow nun, Phuntsok Nyidron, languishing in Chinese jails. I appeal to the international community to help give them freedom." At the time of her release, Ngawang Sangdrol was only 26 years old.

Seventy-two year old Takna Jigme Sangpo was released on 31 March 2002. In April 2003, he made the following statement to the U.N. Commission on Human Rights: "When I was 37 . . . I was detained for remarks I made about the Panchen Lama, which were considered counter-revolutionary. . . . I was sentenced to 41 years of imprisonment. During more than three decades of a political prisoner's life I was tortured . . . beyond human imagination. . . . My dignity as a human being was . . . crushed. My physical appearance today is proof of the immense suffering I endured. . . . Due to prison atrocities and harsh prison conditions I lost my eyesight. . . . Many prisoner colleagues died in prison or were executed. On June 4, 1997, Sangye Tenphel was tortured to death. . . . Two monks, Khedup and Lobsang Wangduk, died after torture sessions in May 1998. A third monk, Lobsang Jinpa, died under mysterious circumstances. . . . Torture and degrading ill-treatment are common practices . . . in Tibet's prisons. . . . I wholeheartedly thank governments and NGOs who urged the Chinese authorities to release me and other . . . political prisoners. This old man from Tibet appeals to all nations . . . to help end the suffering of the Tibetans. I pray for an end to the suffering of all political prisoners in this world."

PLUNDER AND DESTRUCTION FOR CHINA'S BENEFIT

BIODIVERSITY

By remaining undisturbed until the mid-twentieth century, the Tibetan plateau's 2.5 million square km is a storehouse of innumerable species which are necessary to the balance of life worldwide. Due to the variety and complexity of unique ecological niches, Tibet is seen as a final sanctuary for some of the world's rare plant and animal species. There are over 12,000 species of vascular plants, fungi account for 5,000 species of 700 genera, of more than 5,000 higher plant species, over 100 are woody plants of 300 species, and the 400 species of rhododendron account for 50% of the world's total species. Of immense value to medical science are the over 2,000 medicinal plants in the wild.

There are 210 species of mammals in 29 families, and 532 bird species in 57 families. Endemic animals include the snow leopard, blue sheep, giant panda, red panda, golden monkey, wild yak, and Himalayan woolly hare. Today at least 37 bird species among more than 81 animal species are endangered in Tibet.

The Chinese view all wildlife as an economic resource in contrast with traditional Tibetan respect for all living creatures. Mammals are hunted and poached for wool, antlers, skin, fur, and inner organs. Fish are dynamited in lakes and rivers.

The loss of Tibet's unique fauna and flora would be irreversible and the impact on the fabric of the plateau's living system is of grave global concern.

WATER RESOURCES

The Tibetan plateau is source to the world's ten greatest river systems which flow to China, India, Nepal, Bhutan, Bangladesh, Pakistan, Vietnam, Burma, Cambodia, Laos, and Thailand. Forty-seven percent of the world's population depends on Tibet's watersheds and rivers.

China's policies of development, industrialization, resource extraction, and population transfer have led to massive intervention in Tibet's rivers and lakes. Amdo is home to vast dams providing power to cities in Western China. Dams in Kham have resulted in river fragmentation, and wholesale deforestation is destroying hydro-ecology. China plans further large-scale schemes to harness waterways to service the growing shortfall of power in China and provide for further industrialization and urbanization of Tibet.

Fragmentation and stagnation of rivers has led to destruction of fish species and extinction of plants and aquatic species. Dams deprive alluvial plains downstream of fertile soil for agriculture.

Rivers also face pollution from toxic mining wastes. Tailings from large-scale mining operations are a primary source of water pollution in Amdo. Rivers around Lhasa are polluted by untreated sewage, industrial waste, and salts and nitrates leaked from fertilizers used in intensive farming projects to meet the needs of the expanding Chinese population in Tibet. The "TAR" 1996 Environment report stated that 41.9 million tons of liquid waste was discharged into the Lhasa River.

Overfishing, pollution, human intervention, and shrinkage are all endangering the purity and ecological survival of Tibet's legendary rivers and lakes.

AGRICULTURE

Since over 80% of Tibet's population relies on agriculture for its livelihood, farmers and nomads suffer greatly under China's exploitative policies. By a complex system of cyclic grazing, nomads kept grasslands viable for centuries. Organic farming methods sustained soil fertility in a fragile mountain environment.

China's destruction of the plateau's agro-pastoral economy began with the "Democratic Reforms" of the 1950s and 1960s. Livestock numbers declined and food grain shortages emerged for the first time in history. Due to crippling taxation, production quotas, export of meat and grain to China, and experimental agricultural policies based on ideology rather than social and geographic reality, Tibet experienced outright famine. Marginal lands were cultivated to feed China and unsustainable high-yield wheat introduced, leading to extensive destruction of fragile grasslands.

Since 1989 a centralized policy controlling agriculture was aimed at intensifying land use and producing grain surpluses for "the state." Incentives for farmers were minimized by grain quota systems, a multitude of taxes, and intensive farming relying on monoculture. This required heavy outlays on chemical fertilizers which destroy the natural fertility of the soil and lower profitability. Half a century of agro-pastoral mismanagement imposed by China has deprived Tibetans of their previous self-reliance and traditional way of life.

FORESTRY

When the Yangtze river floods of August 1998 caused a national disaster, Beijing finally focused the blame on deforestation around the river's fountainhead in Tibet (Kham). Until 1949 Tibet's forests grew largely undisturbed on isolated slopes, and regeneration was natural since logging was banned.

Having denuded its own forests, China succeeded between 1950 and 1985 in reducing Tibet's forest cover from 25.2 million hectares to 13.57 million hectares. This 46 % reduction had a market value of US$ 54 billion. Deforestation is today recognized as a major contributor to Tibet's environmental degradation. State-owned forestry enterprises are obliged to fill annual quotas, but since they are forced to fell and sell a surplus to subsidize low income resulting from underselling their quota, the forestry sector is in effect destroying itself. In addition, illegal felling is believed to exceed planned production in the "TAR."

The effects of China's rapacious forest felling in Tibet are severe. In addition to siltation, pollution, and flooding of the ten major rivers that feed Asia, Tibet's vegetation controls the plateau's heating mechanism, and this in turn affects the stability of Asia's monsoon. Deforestation also leads to desertification which curtails water flows. China's Yellow river has already suffered an overall 23% fall in water discharge.

With 400 Chinese cities experiencing water shortages, 108 facing water crises, and major crop losses due to lack of irrigation, Beijing can expect further ecological catastrophes caused by a history of official disregard for nature.

MINERALS AND MINING

Tibet's huge mineral wealth was one of the primary reasons for the 1949 invasion, and today Beijing controls what is arguably the last truly great frontier of the mining world. Over 126 minerals have been identified, including significant deposits of uranium, gold, chromite, lithium, boron, iron, and silver. Tibet's oil and gas reserves are also of global importance. Since China's own resources are near exhaustion, Tibet's rich deposits are now of paramount importance to China's industrialization and surplus mineral exports.

The consequences for Tibet have been deplorable. Massive debris, slag heaps, abandoned mines, and slope destabilization blight the overground. Below, the soil is polluted by toxic wastes from materials used in extraction. Massive wastage is also recorded due to improper extraction methods. Social problems have also arisen due to the huge influx of Chinese migrant labor. Illegal mind are also drawn to the benefits of random mining exploitation.

Rather than controlling illegal mining, corruption, and hazardous waste, China is focusing on attracting foreign investment into the mining sector. Environmental protests by Tibetans are kept down, sometimes by lengthy prison sentences.

China is investing US$ 1.25 billion in developing mineral resources in Tibet's Central and Western regions alone. Acceleration of extraction indicates the certainty of mammoth returns. In addition to high-profile oilfields, estimated at 42 billion tons, Tsaidam's natural gas reserves of 1,500 billion cubic meters are an important source of potential energy for China.

The Chinese name for Central Tibet is "Xijang," meaning "Western Treasure House." By promoting mining as a pillar industry, Beijing is finally succeeding in draining Tibet of its once-dormant mineral resources.

NUCLEAR THREATS

Tibet, once governed to the last detail on principles of non-violence, is today a storehouse for Chinese nuclear weapons and a dumping site for radioactive waste. The highest plateau in the world is a natural launching pad for Beijing's ambitions to achieve superpower primacy.

By 1971, the first nuclear weapon was installed in Amdo. Today the arsenal includes 17 radar stations, 14 military airfields, eight missile bases, at least eight intercontinental ballistic missiles, and 70 medium range and 20 intermediate range missiles.

China's DF-4 IBMs (ranges of 4,000-7,000 kms) are stored in Tsaidam. Further DF-4 missiles are deployed at Terlingkha, headquarters of a missile regiment with four launch sites. A fourth nuclear station in Southern Amdo houses four CSS-4 missiles with ranges of 12,874 kms. A base near Nagchuka has underground complexes housing ballistic missiles. An underground complex close to Lhasa stores ground-to-air and surface-to-surface missiles which are paraded through the capital annually on Chinese Army Day. Further missile stockpiles are kept at Kongpo in the southeast.

Nuclear and other hazardous wastes are being dumped on the plateau. China's Xinhua News Agency admitted in 1995 that radioactive pollutants had been discharged near the shore of Lake Kokonor in a 20m sq. dump. Radioactive waste has been dumped in a watershed draining into the Tsang Chu River which becomes China's Yellow river.

China still employs shallow burial techniques for nuclear waste, and remote regions of Tibet are earmarked for recycling of toxic wastes from developed nations. Already an abnormal rate of childbirth mortality, birth deformities, mysterious illnesses, and high death-rates among animals are recorded around nuclear production facilities in Amdo, as also high rates of cancer in children—similar to post-Hiroshima findings. Other reports of deformities and illnesses in humans and animals are linked to uranium mining in the "TAR" and Amdo. Contaminated waste water from Tibet's largest uranium mine, near

Thewo in Southern Amdo, is released into the local river, with victims turning blue or blue-black after death.

POPULATION TRANSFER: CHINA'S "FINAL SOLUTION" FOR TIBET

All the elements of discrimination against a distinct people are present in China's population transfer to Tibet. There is discrimination in housing, employment, education, health care, language, national customs, and political rights. But the gravest threat for the future is that Tibetans are increasingly outnumbered and marginalized on their own soil by the ongoing influx of Chinese settlers.

By skewing the demographic composition Beijing is achieving its policy objectives to incorporate Tibet irrevocably into China. Lhasa is already predominantly Chinese, with administrators, business migrants, military, and security personnel outnumbering Tibetans two to one. In Amdo, cities can be over 90% Chinese.

Beijing's population transfer policy is colonialist, embracing the needs to quash resistance to Chinese rule, exploit natural resources, solve Chinese population and unemployment pressures, and consolidate its hold over a militarily strategic zone in central Asia.

Preferential policies favor Chinese settlers economically, from financial allowances to easy procurement of business licenses. Tibetans are disadvantaged in "modernization" schemes. Few Tibetans can progress to higher education due to education policies weighted in favor of Chinese literacy, which also ensures that Tibetans are excluded from decision-making roles in economic and social development. Admitting that 20.7% of Tibetans in the "TAR" live below the poverty line, the Lhasa administration attributes this to "inherent backwardness and remoteness."

Beijing is stepping up infrastructure and resource development on the plateau, which in turn is used to justify an ever-increasing Chinese labor force. Expanding road and rail networks, easing of residency regulations, free market systems, and exemption from taxes have increased the attractiveness of Tibet for China's migrant workers, petty traders, and small-scale entrepreneurs.

The official population transfer policies which absorbed Eastern Turkestan, Inner Mongolia, and Manchuria into China by massive migration are today being applied in Tibet. Already the ratio is around 7.5 million Chinese to 6 million Tibetans. This, says the Dalai Lama, "is the most serious threat to the survival of Tibet's culture and national identity."

THE STATUS OF TIBET

The ICJs 1997 report on the status of Tibet reads: "Central Tibet . . . demonstrated from 1913-1950 the conditions of statehood as generally accepted by international law. In 1950 there was a people, a territory, and a government which functioned in that territory, conducting its own domestic affairs free from any outside authority. . . . Foreign relations . . . were conducted exclusively by the government of Tibet. Central Tibet was thus at least a de facto independent state when in the face of a Chinese invasion it signed the 17-Point Agreement in 1951, surrendering its independence to China under force. . . . A number of undertakings (in the 17-Point Agreement) were violated by China. The Government of Tibet was entitled to repudiate the agreement as it did in 1959."

On the question of self-determination the ICJ concluded: "Tibetans are a people under alien subjugation, entitled under international law to the right of self-determination, by which they freely determine their political status. . . . [They] have not yet exercised this right, which requires a free and genuine expression of their will."

The ICJ report elaborates: "The U.N. General Assembly debates show that the Tibet question was considered in the context of a distinct people under alien subjugation and domination, entitled to exercise its legitimate right to self-determination. . . . Tibet's status as separate and distinct from China was thus not disputed. . . .

"The PRC and CCP acknowledge that the Tibetans constitute a separate entity. . . . Before Mao gained control of the CCP, resolutions recognized the principle of national self-determination, including full Tibetan power to join with China, with the Soviet Union, or to be independent. The 1947 Constitution of the Republic of China stated that 'the self-government system of Tibet shall be guaranteed.' The 1951 17-Point Agreement recognized the Tibetan nationality as 'one of the nationalities with a long history.' Subsequent PRC Constitutions and the 1984 Regional Autonomy Law recognized the Tibetans as a separate nationality. . . . 'Tibetans did not participate in the revolution that created the PRC. Nor did Tibetans at any time express the will to be integrated into China. . . . After the advance of Chinese forces into Eastern Tibet in 1950 . . . Tibet signed the 17-Point Agreement at pistol point. However this agreement was repudiated in 1959 on the ground of subsequent breach of its conditions by China; a repudiation the ICJ considered legally justified. From the Chinese invasion up to the present, all indications are that the vast majority of Tibetans . . . oppose Chinese rule, which they consider a form of alien domination."

The Conference of International Lawyers put it more succinctly: "The PRC is illegitimate as the government of Tibet. By its conduct of genocide . . . torture, and murder . . . the PRC has forfeited whatever right of territorial integrity it may once have had with respect to Tibet. . . . The Tibetans are entitled not to be subject to the PRC.

"Tibet was a factually and legally independent state when it was unlawfully invaded by the PRC. . . . Tibet remains a legally independent state despite its decades-long occupation by the PRC. The Tibetans are entitled to exercise their right to self-determination, and they should be permitted and assisted to do so."

And in its conclusions, the CIL states ("The London Statement"): "The PRC is required by international law to ensure the respect of fundamental human rights of the Tibetan people. It cannot evade that legal requirement by an appeal to its domestic jurisdiction. On the contrary, the violation of fundamental human rights is an additional justification for the demand by the Tibetan people for the exercise of their right to self-determination."

WHAT TIBETANS WANT

In 1987 the Dalai Lama proposed the following 5-Point Peace Plan:

1. Transformation of the whole of Tibet into a zone of peace and non-harm.
2. Abandonment of China's population transfer policy which threatens the very existence of the Tibetan people.
3. Respect for the Tibetan peoples' human rights and democratic freedoms.

4. Restoration and protection of Tibet's natural environment and the abandonment of China's use of Tibet for the production of nuclear weapons and dumping of nuclear waste.
5. Commencement of earnest negotiations on the future status of Tibet and of the relations between the Tibetan and Chinese people.

In an address to the European Parliament in 1988, the Dalai Lama made the "Strasbourg Proposal," in which he elaborated on the 5-Point Peace Plan:

I have always urged my people not to resort to violence. Yet I believe all people have the moral right to peacefully protest injustice. Every Tibetan hopes and prays for our nation's independence. Tibetans have sacrificed their lives to achieve this precious goal. The Chinese continue to pursue a policy of brutal suppression.

The fifth point of the peace plan called for earnest negotiations between the Tibetans and the Chinese. The TGIE has taken the initiative to formulate some thoughts which may serve as a basis for resolving the issue of Tibet.

The whole of Tibet should become a self-governing democratic political entity founded on law, in association with the PRC. The PRC could remain responsible for Tibet's foreign policy. The Government of Tibet should, however, maintain its own Foreign Affairs Bureau in non-political activities.

The Government of Tibet should be founded on a constitution of basic law, providing for a democratic system entrusted with the tasks of ensuring economic equality, social justice, and protection of the environment. The Government of Tibet should have the right to decide on all affairs relating to Tibet and the Tibetans.

The Government should be comprised of a popularly elected Chief Executive, a bi-cameral legislative branch, and an independent judiciary. Its seat should be in Lhasa. The social and economic system should be determined by the wishes of the Tibetan people.

The exploitation of natural resources should be carefully regulated. The manufacture, testing, and stockpiling of nuclear and other armaments must be prohibited

To create an atmosphere of trust conducive to fruitful negotiations, the Chinese Government should cease its human rights violations in Tibet and abandon its policy of transferring Chinese to Tibet.

Whatever the outcome of the negotiations with the Chinese may be, the Tibetan people themselves must be the ultimate deciding authority. Any proposal will contain a procedural plan to ascertain their wishes in a nationwide referendum.

The Chinese leadership needs to realize that colonial rule over occupied territories is anachronistic. A genuine union or association can only come about voluntarily, when there is satisfactory benefit to all the parties concerned.

The TGIE is willing to consider any realistic initiative by the Chinese leaders which takes into account the historical facts, the changing situation of the world, the legitimate rights and aspirations of the Tibetan people, and the long-term mutual interest of both Tibet and China.

In essence, what the TGIE is seeking is not full independence from China, but a form of genuine Tibetan autonomy in association with China. This is not because the vast majority of Tibetans would not prefer complete independence, but because of China's continued defiance and intransigence on the issue. The Dalai Lama feels that it is wiser to accept a certain measure of Chinese suzerainty in order to expedite the resolution of the human rights crisis in Tibet, the preservation of Tibetan identity and the environment, and the introduction of a genuine expression of Tibetan self-determination.

THE RESPONSE FROM BEIJING

China's "White Paper on Tibet" of 24 September 1992, concludes: "For more than 700 years the Central Government of China has continuously exercised sovereignty over Tibet, and Tibet has never been an independent state. The Dalai-clique and anti-China overseas forces claim that between the 1911 revolution and the founding of the PRC in 1949, Tibet became a country exercising full authority. Historical facts refute such a fallacy. The so-called Tibetan independence which the Dalai-clique and overseas anti-China forces fervently propagate is nothing but a fiction of the imperialists who committed aggression against China in modern history."

In response to an invitation to put its case before the Conference of International Lawyers on Issues Relating to Self-Determination for Tibet (The London Conference), the Chinese Embassy in London replied: "As is known to all, Tibet has been an inalienable part of China's sacred territory since the thirteenth century. The Tibetan people are a member of the big family of the Chinese nation. The so-called Tibetan Question has been fabricated by a very small number of separatists in an attempt to split Tibet from China. . . . This can by no means be tolerated by the Chinese Government. . . . China will not be represented at the conference . . . and we strongly insist that arrangements for this conference be canceled" (Letter dated 14 December 1992).

The Chinese Third Work Forum on Tibet (1994) proposed the following strategies for dealing with the Tibet Issue: "The struggle between ourselves and the Dalai-clique is a matter of opposing split-tism. . . . This is a life and death struggle. . . . The judicial administration should . . . quickly . . . establish laws . . . to fight against the splittists. . . . Striking Relentless Blows is one of the important elements of . . . public security. . . . We must rely on . . . public security offices and . . . the masses in dealing with public security work.

"By attacking the Dalai-clique we must try to gain support . . . in people's hearts . . . by improving the efficiency of propaganda work abroad. . . . We must gradually change the international point of view. . . . Western countries are supporting the Dalai-clique and using . . . the Tibet issue to interfere in our . . . internal affairs. . . . We must defeat their hope of internationalizing the Tibet issue."

A highly classified document quotes a leading Chinese official as saying: "We have no need to engage in dialogues with the Dalai Lama. The Dalai Lama's return to China will bring a great risk of instability. We will then not be able to control Tibet. The Dalai Lama is now fairly old. At most it will be ten years before he dies. When he dies, the issue of Tibet is resolved forever. We therefore have to use skilful means to prevent his return."

On 2 April 2003, the 59th U.N Commission on Human Rights began its debate, with several delegates raising the question of Tibet. The E.U., Australia, Canada, New Zealand, and Norway expressed concern over the human rights situation in Tibet. According to World Tibet News reports, the Chinese Ambassador "delivered a very noisy and angry statement, telling . . . Western countries that it is his govern-ment which cares most for the human rights of the 1.3 billion Chinese . . . and they are satisfied with the Chinese government. So long as they are satisfied, the Chinese government will not change its policies.

Whether you (Western countries) are concerned or find it acceptable or not is entirely unimportant and even meaningless. Nobody on this planet can hold back the Chinese people from marching forward along the path of their choice."

Sources:

1. International Commission of Jurists: "Tibet: Human Rights and the Rule of Law" (December 1997).
2. Conference of International Lawyers: "Tibet: The Position in International Law" (The London Conference, 6-10 January 1993).
3. International Committee of Lawyers for Tibet: "A Generation in Peril" (March 2001).

TGIE: Department of Information and International Relations:

4. "Tibet Under Communist China—50 Years" (September 2001).
5. "Tibet: Environment and Development Issues" (April 2000).
6. "China's Current Policy on Tibet" (September 2000).
7. "The Dalai Lama—Statements 1987-1995."

The Dialogues

THE KARMA OF TIBET

DR: For many spiritual people the question needs to be addressed: How was it possible that a culture of violence, greed, and materialist expansionism was able to triumph over a culture rooted in the spiritual values of compassion and mindfulness striving towards Enlightenment? Doesn't this part of Tibetan history clearly illustrate the impossibility of establishing a spiritual society on earth? Does it not confirm what most people already suspect about the global order, that the realistic and pragmatic way is the pursuance of power?

Does it not also undermine the notion of Karma in the sense that those who attempt to amass Kushala Karma through the practice of righteousness and wisdom merely become more vulnerable to those whose philosophy is based on the mundane principles of avarice and power? Is there not a balance to be struck here, and did Tibet fail to strike that balance in its pre-invasion history?

RINPOCHE: By design of the collective karmic force it appears to me, or I am inclined to believe, that each nation or each country—or we can dispense with the terms "nation" or "country"—we may speak of a particular race of people—has its unique universal responsibility, by the design of collective karmic force.

This is quite evident or visible if we observe the various and differentiated races in this world. And Tibet, situated in a very remote area, almost unapproachable by its neighbors, a very high and dry land, surrounded by high mountains, and very thinly populated: this people, the Tibetan race, has as its responsibility to preserve, promote, and disseminate a certain spiritual heritage, and this has been the case for the last 1500 years at least. Its particular responsibility or job has been to preserve a Buddhist-related spiritual heritage and Buddhist culture, for their own people and for the neighboring peoples: Mongolia, Manchuria, China, India. These neighbors were being benefited by the Tibetan people, and the Tibetan people were not meant to build up economic power or military power or political power. Their main responsibility was to the Buddhist spiritual and cultural heritage.

Until recent times, by and large with a few exceptions, the Tibetan people were able to perform their responsibility and able to remain within that limitation of their performance. And they were quite happy and content.

But in the last 100 or 150 year period prior to 1951 the Tibetan people failed to perform their responsibility as they should have done. And they were much influenced or overpowered by negative defilements, and they became greedy for power and wealth, and spiritual influence was reduced day by day, and material influence was increased tremendously.

And the nation became much weaker since the 8th Dalai Lama until the 12th Dalai Lama. The 9th, 10th, 11th, 12th Dalai Lamas had very short lifespans and were not able to look after the state governance of Tibet. And for around 100 years—a little less than 100 years—the country was ruled by unenlightened regents. Some of the regents who were enlightened were rendered powerless by other officials. And therefore the spiritual strength of the nation became completely rotten.

And the 13th Dalai Lama did his utmost to revive this strength, but he was also not able to find any good functionaries who could understand his policies and how to implement his policies and programs. He found himself alone, no-one around him was able to understand him and work according to his vision and wisdom. Then finally he was a disappointed person and before he passed away he wrote the famous pronouncement, and in that also he very clearly stated that Tibet may not be able to defend itself against the influence of communist China, and he cited the examples of Mongolia and other countries, saying that the same fate might befall Tibet. So he very clearly foresaw this—if somebody believes in his spiritual power, it was and remains very easy to believe him; but even a secular person with no belief in his spiritual power must admit his ability to foresee the future. And we understand that he was a very extraordinary political analyst: he saw the rise of communism and the changing China, and he saw how Tibet would be occupied by the Chinese communists. It was a very foresighted political analysis.

So therefore I do not give the credit for the occupation of Tibet to the communist Chinese military power or to the Chinese power as a whole. I give the credit—or perhaps the discredit—of losing Tibet to the weakness of the Tibetans themselves.

And it was open to communist China; we could say that we very happily invited them to come and occupy Tibet. So it was not the power of China, but the weakness of Tibet which led us to the present situation.

We had committed so many mistakes and we had accumulated so much negative collective karmic force for the people—and the upright people had become completely excluded and helpless in the management of the state, and the monasteries had become corrupt. And the government officials had become corrupt and the regents had become corrupt. And this corruption and lack of foresight, and then particularly ignorance of the international political situation—we had lost so many golden opportunities. The Tibetan leadership of the previous 100 years never understood the world or how to govern a nation or country. They thought only to collect and misuse taxes. Beyond that they did not know anything: how to build up international relations and so forth.

In 1913 when a small Chinese military force was expelled from Tibet and the 13th Dalai Lama restated Tibet's independence, from then until 1951 there was ample time to assert Tibet's sovereignty and independence in the international community of nations. At least they could have set up diplomatic relations with India, Nepal, Bhutan. This would have been so easy to do. Or they could even have applied for membership in the United Nations in the beginning; and throughout the Second World War Tibet was recognized as a neutral nation by the British and by the other side as well. But we were never able to take advantage of these things. Somebody suggested to Shakyapa, when he was about to send a delegation to America after the Second World War—the American people solicited him to apply for membership in the United Nations, and he informed the Kashag (Tibetan Cabinet) and the Kashag replied: "Mind your own business and don't do anything which you have not been instructed to do." [Laughs] You might have read it somewhere. So he was prevented from initiating anything to assert Tibet's sovereignty.

On the other hand, Nepal gave evidence of her sovereignty by quoting her treaties with Tibet. Nepal only had treaties with Tibet, and with no-one else. And on this basis they recognised Nepal's sovereignty in the United Nations.

And all this process and progress of affairs did not come about by accident, but was due to the foolishness of the leadership at that time. And nobody knew how to manage the whole affair, and so it went to China. So this does not contradict the principle of causality and the theory of Karma. It also does not contradict that spiritual and righteous governance can remain stably and can be protected by its principles from the evil side. Tibet did not have all these virtues and the vices were accumulated, and it went. And even today the majority of the Tibetan people could have a purer mind and power of love, and reduce the hatred and anger towards the Chinese rulers. If this were to happen, we could have autonomy at least within no time, the genuine autonomy which His Holiness is pleading for.

But we are not able to achieve it, not because of China's power, but because of our weakness of the positive karmic stance, and that is quite evident. And this happening, the Tibet incident or the Tibet issue, is enforcing the law of causality and the theory of Karma.

And you will see that if the Tibetans will be able to accumulate positive collective karmic force, that change will occur, unexpectedly and easily. But again, how long will it last: if a good situation arises, how long it will last will again depend on the people's behavior and the extent of their positive karmic force.

Particularly in the case of a small nation like Tibet, no military and no political power can do it any good. Only positive karmic force and strength of morality and the spirituality of the people can help them.

TIBET AND TAIWAN: CONTRASTING STANCES

DR: In terms of the philosophy of Satyagraha and Ahimsa, how can the world seriously believe in the value of non-violent struggle and resistance which has failed to achieve anything for Tibet over the last 50 years?

For instance, is it not true that Taiwan, with its military capacity and worldly political methodology, has been more successful in holding off the threats of the PRC than Tibet with its more spiritual views? Again it seems that the principle of power must triumph over the principle of compassion. Is it enough to believe that the most important task of spiritual people is to continue to shine a light into the prevailing darkness of the world, even if that light itself never overtakes and achieves victory over darkness?

RINPOCHE: There is no fault in the principle or philosophy of non-violence or Satyagraha. We cannot compare Tibet and Taiwan. Of course it is very difficult to compare the spiritual and non-violent force of the Tibetan people with the tactics of the Taiwanese people—that may not be the real question at this moment.

But things were different: Taiwan could maintain its separation from mainland China for all this time, not only due to their own military and material power, but due to a degree of international and foreign support.

In the beginning China did not and could not invade Taiwan by military force due to threats held out by the Americans. And in that matter, yes, we can argue that their rescue was due to political and military force. I can say: yes, it happens. Both sides are a negative force. Mainland China had no positive force and similarly Taiwan had no positive force, both being based on military and violent power—it was a modern military/political power struggle, and the result was that Taiwan could remain separate but not independent. Yet they are functioning as a de facto independent country. But the military and political struggle still goes on, with constant threat of war and intimidation.

But in the case of Tibet we were completely lost and submerged under communist Chinese force due to our weakness. To fight against the modern Chinese force we may also try to build up a worldly force, political or military. Perhaps we could completely surrender ourselves to America to help us, or we may completely surrender ourselves to some other power—but in that case, just for argument's sake, if we accept that some other power could help us militarily, and that they dispel the Chinese force from Tibet, again we would have to remain under that military power's occupation. We can't say, "Now China has gone away, you must also go away" because, if they go away, China will come back. This is again according to the principles of worldly power. Unless we keep one side over us, we cannot keep the other side off! If we accept those principles, then I don't think there is any difference; either we remain under Chinese occupation or under someone else's.

The government or administration of such a country would be neither independent nor genuinely autonomous. It would always remain dependent on the pleasure of the "liberator" and its directives. So here again the Tibetan people cannot rely on worldly power, and they do not have at this moment a non-worldly or spiritual power— we have given it up voluntarily by ourselves. And the only possibility and option for us is to regain our moral and spiritual power and through that energy to engage in direct and non-violent action. There is no other way to change our future. And, again, this does not violate the laws of causality.

PRESERVING DHARMA AND BUDDHIST CULTURE IN TIBET

DR: How can Tibetans within Tibet return to their true task of preserving Dharma and Buddhist culture while this task is being carried out by Tibetans in exile who have no access to Tibet? How will Tibetans inside Tibet regain their lost knowledge of these things?

RINPOCHE: Greater communication between Tibetans in exile and Tibetans inside Tibet became possible during the 1980s and many Tibetan teachers living outside Tibet were able to visit Tibet and to rebuild some of their monasteries, and also to revive the tradition of study and the tradition of practice, and in a number of places good centers of learning and good centers of meditation were slowly rebuilt.

Of course, quantitatively it was not like before. But, nevertheless, there was a period of some revival. And this process was set back again in the late 90s and even today, after the demolition of Sitar Monastery and after the imprisonment of some of the very famous and very spiritual teachers.

But still, the people, the students, young monks, keep coming from Tibet to join the monasteries in India, and also some people who have completed their courses of learning in India are willing to go back and teach in Tibet. A kind of very thin lifeline is still there, and we are trying to improve it and trying to encourage scholars and practitioners who have completed their study in India to go back and settle in Tibet or to remain there for a couple of years to improve the standards of teaching.

But this is neither sufficient nor easy at this moment. Since we have reestablished direct contact with the PRC, there have been only three visits by His Holiness' envoys. One of the points they are trying to emphasize today is how to sufficiently restore religious freedom and to facilitate exchange between exiles and Tibetans inside Tibet, to make this easier.

And we are working towards the aspirations of His Holiness as far as possible. But one thing we must keep alive is the in-depth study of the subjects in India, with the hope that a time will come when people can go back and reestablish the traditions and the lineage in Tibet.

So His Holiness and all the enlightened scholars and spiritual teachers are working very hard in India, Nepal, and Bhutan to keep the tradition alive, and when the time comes they may be able to go back and revive the tradition inside Tibet—and for that matter, His Holiness is willing to accept autonomy rather than independence. One of the reasons for his decision to accept autonomy is just to regain the possibility of the revival of the spiritual and Buddhist cultural heritage without too much delay and without the unnecessary postponement of drawn-out political change.

Within the context of the Chinese occupation we might be able to do some positive work inside Tibet so that the lineage or tradition which is now becoming very weak and on the verge of extinction, could be kept and revived.

THE FUTURE VISION OF TIBET

DR: In the past Tibet was a hidden, mysterious land from which many myths and fantastical tales were brought back to the West. After the Chinese invasion, with its brutality and dehumanization of the populace, Tibet has, it seems, been largely written off as a sort of permanent gulag.

Yet we hope, almost against hope, that Tibet will one day be re-established as the great seat of Buddhist learning, what His Holiness has called the Fourth Refuge of Dharma. What is your vision for a future Tibet?

RINPOCHE: Several years ago I wrote a small pamphlet on a future vision for Tibet and at that time my ideas about autonomy were not very clear. That pamphlet was based on the idea of an autonomous or independent Tibet and dealt largely with cultural issues and ways of life. By now His Holiness' vision of autonomy is more clearly defined and a number of things may still depend on the statement he has written. It is very short and is a broad outline of a future autonomous Tibet.

And it is a big question, and I don't know how I can organize my mind to speak about it in this one session, but I will try.

The ultimate objective or vision of the Tibetan people would be the establishment of a non-violent society. And the establishment of a Tibetan non-violent society would be a kind of modern example to the world. His Holiness has characterized this objective as "a zone of Ahimsa."

This vision of Ahimsa is broad and far-reaching. Tibet is situated at a very high altitude: "The Roof of the World," and the sources of many large river systems are located in Tibet. Thus Tibet is very important in terms of non-harm to the environment also. The south Asian continent monsoon rains also come from the cloud formations over the Tibetan plateau—for these and other reasons it is a very important nerve-center of the total Asian environment.

And of course the basic collective responsibility of the Tibetan people is to show the path of non-violence and the path of compassion to the world, to humanity, and for that we must organize ourselves in every way as a non-violent society.

A non-violent society does not mean a Buddhist society or a Hindu society or any particular religious society. Such a society may be a non-religious society, yet it can be a non-violent society. On the other hand, if it is made up of many or any religions, yet it can be a non-violent society.

How to establish a non-violent society at this moment in the modern world depends on two issues, I think, which have become extremely important: the political system and the economic system. These political and economic systems become conducive to stability in society, and then non-violence is ultimately possible. Because most violence, at this moment at least 90% of violence, has economic causes. At the present time economics is perhaps *the* root cause of most of the violence practiced by human beings in their societies. Then that is a little supplemented by political systems; not only the economic system, but the political system also contributes to the escalation of violence in human society.

So with regard to the future of Tibet, keeping within these 2 objectives, to achieve a zone of non-harm and to establish a non-violent society, we need a democratic community, a genuinely democratic community. And I think this is an obstacle for the present PRC—they may agree to allow a degree of autonomy, but to give a democratic system which would not allow a single party—the communist party—to hold absolute power, is beyond their thinking. In our thinking, the communist party could be one of the parties in a multi-party democracy. If possible, we would prefer a partyless democracy, but, if this is not possible, we can accept a multi-party democratic system. That is the vision for the future of Tibet.

But we need to remember that democratic systems are not perfect; they have their own limitations and defects. But of all the political systems or systems of governance available in the world today, democracy is one of the best or perhaps *the* best. I think it is the best of all the systems in the world today. So therefore we envision a demo-

145

cratic system, and then we also have a number of our own inputs: how to make a democracy for the Tibetans; most people believe it should be partyless—not divided along party lines—so that each individual voice can be given an audience, that individual ideas are given the most importance. And through dialogue and discussion the people can find common ground, and thereby they can truly govern themselves as a community. So this is an important aspect of the political vision of a future Tibet.

And then, secondly, they must have a properly balanced economic system, not based on greed or consumption, but on need and utilization. And that means a lot of hard work to be done. First of all, we shall have to make ourselves self-sufficient and self-supporting. The population of Tibet is not so big and the land available for Tibetans is more than sufficient, and we shall make a policy on the proper utilization of land. Land should not belong to any individual but should be the common property of all the Tibetan people, and whosoever is using the land, as long as he or she cultivates or afforests or gardens—or whatever productive use it is put to—they should have available to them as much land as they can properly utilize. And if by some chance they are not able, or do not wish, to work on the land, then they should not have any hereditary holding on the land.

So agriculture, animal husbandry, and corporate industry should be the basic pillars of the economy, and agriculture should be given top priority. And it should be a non-violent agriculture; a natural and purely organic agriculture should be reintroduced as it was in Tibet in the past.

By now there has been a lot of chemical abuse of the land under pressure of the strict orders of the Communist Party or the PRC. They are using a lot of chemicals in several parts of Tibet, and that should be reversed. And everybody should return to organic agriculture so that agriculture should be non-harmful; and, then, as we used to have before, Tibet must have surplus food production which can be used to help the Chinese and Indian population if the need arises, and this applies also to Nepal and Bhutan. They could benefit from our surplus production of agricultural and dairy products.

And in Northern Tibet, which is very good for animal husbandry, the traditional nomadic way of life should be revived and the grasslands should be preserved, and areas where desertification has taken place should be rehabilitated to grasslands. For this purpose certain organic methods can be used. And then the animals would be treated traditionally and their health would be restored. In these ways, dairy products and green foods can be restored, and these two should be sufficient for the Tibetan people.

All the other traditional industries should also be revived, such as the manufacture of very high quality clothing and other traditional handicrafts of a very fine quality, which can be used domestically and exported for foreign exchange. But this should be a system of equality. There should be no imports exceeding the value of exports.

There must be this balance and localization should be given top priority. Transportation of raw materials and transportation of finished goods should be an unnecessary job—transportation and the need for transportation should be reduced as much as possible. By reducing the need for transportation, the total environment is to that extent saved from pollution.

So the idea is as much localized production for local consumption as possible, and then a little transportation for export of surplus or conveying of surplus to needy areas. And for transportation we have very good river systems in Tibet, and these should be used for transportation of goods in the traditional way, using the natural flow of the rivers and manual propulsion rather than pollutive mechanisms. These always were our traditional means of transportation, and we can improve the river systems by non-harmful and eco-friendly means.

And then, with regard to people's communication and travel, that could be achieved by public transportation systems largely based on smokeless gasses used for buses and a good network of roads to make the entire population accessible to each other. These are the kinds of things we have envisaged.

At an economic level, there are so many things that we can do by small-scale cottage industries. For example, the cutting of precious stones and assembling of watches, and even the assembling of computers. These things do not need a huge industrial infrastructure. They can be done in separate cottage industries. For example, diamond cutting can be done: hundreds of diamonds can be carried in a small package; there's no need for huge industrial workspace or intensive transportation, so there's no problem. It is the same with the assembling of small electronic components and so forth—these are just a few examples to illustrate the principle. Eco-friendly and not in need of giant industrial production teams—because Tibet's population is small, and we can regulate these industries so that the local people become self-sufficient, and these are the guidelines we insist on.

Then the use of money must be discouraged and the banking system should also be discouraged. The barter system and exchange of goods should be improved and money should be used only as a last resort for indispensable things; otherwise people need not indulge in the greed associated with money. There may not even be a Tibetan currency. Chinese money can be used in small quantities so that people do not indulge themselves with money. People should rather be in a position to manage their lives without using money at all.

Now with regard to education: up to university level the state should be responsible for the education of the people, and education should not result in incapable people. The highest educated person should be able to go back to their home and continue with their work and, as a result of their education, that work should be improved and increased. We should have sufficient professionals to carry out their tasks so that we can remain independent, not dependent on others. For instance, we should not have to import human resources.

Then there should be a preventive-based health policy using traditional Tibetan medicine. All forms of traditional medicine and health practices such as yoga and so forth should be made the common knowledge of all the people and constitute common treatment. General health should be kept sound and the medical system should not become a form of trade. There should be no question of some being able to afford complicated medical treatment while others cannot. Everybody should get the best treatment whenever it is needed, but health in general must be taken care of by the state, using traditional methods and cures and working to improve these. At the same time we must have the most up-to-date medical facilities throughout the country.

And then most important is the reestablishment of religious and cultural traditions, and each religious tradition should have the fullest freedom to preserve and promote its own practices and teachings, but at the same time the monasteries must come under strong control and be restricted by law so that only genuine practitioners should have protection and the right to live the monastic life. If someone is not very serious about Buddhist practice, he or she must return to secular life and not lead a monk's life, dependent on the generosity of the lay-people. So monkhood should not become an escape from hard work and just living on the charity of others—that demerit has been part of Tibet's history over the past 700 years, with many monks and nuns living an unprofitable life on the backs of the lay community.

Religious freedom should be absolute in totality but there should be some kinds of checks and balances. The commercialization of Dharma and the misuse of Dharma should be prevented. His Holiness has several times said that monasteries should not depend on the quantities of monks but must have monks of quality; real scholars, really good practitioners. In that case, of course, the several thousand mediocre practitioners should not be allowed to remain in the disguise of monks and nuns. And in the case of religious teachers there should also be checks and balances so that only capable teachers should be allowed to teach so that the transmission of impure teachings be prevented.

Of course the state cannot carry out this task, but the religious institutions themselves have knowledge of their own traditions. There should be a council of religious affairs which shall have the legitimacy and degree of authority over all the monasteries and nunneries and religious institutions and centers so that these can be kept in their purest form, and separate from the influences of non-religious social forces.

I think these are things which will be good for the future of Tibet. Then, of course, we should have a very cordial relationship with the Central PRC Government and Local Tibetan Government and the entire Tibetan people, as also the minorities, should enjoy an equal degree of autonomy and in this way they could live as one community, each enjoying their own traditions to the fullest.

DR: What about Tibet's mineral resources, for example, natural gas and oil? Should these remain untapped or should they be put to use in a free Tibet?

RINPOCHE: This is a very crucial question. The use or non-use of Tibet's mineral resources should basically be decided by the Tibetan people. As I said, we must have a genuine democracy, and if we have a genuine democracy these things will not be decided by Central Government or the PRC, neither will these things be decided by a few people who have large companies or multinational corporations influencing the economy. I emphasized that Tibet's economy must be a localized economy, not a globalized one; and in a localized economy the people living in those areas must decide whether or not to make those resources available, and the local people should have the first voice as to whether the resources can be used or not.

Our vision is that Tibetan people should be able to live at a very high standard of living in today's context, in the context of the modern world—but that quality of life does not depend on globalization. That kind of life can be provided by these means: agriculture, animal husbandry, and small-scale industry. These three things should suffice to supply a good earning and a good lifestyle. Of course I am not speaking about the type of lifestyle where one has hundreds of millions of rupees or dollars, not knowing what to do with them. But each person should have more than enough food, a very decent house with electricity, water, and all modern amenities, a good transportation system, and a very efficient communications system. All these modern facilities can be had through our own agriculture, animal husbandry, and small-scale industry. Realizing this, people would know that we need not exploit the minerals and natural resources, and for the sake of balance and preservation of the environment we should try not to use these materials because we can have our needs met by other traditional resources. That would be possible for us.

But if there really is a need among the people and we need more money for certain projects such as large-scale construction or something similar, or we need more money for education, then our vision is that, instead of taking grants from outside or taking outside loans, instead of indulging directly or indirectly in structural violence, we can opt to use our own mineral and natural resources as a last resort, in a very expert way and with expert advice on how to use them without harming the environment or causing ecological imbalance. If there is the slightest possibility that using them may cause environmental or ecological damage, then the people should be prepared to accept some inconvenience or even relative poverty, but leave the resources intact. But it is very early to discuss these things at this stage without knowing the local conditions and the local situation.

Today many people give opinions: some minerals are self-replenishing, for instance. In the case of such minerals there is no harm in using them; rather, it is a good thing to use them. In a well of water, the same amount of water you take out, that amount comes back. That is the natural way. That kind of mineral we cannot hesitate to use.

But there are other kinds of minerals or natural resources. You take them out and this action degrades the entire soil or causes imbalance to the ecosystem. They are necessary to retain the wholesomeness of the environment. This kind of discriminating wisdom must be brought to bear by the local government on the question of minerals and other natural resources.

DR: How do you envisage the justice system in an autonomous Tibet? At present under the PRC the system is little more than a Kangaroo Court. In a free Tibet will the justice system be in Tibetan hands or remain under the control of the PRC? And how would the system work?

RINPOCHE: As I mentioned before, for an autonomous Tibet, in accordance with the Strasbourg Proposal, we have three uncompromising demands: One is for the entirety of the Tibetan group; the second is for a democratic system. Third, when we speak about a democratic system, an independent judiciary is inbuilt in that system. Therefore we will have an independent judiciary within the basic law of Tibet—the separate basic law of Tibet.

And it will be a little different than in the case of Hong Kong. Hong Kong had a judicial mechanism before it was handed back to China, and that judicial system continues until today. And therefore they started out with a rather better judicial system than China, but which is now being very much handicapped with the new basic law and its interpretation by the Central Politburo of the communist leadership, which has compromised it so that the whole judicial system in Hong Kong is now paralyzed; it is not able to function properly. We know about their experience.

So an independent judiciary within an autonomous Tibet should deliver justice over most disputes, including criminal and civil disputes and interpretation of the basic law—all these must be within the exclusive jurisdiction of the Tibetan judicial system.

And of course there may be some relation between Central Government and local Autonomous Government or certain common cases which involve the interstate or intergovernmental institutions, and for those matters we might depend on the judicial system of the PRC. But for the majority of judicial cases we must have an independent judiciary separate from the PRC, and that separation must be more complete than in the case of Hong Kong. And the High Court of the Tibet Autonomous Region should be the competent judicial institution to interpret the basic law of Tibet. That is very crucial. And if this High Court is not allowed to formulate or interpret the basic law, then the same experience of Hong Kong will be repeated in Tibet as well.

And our judicial system must be largely based on natural justice, and it must be a justice which does not concentrate on punishment and reward, but a system aiming at the transformation of the minds of people: a way of justice which becomes instrumental for the transformation and enlightenment of people's minds. For example, in criminal cases, there should be consistent teaching and counseling of those criminals instead of giving them cruel treatment or torture. Human rights violations and torture of humankind must be completely abolished from this system of justice. Genuine Ahimsa must be established.

So there are many things which will have to be taken care of by the people managing the justice system, especially in the areas of removing cruelty and replacing retributive justice with education, mercy, counseling, and improvement of the criminal mind. But the judiciary must be of the highest degree of autonomy and must be left to function autonomously within the guidelines of a non-violent approach.

DR: With regard to international relations, will Tibet be more aligned to Asia or to the West which has been largely ineffectual but at least very vocal in its support for a free Tibet? Or do you see yourselves as more aligned with your neighbors, including the PRC? And secondly, would Tibet want to be part of international structures such as the U.N.O. and other international NGOs and judicial structures?

RINPOCHE: In the Strasbourg Proposal it was envisaged that diplomatic relations with other countries would be exclusively the prerogative of the Central Government, that is, the PRC. But the local Autonomous Tibetan Government shall have a certain freedom to have educational, cultural, and religious ties with other countries. But China, the Central Government, was not in agreement with this proposal. This was one of the proposals to which they objected.

We can reduce this demand also, if China insists, but what we envisage in a future autonomous Tibet is: any student or any person who is interested to study culture or religion in Tibet should be able to visit Tibet without any impediment. Any Tibetan teacher, artist, or performer who is invited by any other country for a short or long term, or for any period; this should not have to be cleared by Central Government. It should be a Local Government decision, and people should be free to come and go. And, similarly, any academic and cultural exchanges should be decided by Local Government. That is our vision: it would be more expeditious if we had the authority to decide these things.

But to participate in the institutions of the U.N.O., I personally do not see much importance. Definitely Tibet cannot become a member of the U.N.O. We will remain an autonomous province of the PRC. Only the PRC will be a member country. But there may be a possibility to have our representatives or ambassadors in UNESCO or other such institutions, but we are not very interested to participate in these institutions because most of them are not very effective and not very democratic. Therefore it is better to limit ourselves and do individual and effective work in these areas.

But this is very flexible. The important thing is that the spiritual and cultural tradition of Tibet can reach outside without any hindrance from the Central Government. That much freedom is definitely required.

Within the above-mentioned parameters, our relations with other countries will be equal and reciprocal. Tibet will not be particularly aligned to Asia or to the West, nor with its neighbors; it will be friendly with all and aligned with none.

DR: Certain Tibet Support Groups are calling for His Holiness to return to Tibet, voicing the view that this would expedite the achievement of Tibetan autonomy and would be of great encouragement to the people inside Tibet to work more openly, more persistently towards autonomy within the PRC framework. Is there any possibility, or are there any hopes or plans that His Holiness may return to Tibet?

RINPOCHE: We all believe that His Holiness will return to Tibet in this lifetime, and that return may be permanent or it may be a visit. That no-one can decide at this moment. But everyone believes that His Holiness will definitely visit or return to Tibet in his lifetime. We all believe in that.

And that is very important for the people inside Tibet, those six million Tibetans who live inside Tibet and have no opportunity to come to India to see His Holiness. To see His Holiness and to receive his blessing and to be in his presence is a fundamental right of the Tibetan people. And this right should not be subject to politics.

So we always hope that His Holiness, even for a short spell of time, should visit Tibet, the major areas of Tibet, so that the people living in Tibet may have the opportunity to see him, to receive his teachings, and to have his blessings.

But this should not be mixed up with politics. The PRC Government tries to project in the international scenario that there is no problem in Tibet; everything is settled. According to the PRC the one question to be settled is how His Holiness can return to Tibet. According to them the only outstanding problem is to negotiate or discuss the return of the Dalai Lama. In their view everything else has been settled: the Tibetans have been given autonomy, this autonomy is working smoothly, and so on and so forth. But we must not confuse this matter.

His Holiness' return to Tibet is not an issue which needs to be negotiated or discussed, or which needs the persuasion of the Chinese Government. And His Holiness has made it absolutely clear that there is nothing to discuss with regard to the status or the facilities or whether he returns to Tibet. These things are irrelevant to the Tibet issue. So these two, the political status of Tibet and the status of the Dalai Lama, should not be mixed up.

The issue of Tibet is the future of the six million Tibetans in Tibet, not the future of the Dalai Lama. The six million people of Tibet need the Dalai Lama's leadership, and this is a spiritual issue which is also a separate issue. And during his lifetime, if the exiles can return to Tibet and Tibet can enjoy full autonomy as we are demanding, His Holiness has very clearly said that he will not participate in politics or hold any political office in the new arrangement. He will be a religious teacher only, dealing with spiritual matters: "Just a simple monk," as he always says.

And that is not deceptive language: it is the naked truth; His Holiness means what he says, and we should respect that. So His Holiness' return to Tibet and the settlement of the Tibet issue are two completely different matters, two different issues which need to be dealt with separately.

If the Tibetan issue is settled and His Holiness, without any political participation or political post assigned to him, returns to Tibet, he has every right to do so in order to teach Buddhism to his disciples. Even if the Tibet issue is not resolved and His Holiness wishes to return to Tibet for spiritual, non-political reasons, and if China does not object, it can be done. But even if everything is settled and His Holiness chooses not to go back, if he chooses to remain in India, if he chooses to remain till the end of his life in India, that is his freedom and his right. So we do not want to use His Holiness or the institution of the Dalai Lama in order to resolve the Tibet issue. We cannot use the Dalai Lama for these purposes.

Of course, his leadership is very important and very real. He will try his best; he will do everything for the resolution of the Tibet problem. But from the side of the Tibetan people, if we use His Holiness as a strategic instrument for placing pressure in order to achieve autonomy, I don't think that would be fair, and it would confuse the issue.

LOSING PATIENCE WITH NON-VIOLENCE

DR: A number of young Tibetans in exile and the Tibetan Youth Congress itself are beginning to express their discontent at the lack of progress towards a free Tibet. Their contention is that non-violence has proven itself ineffectual in the Tibetan struggle, and that the time has perhaps come to awaken the world to the plight of Tibet by engaging in acts of violence against the PRC and PRC institutions around the world. How do you respond to this feeling?

RINPOCHE: The Tibet struggle, as you mentioned, was started as a violent resistance right from 1949. And until, I think, the mid-70s violent resistance or rebellion continued in many pockets of Tibet. But one thing we must remember is that all this armed rebellion and resistance was not state-sponsored or state-organized. The state supported armed resistance for a very short period before the capture of Chamdo in 1950. And that was a very poor show and was crushed within a few days. That was the end of state-sponsored resistance. State-sponsored resistance was also not within the regime of the 14th Dalai Lama as he was not yet old enough to reign.

After crushing the Chamdo rebellion the occupation was completed. Only then was the state power given to the 14th Dalai Lama two years before the usual age of majority. And I think since then, from day one of his reign, his position was one of non-violence. He tried to negotiate with the Chinese and the 17-Point Agreement was concluded, and when violent rebellion was continued in 1958, the Government officially sent two abbots and two officials to persuade the Khampas to desist from violence, but it was not possible to convince them to give up their arms. And at that time circumstances were quite different.

So the point I am making is that, under the leadership, the political leadership of the present Dalai Lama, there was no organized or no state-approved violent action. That is a fact of our history.

Previously the Tibetan Government did have a small organized military force, but this force was only for the protection of His Holiness and the palaces—really a form of personal security; nothing more than that. They were never engaged in violence.

On 17th March 1959 when His Holiness escaped under threat to his life, Lhasa was bombarded by the Chinese military force on the 20th and morning of the 21st. And then of course at that time all the military and civilian force in and around Lhasa reacted very sharply—but this too was not state-ordered: it was all spontaneous. There was at that time no communication beyond Lhasa, and no state orders could be given. It was an unorganized public reaction. But these things are not noticed or not known.

Thereafter His Holiness chose the path of non-violence, and the path of non-violence has proved very effective and has delivered results beyond our expectations. That is also to be understood.

It should be understood in this way: If we were not engaged in the non-violent path, but in the path of violence, and armed struggle was encouraged to continue and was supported by the TGIE, then we should evaluate what sort of result could have been achieved by this. It was absolutely clear that none of the world governments would help the armed struggle nor sympathize with it. And the entire cause would have been completely swept away from the international scenario by this time, fifty years on. The Tibet question would have been completely forgotten and the armed rebellion would have been crushed very easily by the PRC. By the time unrest began again in the 70s the PRC brought more armed force into Tibet, so there was not the slightest chance of winning an armed struggle.

Then we come at a later stage to the 1987 and 1988 uprisings in Lhasa. All of them were by and large of a non-violent nature and the people did not even use the arms snatched from the Chinese military forces. These were just destroyed. I can't say it was completely non-violent, but I say by and large there was less violence than non-violence.

Therefore China found it difficult to repress that uprising very easily and it also helped to turn world opinion in favor of Tibet. There was much sympathy for the largely non-violent nature of the uprising.

And now coming to the question of patience. There can be no limitation on patience or the notion that we should only be patient up to a point, and then if we have still not achieved autonomy we should turn to violence. I don't think that this is the right approach to any kind of national conflict or struggle.

We have to consider both approaches. If we had opted for the violent way, what would we have achieved by this time? But we opted for the non-violent way, and we must ask what this approach has achieved as well as what it has failed to achieve until now. And if these two comparisons give you the result that the violent way might have been more effective, then of course there might be some dispute and loss of patience.

But that is absolutely not the case. The international political scenario and Chinese power are both abundantly clear to everyone and anyone can understand, can evaluate where, had we chosen the violent path, we would stand today. That needs to be analyzed and clearly spelt out. Then the question of losing patience can be discussed and justified.

Otherwise we remain firmly convinced that it was the right choice by His Holiness to choose the non-violent path. It is the reason why the Tibet issue is still alive today, and growing stronger, and there is a lot of concern for Tibet. Also, China is not able to ignore the insistence of the Tibet issue, and they cannot completely ignore His Holiness or the TGIE. They need to respond, and they need to deal with us. That has been the result of the non-violent struggle.

Now many say that 45 years have passed and nothing has changed. Forty-five years is a very long period for the lifetime of an individual, but for the lifetime of a nation and a people I don't think 45 years is that long. India needed to fight for her freedom continuously for more than 200 years, from the British and from others.

And even if we look at the present conflicts which we are witnessing, for instance, Israel and Palestine. For the last 50 years this struggle has existed there and they are not able to bring their freedom struggle to a conclusion. Both of the parties in this conflict are not non-violent; they chose the path of violence, and this has brought no good result.

In the case of India and the struggle in Kashmir: it has not been resolved in 55 years. All of them chose the violent path, and there have been three wars between Pakistan and India, but the issues still remain; nothing could be achieved. Yet, on the contrary, if right from the beginning India and Pakistan had sat together and sincerely discussed through a non-violent dialogue, I am sure that the question of Kashmir and other border issues might have been solved by now. Or even had they not been solved, they would not have sacrificed hundreds of thousands of human lives in vain, including the lives of civilians. All violence has achieved is to have made these issues harder to resolve.

And these are only a few examples we can use to illustrate our standpoint. Therefore a practitioner of non-violence and compassion should not become impatient and should not lose the patient path of non-violence or make comparisons with situations similar to ours but in which there is no hesitation to use violence, and where they are also not able to resolve their conflicts in spite of the expense of human life and resources.

Due to our non-violent approach, not only is the Tibet issue still alive, but not a single PRC or Tibetan life has been lost as a result of non-violence. That is also a great achievement: to preserve human life is very important and very sacred.

So my answer to this question would be: By its nature patience means patience forever, not for a limited time. If somebody practices patience for a period of time and he or she does not get the desired result and then loses patience, that kind of mindset is not patience, it is not the endurance of patience. It is just a temporary strategy. So, whosoever has real patience should never let go of it.

PART V:

SATYAGRAHA AND AHIMSA (TRUTH-INSISTENCE AND NON-HARMFULNESS)

INTRODUCTION

The Gandhian philosophy of Satyagraha has been translated as "the grasping for and holding onto Truth," and by its tenets the essential truth of any situation or problem can only be clearly discerned by a peaceful mind and a determined attitude of non-violence.

Satyagraha advocates openness and complete honesty rather than tactical duplicity, even if such duplicity may be the most efficient route to achieving one's personal or socio-political ends. But Satyagraha is not focused on victory or the achievement of goals in the ordinary sense. It relies, rather, on the inevitable triumph of Truth itself over falsehood and injustice: that is, Truth overcoming obstacles and adversaries through its own inherent power over the minds of people.

In the development of this philosophy, Gandhiji drew on elements derived from Tolstoy, Thoreau, Christianity, and the Gita and other Hindu writings. From this point of view it can be said that Satyagraha is the expression of a universally derived and universally appealing ideal. In Rinpoche's case, Buddhism has added its own dimensions to the view of Satyagraha.

The following extract from the speech on Satyagraha which Rinpoche delivered in Prague in 2003 provides the best introduction to the basic ideas of the Satyagraha-ideal:

> . . . It is a difficult task for me to brief you about Satyagraha due to three reasons: First, Satyagraha is a vast subject that cannot be dealt with in 15 minutes. Second, I have not prepared my presentation in writing, so now I cannot sum up things easily. And third is my language limitation. I find it difficult to express myself in a foreign language. Nevertheless, I will try my best.
>
> . . . In Satyagraha there is no victory or defeat. The objective is to find the Truth. So if, while making comparisons between defeat and victory, or success and failure, one chooses one or the other, perhaps one may not become a true Satyagrahi. A Satyagrahi looks only for the perception of Truth—nothing else. Victory is partial; it is compared with defeat. And if one has the perception of victory and defeat, then there is fear and desire. As long as fear and desire remain in one's mind, one may not be a completely true Satyagrahi.

So we have to rise above desire and fear. But the intention to find the Truth only, and to remain with it—to insist upon it—is Satyagraha.

Truth, according to the Buddhist viewpoint, has two levels: Absolute, and relative or conventional. In politics or social justice, the Absolute Truth does not work; we have to find out the relative truth upon which we have to work. And relative truth can differ from person to person, situation to situation, or time to time. As your perception of truth changes, your insistence will also change. Satyagraha is amendable and reversible. Once your perception of a relative truth changes, your insistence will also accordingly need to be amended. Therefore Gandhi said, "I do not try to be consistent. My experiment with truth is always progressing and improving. If and when my perception of truth changes, my actions and insistence will also accordingly go with it." Therefore Gandhi did not care about being inconsistent in his action and speech. What he cared about was that there should not be inconsistency between his perception of truth and his action. That is of utmost importance, whatever one considers. If we perceive truth, our action, speech, and thoughts must be in accordance with that truth. There cannot be any compromise or inconsistency in this regard. As soon as such inconsistency comes in, then we are no longer Satyagrahis. . . .

What I consider a more appropriate example of Satyagraha in action is what His Holiness the Dalai Lama and his Tibetan Governement-in-Exile are practicing. This might be more suitable and perhaps more useful for this occasion.

The English translation of Ahimsa is a bit inadequate, so I would like to explain my understanding of this term. Ahimsa includes a much wider spectrum of action and activism, whereas non-violence only negates violence. Truth and Ahimsa are the two sides of one coin. When one perceives a truth, the perception itself leads one to Ahimsa. And one becomes "Ahimsak"—one perceives the Truth more clearly. The two are interdependent. The practice of Ahimsa is the persuasion of Truth, and the persuasion of Truth is the practice of Ahimsak—they go together. Then all our actions in our day-to-day life need to be consistent with what we perceive to be the Truth.

To give a simpler illustration, His Holiness and his Government-in-Exile perceive that a genuine self-rule for the entire Tibetan nationality within the Chinese Constitution is an aspect of truth. Briefly, we perceive that to remain in association with China with full self-rule for the entire Tibetan nation is an aspect of truth, and we pursue it. When we pursue it, we cannot be diplomatic or adjustable. We cannot compromise many things that might be apparently useful in the pursuit of our goal. For example, to achieve that self-rule, we need to negotiate with the authorities of the People's Republic of China who very clearly and vigorously tell us: "OK, we are ready to negotiate with you, but first His Holiness must accept Tibet as an inseparable part of China. He also must accept Taiwan as a province of the PRC. And thirdly, he must give up all kinds of separatist activities." Many people think that His Holiness and his people are fools, and that, if we want to arrive at negotiations we should accept these things. They wonder why we do not go ahead and say Tibet is a part of China. Today it is, indeed, a part of China; the world accepts that. Then, they say: "What is the use of shying away from it?" They say we are absolutely undiplomatic and idiotic.

We are told: "What is the harm in saying that Taiwan is a province of China? It was, and it may be again in the future. And what is the harm to the Tibetan cause in agreeing to this? Accepting Taiwan as a province of the PRC does not make it happen tomorrow. PRC cannot occupy Taiwan the next day. It is simply words, but you can't pronounce them. Then there would be a good opening. After that, if China does not come for negotiations, then you can tell the international community that you have accepted all the preconditions for talks, but yet China is not coming for negotiations. Then your case will be much stronger."

But we insist in not accepting the untruth. In accordance with our perception, His Holiness cannot rewrite the history of Tibet. He cannot say that Tibet was, will be, and is an inseparable part of China—it was not. So we have to say: "Look, we cannot accept these preconditions whether we may achieve a negotiation or not. We want negotiation, but we cannot accept an untruth according to our perception. That is our insistence on truth."

As far as Taiwan is concerned, we have no business in its matters; it is an internal or external matter between mainland China and Taiwan. Who are we to accept or reject matters involving a nation with which we have no connection, relation, or business? If we interfered in their business, that would be because we did not perceive any truth about it. So we are not able to accept that precondition either. Of course, as far as giving up all kinds of separatist activities, we have not, do not, and will not engage in them—that I will say.

So this is one kind of Satyagraha which we are practicing now. Not compromising with truth, yet insisting on achieving the negotiation through which a solution to the Tibet problem can be found.

Similarly, in day-to-day administration we insist on truth, nonviolence, and genuine democracy. Many of my civil servants and colleagues find this very harmful for running the administration institution smoothly, particularly in a place like India where there are many things that need to be done illegally and through unfair means. If we stop resorting to unfair means to get things done, it is certain that there will be a lot of delay and inconvenience even in small things. For the last two years we, particularly my administration, very clearly have refused to do anything which infringes the law of the land—the Indian law. It is a Himalayan problem—huge obstacles are there, but we accept the inconvenience. One aspect of Satyagraha is to accept the torture, the problem, the suffering, yet not to compromise with untruth. We experience difficulties day in and day out, but we have not given up. I cannot say that every department and every civil servant of my administration is working on it, but by and large we are trying to do it. This is another kind of Satyagraha we are practicing.

To conclude, since my time is up, there is another important aspect of Satyagraha we are practicing—among its many aspects—and that is to resist injustice, and to resist or react to violence. Gandhi was not happy with the expression "passive resistance." Passivity implies laziness or idleness; and there are many religious traditions which teach non-resistance to evil. Resistance is also considered a kind of violence, but this is a dangerous misconception. Many people think non-violence means non-resistance or non-reaction to injustice. Justice is an aspect of truth. To do everything possible within one's power to protect and preserve justice—that is the legitimate duty of a Satyagrahi.

Wherever we see or encounter violence and injustice, we have to resist it compassionately, lovingly. Without any trace of hatred or vengeance, we have to resist physically, vocally, and mentally—going through all the threats and dangers. Resistance means an opposite action. If there is violence and one resists it by counter-violence, one just falls into the trap of the opponents. They are promoting violence, and we help it by contributing counter-violence. The Satyagrahi thinks that violence resisted by counter-violence is a big contribution to that violence because it will not do anything to reduce or bring about the cessation of violence. This is a law of nature.

Sensible people can see that if there is a fire, and they want to extinguish it, they have to add something of its opposite nature. It cannot be extinguished by adding more fire or fuel to it. If there is a flood, we have to reduce the amount or stop the source of water. To fight a flood we cannot put more water in it. It would be absolutely illogical and there would not be any hope of countering the problem. This is a very clear law of nature which needs to be understood. So we have to resist injustice or violence by applying the opposite force to it. That opposite force can reduce and eliminate the violence because it eliminates the cause of violence.

Buddha's first teaching is the simple fact that we should be aware of the existence of misery, we should search for the cause of that misery, and we should understand the possibility of eliminating its cause. And the method—the path for eliminating that cause—should be practiced or adopted. These are the simple Four Noble Truths, and they are applicable to every human action. Whatever we do, we have to act accordingly.

If we are suffering from a disease, we have to discover its root cause, then we have to find an antidote for that cause, and by eliminating the root cause we will be cured. Only treating the symptoms, as most of the modern allopathic drugs do, will not cure us. We may be instantly relieved of the symptoms, but the disease will remain.

Satyagrahis must be able to search for the cause of a problem and eradicate it. The present Tibet situation is caused by a few dictators of the PRC, due to their ignorance, hatred, and greed, which are caused by their negative emotions. If we are to resolve this problem, we have to deal with the negative emotions of the Chinese leadership. Those negative emotions can be reduced and finally eliminated if we apply the opposite force to counter them. Those opposite forces are love, kindness, affection, caring, and desirelessness. This attitude can directly affect the mindset of the Chinese leadership. Once their mindset is changed, the problem can be automatically solved. And it would not only be temporarily solved; the solution to the problem through Satyagraha would be a permanent solution, and we are looking forward to achieving that solution. Thank you.

The Dialogues

DR: Satyagraha or "Truth-Insistence" is a concept associated mainly with the non-violent independence struggle led by Mahatma Gandhi, the guiding philosophy behind the struggle methodology of Gandhiji and his followers. As a result of this association, Satyagraha is viewed by most people as a socio-political view related only to India in the specific context of the Gandhian independence movement.

But Satyagraha is much more universal and far-reaching as a philosophy of life, is it not? It can be applied not only to all areas of our endeavor, but is an indispensable aspect of authentic spirituality. In your own case, your vision of Satyagraha must have been colored by Buddhism. But can we say that the principles of Satyagraha are compatible with all religions and with all moral philosophy?

RINPOCHE: The concept of Satyagraha, practiced by Mahatma Gandhi, was indeed a combination of many traditions, including Indian spirituality and the Indian philosophical traditions in which Gandhi was born and brought up.

And at the same time he was most inspired, with regard to formulating Satyagraha as a formula for political and social justice, by Thoreau, Tolstoy, and many other non-Indian traditions and sources. I think the practice of Satyagraha is a very old technique, existing everywhere in the world and used for the realization of Truth or in defense of Truth or for achieving justice on the basis of Truth.

And speaking personally: yes, as you mentioned, my own view of Satyagraha is much conditioned or influenced by Buddhist teachings. I sometimes think that Siddhartha's endeavor and experience in enduring six years of very difficult conditions in search of Truth, his practice of severe austerity, giving up all care of his body and pursuing meditation so as to reduce himself almost to a skeleton, until he gave up without having attained realization—until he gave up his practice—was a kind of Satyagraha: determination in holding onto the search for Truth.

But he realized that this was not the correct way. Again he nourished his body and refreshed his mind and found the middle-way approach, and he returned to the Bodhi Tree where he sat down and determined that he would not get up, no matter what, until he had attained Enlightenment. And that, I think, is also a form of Satyagraha in search of Truth. Of course, during that session he attained Enlightenment through his determination and was able to share his experience with the world.

And in the Western world there was Socrates, who consumed poison rather than compromise his search for Truth and his findings, to make compromises with the viewpoints of others in order to survive. In defense of his own conception of Truth and justice, whatever it meant to him, he chose to give up his life instead of giving up his Truth, his authentic philosophy and the way of life that flowed from these. And we find many other people who did the same.

Jesus chose to be crucified, yet did not condemn his tormentors, and prayed that they might be forgiven. And this is, I think, the essential quality of Satyagraha—that it is practiced in defense of the Truth or a specific truth. And Jesus chose pain and suffering rather than compromising the Truth. I think that all these were a source of inspiration for Mohandas K. Gandhi, demonstrating how to employ this technique in search of social truth and social justice.

He was much inspired by Thoreau as well, and also by the various writings that are usually regarded as the province of the Christian community, and followed and practiced by Christians. And in his correspondence about Tolstoy we also find a background to the formulation of his ideas on Satyagraha.

So I would say that Satyagraha is an inviolable principle of all religious traditions—as far as my knowledge goes—no spiritual teaching would say that you can or should compromise the Truth. It cannot be given up to the convenience of worldly life. No teacher of Truth would teach against this principle.

The explanation of Truth may differ from religion to religion, but the importance of Truth and of remaining with that Truth: in this regard all religions are the same. And particularly when coming to Buddhism, we have more to consider. Buddhist teaching is unlike most of the other religious traditions in that it speaks of two different truths: the Absolute Truth and the relative or conventional truth. When you merge with the Absolute Truth, then, of course, all differences and inconsistencies cease and there can be no conflict because there is no duality or diversity. The Absolute is beyond the religious conventions and disparities which we encounter in everyday life.

But as regards the relative truth we should give equal importance to all the various religious groups, even though there are so many alternative interpretations of Truth and untruth, justice and injustice, good and evil, and so forth. So in that matter we have to hold onto what is considered to be good and true in our own religion. And in the

Jatakas many stories are told of the life of Siddhartha, of his determination and refusal to be separated by circumstances from his search for Truth, and that should also inspire us to hold onto what we consider to be Truth.

So I would say that we must abide with the truth that we consider to be true, holding on with a pure mind to what we consider to be true—which may be the exact opposite of what someone else considers truth to be, because such truth is relative—if we hold onto it with a pure mind, it will lead us to Absolute Truth. What is important is to hold onto our truth without any mental defilements—and this is universally applicable, even in today's hurried and complex society. In fact, it is more applicable today than before, and also is in consonance with all the religious traditions.

DR: How does the practice of Satyagraha for its own sake differ from the practice of Satyagraha for a specific goal or aim? Does Satyagraha predict a predetermined result of its practice in socio-political endeavor or struggle? Does it predicate a defined outcome or does it operate more freely, along dialectic lines perhaps, towards an ideal society whose exact dynamics it does not pre-formulate? In other words, does the practice of Satyagraha make clear promises regarding its socio-political and individual results, or does it only make the statement that "because the practice is clearly wholesome, the result must in some general sense be beneficial"?

RINPOCHE: I think this question cannot be answered in a general way. We cannot generalize in this case. There is Satyagraha which has a specific goal to be achieved, and one can cease from that particular practice of Satyagraha once the goal has been achieved. And this kind of Satyagraha can be considered as a specific and temporary practice.

But that is not the whole of Satyagraha. And, for the most part, you cannot specify the particular aim of Satyagraha practice, one or another objective to be achieved by the practice of Satyagraha. There may be a particular social objective, but the crucial point is that the objective is secondary, whereas the method is principal: more important. However noble or great the objective may be, if your method is not perfect you cannot achieve the aim you have set out to achieve. You may achieve something, but it will have been achieved outside of your truth-vision of it. And even if the objective is partially achieved, it will be negatively affected by the law of causality, particularly in the way in which the nature of causality is understood by Buddhism: the result would be completely determined by the nature of the goal, together with the methods employed to achieve it. A bad goal and a bad method would bring about a bad result; that principle is accepted by all schools of Buddhism. This applies also to the purity of the practice of Satyagraha—even a little defilement would be reflected in the end result.

Therefore, whether you achieve a particular goal or not is not the question of prime importance for the Satyagrahi. The matter of highest concern for that individual is how perfect the method is, and how perfectly it is employed.

The most difficult aspect of Satyagraha is, indeed, when you practice Satyagrahi for a specific social or political goal. It is extremely difficult to practice Satyagraha for these ends in modern society. Among the Tibetans in exile, for instance, we are not able to develop a real Satyagraha among ourselves because of distrust and fear and frustration. All these diminish the force of Satyagraha and, in fact, make it a non-Satyagraha. And therefore it has no result.

Satyagraha must be first of all a compassionate mind towards the opposite side, the opponent from whom we are demanding something. In our case it should be the Chinese authorities who are the object of our Satyagraha. But we are not able to achieve a compassionate mind for these people. On the contrary, we have vengeance or hatred, and that makes all our effort seemingly non-violent, but yet it has no effect and it is rendered defective due to the smallest defilement of mindset which spoils the whole thing.

So, understanding this, we need not pay any attention to the objective. The objective is clear and the objective is good. The objective is good for China and it is good for Tibet. That can be quite easily understood. But we have to focus our whole attention on the forces, the method, the path on which we are moving—the Satyagraha itself.

So unless the effort is really based on Satyagraha, with no mixture of untruth and no mixture of mental defilements, it becomes a non-Satyagraha. Therefore I can say that Satyagraha is not in the first place for the achievement of any particular aim. Satyagraha is an achievement for its own sake: once you achieve Satyagraha, then you need not look for anything more. It is both the means and the end. And if the means is pure, then the end is bound to be pure. This is the right perspective in which to view Satyagraha.

DR: What is the role played by Ahimsa in the complete context of Satyagraha? Is Truth and the practice of Truth in individual and social affairs always compatible with non-harm? Is there no room for a "sword of truth"?

RINPOCHE: I would say very decisively that Satyagraha and Ahimsa are two sides of one coin. They cannot function separately. If you are true to Ahimsa, you are already practicing Satyagraha, and the true Satyagrahi is practicing Ahimsa. And there is absolutely no room for harm in the process of Satyagraha.

But coming back to the question: "What is harm?" As I mentioned some days ago, killing might be considered harmless in a given context and in a specific situation. Taking the life of an individual can in certain cases be considered a non-harmful act, and the very act of killing might perhaps be beneficial to that particular person.

It is very debatable in the Buddhist Canon, but generally the Buddhist accepts that Himsa and Ahimsa cannot be judged only by the appearance of the action. For example, cutting off a limb from a person could be of great harm to that person, but the surgeon might need to amputate an arm or a leg in order to save the life of an individual, and in such a case cutting off one component of the body is not an act of violence because the intention is to help the patient and the result is the saving of a life.

So in this way, you are hurting him, but the hurting becomes a positive action rather than a violent action. So I would say that the sword may have a role in the practice of Satyagraha but that violence would have no place.

Appendix: Extracts from "Satyagraha-Truth Insistence" by Samdhong Rinpoche (March 1997)

Required Qualifications of a Satyagraha Activist:

1. Through unshakeable faith and confidence in Truth and the non-violent path of peace, one must maintain proper ethical conduct (as is specified separately), which consists, in part,

of never speaking falsehoods and never harming others. This conduct must have been maintained for not less than three months before entering the movement.

2. One must have no anger, hatred, or intent to harm the objects of our resistance, the government officials and workers of communist China and all those siding with them.

3. When engaged in Satyagraha activism, one must have the courage never to respond to violence with violence, nor to use violence to protect oneself, no matter how much one is beaten, imprisoned, tormented, and tortured.

4. When undertaking the Satyagraha movement to restore Tibet's independence, one should not consider it a political movement, nor some mundane activity, nor a campaign calculated to hurt the Chinese. Instead, one should recognize and believe that one is engaged in the spiritual practice of restoring Tibet's freedom for the sake of all sentient beings.

5. While participating in the movement, one should in no way expect to gain fame, glory, political or economic profit, or recognition for one's notable accomplishments and the like.

6. One should not at any point remind others of one's contributions nor expect to receive credit, for one has abandoned all such notions. In particular, after the restoration of freedom one must have no expectation whatsoever of any political position, social status, financial support, or any other benefit for oneself in one's relations. And even if such an offer is made in free Tibet, one must firmly vow to decline it unless there are some clear and pressing reasons.

7. In all matters such as clothing, lodging, furnishings, and so on, one must lead a life free of extremes; one must not participate in unethical ways of making a living, and one must have little desire for wealth.

8. One must never participate in any activities whatsoever, whether public or private, that are dishonest or untruthful.

9. One must see to it that one's family members, such as children and aged parents, are not dependent upon oneself for support; if they are dependent, then one must receive their permission.

10. One must have no outstanding loans, no accounts to be settled, no liabilities to manage, and no other such responsibilities to be met.

11. One must never break one's vow of truth and non-violence, even at the cost of one's life.

12. One must not transgress those rules which from time to time are legitimately drafted by the leaders of the Satyagraha Movement.

Decisions Required of a Satyagraha Activist:

1. From the moment that one enlists in the Satyagraha Movement, one must never abandon it until the Movement's announced goals have been met or every single activist has perished without exception.

2. No matter how much misery and hardship one faces in body and mind, one must persevere and never abandon one's activism as long as one lives.

3. Regardless of how much one is praised or reviled, if one's motivation is flawless, then one can never be dissuaded, no matter how many comments others make.

Points to be Understood:

1. One needs to understand from the very beginning that not only is it quite likely that one might well have to die soon after beginning one's activism, but it is possible that all of the members of the movement will die, or that the goals of the movement will not be achieved. But in any case, all members of the movement will die within some seventy years. Hence, inasmuch as one must die either way, rather than dying a few years later without fulfilling one's birth-duty, it is clearly preferable to die a few years earlier while in the process of fulfilling one's birth-duty. Even if one is not willing to die right now, how can one be guaranteed that one will live for any extended period of time?

2. Our goals may not be achieved, even though everyone in the movement has perished, but all the contemporary Tibetans will one day die even if we do not begin a Truth Movement.

More importantly, whether the movement is unsuccessful or we fail to engage in a movement, our culture and our ethnic identity will perish in either case. Inasmuch as all would be lost one way or the other, rather than doing nothing and waiting for everything to be destroyed on its own, it is clearly preferable—no matter how one argues—that we lose everything while attempting to fulfill our birth-duty.

Inevitable Obstacles to the Satyagraha Movement:

The Satyagraha Movement is likely to face many possible impediments and obstacles, but most are little cause for concern. However, the two most serious obstacles could prove problematic. They are:

1. Satyagraha activists will face immeasurable torture and torment, and our tormentors will use every conceivable method to arouse our anger. In doing so, they will attempt to incite activists to employ violence and falsehood, and it is possible that some will break their vow of non-violence. Another possibility is that our opponents will recruit and infiltrate their agents into the Satyagraha Movement. These agents will then attempt to incite others to violence.
2. Through vague and false statements, and with the pretext of seeking some means of arriving at a settlement, time will be wasted in meaningless discussions that are intended to stop the Truth Movement.

We will need to face these two eventualities with great skill and vigilance.

A Response to Skepticism About Satyagraha:

Although many people do not think this way, the fact remains that if the Path of Truth and Non-Violence is truly powerful, it must be capable of overcoming anything it faces. And if it is faced with lawless brutality, the Path of Truth and Non-Violence will necessarily become even more potent. When Truth confronts falsehood and non-violence confronts violence, the stronger force will be the one that is more valid; the fact that one's opponents have more brute force does not mean that they will thereby have greater strength. When we say that Buddha Shakyamuni overwhelmed billions of demonic forces with a single meditation on love, we are not recounting a simple story; instead, I feel that we are speaking of a rationally supported symbol of the power of Truth and Non-Violence. Finally, even if participating in such a movement were to be tantamount to suicide, I have already remarked that we must die one way or the other. So rather than die having led an empty and meaningless life, it is far more meaningful and more in keeping with the demands of history to die while engaged in the spiritual practice of Truth and Non-Violence for the sake of our nation and its spiritual traditions.

PART VI:

THE FOUNDATIONAL
VIEW—BUDDHADHARMA

THE LIFE OF SIDDHARTHA GOTAMA

The life of Siddhartha, Prince of the Shakyas, is known generally by many people. He was born into royalty and the prospect of vast wealth, power, luxury, and refinement. Throughout his childhood years, he was shielded from all sight of misery in the world, growing up in a deliberately manufactured environment of illusory pleasure and happiness. As a young man, on leaving these palatial environs for the first time, he was first exposed to the truths of human suffering, presented to him in the form of sickness, old-age, and death. His initial shock at these revelations drove him to the contemplation of his own privileged situation and its essential powerlessness to overcome these inevitable human afflictions and the final extinction of death.

Realizing that wealth, youth, and privilege could not prevail over the afflictions and stresses common to all of humanity, he exchanged the palace life for that of a homeless wanderer—a seeker after true liberation.

On this path of learning and experimentation, probing through his own experience the practices of asceticism as the opposite pole to his earlier life of luxury, and subjecting himself to many deprivations and much mental anguish, he relinquished these extremes as well, realizing the Path of the Middle Way, which he later summarized in his teaching as the Noble Eightfold Path: the avoidance of extremes through wisdom, mental development, and morality or virtuous conduct.

In our contemporary world, especially in developed countries, many of us are caught up in the "Siddhartha Dilemma." Not only do we generally have more widespread opportunity and access to wealth, but there is also the chase after prolonged youth and the contriving of increased and varied pleasures, entertainments, and distractions. Medical science has significantly decreased the threat of fatal illness, a host of pharmaceutical products keep us younger for longer, and advances in genetic manipulation are making cautious promises around the possibility of significantly increasing our lifespan. Thus, instead of being prompted by the experience of illness and old-age to reflect on life's unsatisfactory outcome and the impermanence of shallow pleasures, we apply ourselves to more ingenious ways and deluded hopes of keeping suffering away for longer periods. And in the inevitable case of death, we turn away from it by various forms of denial and distraction.

THE FIRST NOBLE TRUTH: THE TRUTH OF SUFFERING

The First Noble Truth is the truth of life in Samsara, our complex realm of cyclic existence, as seen from the perspective of enlightened beings. In essence it makes the statement that all life in this realm is suffering, and we sometimes see this statement augmented into such forms as: all life lived in the ego (or selfishly) brings suffering, or that all our life experience, including transient pleasures and happiness, ultimately reveals itself as unsatisfactory, unfulfilling, and delusory. The First Noble Truth taught by the Buddha has also been expressed as "all life is stress," implying that our mental states and our activities inevitably involve uncomfortable and painful stresses which we simply cannot avoid.

We could say that this truth is acknowledged in the emphasis of modern psychological practice on guilt, anxiety, and depression—the most common components of neurosis. We feel guilty on account of our past and present failures, anxious about the future and our place in it, and depressed for any number of reasons. These neurotic manifestations play so big a role in our societies that sedatives and anti-depressants constitute a huge component of the pharmaceutical industry and of medical prescriptions—and, of course, there is the increased tendency to seek out every form of escapism, including alcohol and drug abuse and promiscuity generally. And there is the constant resort to psychotherapy.

There are also refined and less neurotic forms of escape, exemplified by the resort to an ever-more complex and ultra-profound intellectualism or to the arts or the accumulation of wealth—and even to shallow emotional religious experience. All of these things, properly understood, are proofs of the First Noble Truth.

THE SECOND NOBLE TRUTH: THE TRUTH OF THE CAUSES OF SUFFERING

The Buddha revealed that the root cause of suffering is ignorance of the true nature of the realm in which we live, and of ourselves. From this ignorance arise the notions of an inherently existent "I-entity" and the inherent existence of phenomena. These ignorant notions in turn result in the dynamics of attachment and aversion, expressed as the desire to have and enjoy what we want and not to have or experience what we do not want or do not enjoy.

There can be no real understanding of the Second Noble Truth without close and determined examination of the nature of "I" and of phenomena, and such examination requires much effort and penetrative concentration. We will try to look more deeply into this subject later in this section. For now we must simply try to view the "I" or self as a flux of interdependent processes which do not constitute in any ultimate way an inherently existent entity, a thing in itself. We should try to view phenomena in the same way; as dreamlike perhaps.

But the more we try to see the true nature, the openness, the transience, the voidness, in the deepest sense of self and phenomena, the more stubbornly we are confronted with the "legitimacy" of the view that things really are the way they appear to be: I seem to myself to be as much a self-existent entity in possession of my attributes as does the chair on which I am sitting. My attachments and aversions seem so inalienably a part of me, together with everything else that constitutes my identity.

And the stubborn "obviousness" of this view leads to the conclusion that I have only three choices: to strive to cultivate a "good self," to allow myself to slide into becoming a "bad self," or being content to remain an uncomfortable combination of both, propped up by personal and social mores. These limited choices are influenced and encouraged by the prevalent cult of personality, the role-model syndrome, and the social rewards attached to being this or that kind of person.

Central to this dilemma is the question of being loved and accepted, or despised and rejected as a person. This forms the foundation of the psychological well-being of the individual and society in our psychological theories.

For these and other reasons the truth of not-self is difficult to see, and even when understood, difficult to accept and practice. It is of the utmost importance to be led in this regard by a qualified teacher.

THE THIRD NOBLE TRUTH: THE TRUTH OF THE CESSATION OF SUFFERING

In the Third Noble Truth the Buddha proclaimed cessation from suffering through the overcoming of ignorance (that is, ignorance of the true nature of self) and the dissolution of attachment and aversion. In short, suffering ceases together with the cessation of craving: craving for existence and craving for non-existence, and craving for the kind of happiness which depends on having the myriad conditions which we desire in our life experience. The extinguishing of all craving is the only possibility of complete liberation from suffering in the world.

But our world order thrives on the dynamic of craving. In fact, we are constantly encouraged to crave after such things as success, wealth, convenience, power, and so forth. We are exhorted to crave after admirable personalities, capable minds, and even beautiful bodies which together heighten our sense of self-worth. We are expected to be self-confident and to grasp at every opportunity for mundane self-development.

Ethologists speak about instinctual and inescapable drives which, in their view, are psychologically destructive if not heeded or fulfilled. But there are also cultural, social, and individual drives arising from our conditioning in these areas. We believe that our happiness (expressed as self-fulfillment) depends very heavily on satisfying these cravings.

The mental work (especially study and meditation) requires the willingness to go deep, to employ intense concentration and perseverance. We need to look earnestly at our condition in order to find the inclination, the motivation, and the time needed for these practices.

THE FOURTH NOBLE TRUTH: THE EIGHTFOLD PATH

In the Eightfold Path the Buddha set forth the method for the attainment of liberation, of cessation from suffering. It is a path which leads gradually to the realization (making real in one's own experience) of wisdom and compassion. It addresses three crucial areas of development: morality, mental development, and the unfolding of wisdom. These three are intimately interrelated and reinforce each other on the path to liberation.

MORALITY: RIGHT SPEECH
This is an exhortation to avoid lying, slander, harsh speech, and idle talk. In other words, to discipline our use of speech away from harmfulness and towards benefit for ourselves and others.

As communication technology becomes more sophisticated and globalized, the power and influence of speech grows greater—and yet it seems that these potent channels of communication, particularly the media, are used almost exclusively for the propagation of "spin," political correctness, and trivialities, to the point that we have come to accept, even with humor, that political and other forms of power and influence are inevitably coupled with deceit and delusion. We see irresponsible emotional speech being used in the promotion of religious doctrines and causes. It seems that only scientists are required to be reasonably precise and honest.

In our individual lives speech is regularly used frivolously, glibly, or aggressively, with little concern for the benefit of others.

MORALITY: RIGHT LIVELIHOOD (OR, RIGHT LIVING)
Right living implies using non-harmful means to sustain ourselves, our families, employees, and so forth. By extrapolation we can see that this principle extends to the entire society in which we live, both locally and globally.

And non-harmfulness in this regard can be a very subtle question: for instance, some activities which appear non-harmful in an immediate context may have extremely harmful consequences in the long-term or in a broader context. Harmful effects can also be indirect, such as the gradual degradation of the environment in which we live.

MORALITY: RIGHT ACTION
The essence, again, of right action is that it be at least non-harmful and at best beneficial. Buddhism identifies the minimal aspects of right action as refraining from theft, killing, and illicit sexual conduct. These are refined by the cultivation of wisdom and compassion.

MENTAL DEVELOPMENT: RIGHT MINDFULNESS (OR, RIGHT ATTENTIVENESS)

Right mindfulness is of four kinds: mindfulness of the body, of feelings, of the mind, and of objects of the mind (mental or physical phenomena). It is a practice for sharpening awareness of the true nature of our reality and of ourselves, of what we are doing, thinking, feeling, and perceiving, and why we are doing, thinking, feeling, and perceiving as we do. It deepens our understanding and helps us to cultivate an attitude of meticulousness in our moral outlook and in our analysis of our world and of ourselves.

Actually, most of us live our lives in almost complete unmindfulness. We respond to inner and outer stimuli with conditioned, automatic responses, hardly ever subjecting these to examination. The result is mental turmoil which is reflected in our frenetic lifestyles. At the social level this absence of mindfulness manifests in a corresponding absence of compassion. We are blind to each other's welfare.

MENTAL DEVELOPMENT: RIGHT EFFORT

Right effort is of four kinds: to avoid the arising of unwholesome states of mind, to overcome unwholesome states which have arisen, to develop wholesome states, and to maintain whatever wholesome states have been developed. As one grows in this practice, inner tranquility is correspondingly cultivated.

But we are so driven to frantic activity under the pressures of economic, social, and personal imperatives, that most of our mental effort is devoted to overcoming fatigue, anxiety, and depression. The system in which we are caught up, and our understanding of personality, leave us with little time, energy, or inclination to practice the right effort which leads to a peaceful mind. Again, the shallowness which accompanies our mundane endeavors is, for the most part, unwholesome and strongly bound up with the ego-identity.

MENTAL DEVELOPMENT: RIGHT CONCENTRATION

It is taught that right concentration is fixing the mind to a single object, that the prerequisites for right concentration are the four kinds of right effort, and that the objects of concentration, at least initially, should be one of the four objects of mindfulness: body, feeling, mind, or mental objects.

The benefit of right concentration is that the mind becomes capable of penetrating through the appearances of "self" and phenomena, to see their essence or their real nature. In other words, right concentration enables us to recognize more clearly the impermanence and interdependence of so-called entities, including the entity of ego, and ultimately empowers us to penetrate their "emptiness" or lack of inherent existence. It helps us towards the undeluded seeing which can liberate us from suffering.

Developing right concentration is dependent on meditative practice and study, which is again an indication of the central importance which Buddhism places on the cultivation of mind, or bringing the mind to its true potential and to the realization of its true nature through a process of systematic exercise.

WISDOM: RIGHT UNDERSTANDING

In its final sense, right understanding means understanding the Four Noble Truths in such a way that they motivate and transform our lives. It is the difference between merely comprehending the doctrines of a religion and being infused or energized by the living or spiritual Truth on which the doctrine is based.

Thus right understanding is actually the prerequisite for adequate practice of the Eightfold Path. For instance, to practice right action without right understanding would be to obey a convention without being able to penetrate or explain its rightness or usefulness. And this is true of all the other aspects of the path.

There are degrees of right understanding, and to the extent to which one understands clearly and penetratively, only to that extent can one practice the Eightfold Path with real benefit.

WISDOM: RIGHT THINKING (OR, RIGHT MINDEDNESS)

Thoughts free from lust (or craving), malice, and cruelty, are called right thinking. And, in a higher sense, all thinking which rejects negative patterns and maintains positive or wholesome tendencies is called right mindedness. This practice proceeds from and increases right understanding, right effort and right mindfulness.

And surely it is right thinking that is at the very interface between our motives and the external manifestations of our motives: our speech and general conduct. It seems obvious that wrong thinking is the immediate predecessor to the harm we cause in the world.

But it is impossible to catch hold of the subtleties of right thinking or to train our minds to distinguish clearly between wrong and right thinking without concurrently attending to all the other aspects of the Eightfold Path. And without right thinking we simply cannot speak and act in accordance with the way things really are. We are left without skill in these outward expressions and activities.

The more one considers and practices the Eightfold Path, the clearer it becomes that it is, in fact, one seamless process or practice of development in which the eight components are tightly and indispensably interdependent. Each contains both the seed and fruit of every one of the others. If one or more are absent, those which have arisen in our mental domain will seek them out, call for them and inevitably find them because, unless they are all active, we cannot travel any further on the path to Truth.

KARMA

In Christian belief there is some idea of Karma expressed as a "morality of compensation" based on the Christian maxim, "As you sow, so shall you reap." Many people unconsciously act on this principle, but view it as a transactional philosophy for dealing with relationships: the harm you cause to others will return on your own head.

On the other hand, we often seem to see this principle failing completely: we see wicked and unscrupulous people succeeding, gaining power, renown, and wealth—and, apparently, even happiness in this life. We remember King David's frustrated cry, "Why do the wicked prosper?" The problem here is that we do not understand the depths, the levels of complexity, and the time spans at which Karma (the law of action, or of cause and effect, or of becoming) actually operates.

In Buddhism it is taught that Karma is a dynamic which shapes or develops the way self or ego views the world and acts in it. It is the force which shapes our ordinary or ego-mind and is responsible for the way we perceive ourselves, others, and the phenomena of Samsara. It is like a distorting lens which we have developed through countless lifetimes, and it will continue to cause suffering to ourselves, others, and our realm in general, unless we learn to correct the distortion. This is achievable through study and penetrative meditative practice. In this case, it is important to find a skilled and trustworthy teacher.

REBIRTH

In the Buddhist view sentient beings are reborn countless times into cyclic existence (in any of the Six Realms). In this case "cyclic existence" means the drudge and suffering of birth, old age, sickness, and death. The realm in which the person is born is due to the accumulation of their Karma from previous lifetimes and their ignorant clinging to an "I-existence." Rebirths can be into good or bad circumstances, depending on the Karma generated during previous lifetimes.

There is an obvious relevance of the belief in rebirth to ongoing spiritual development, since the Buddhist view is that it usually takes many lifetimes to achieve Enlightenment. The serious Dharma practitioner wants to make each lifetime as useful as possible in the determined pursuit of final Liberation.

INTERDEPENDENT ORIGINATION

The concept of interdependent origination lies at the heart of the view of Emptiness (Shunyata): the view that all entities, although having apparent self-existence from a conventional or relative standpoint, in fact are devoid of existence from their own side. It is taught that their existence as entities is imputed by the observer on the basis of their interdependent parts, interdependent before-and-after moments, the mental formation processes, various sense consciousnesses, and so forth.

Thus, since they depend on a myriad of interdependent factors for their apparent existence as entities, they cannot be said to exist in and from themselves (i.e. their existence is not self-sufficient), and the main extrapolation made from this argument is the Emptiness or non-inherent existence of "I."

The philosophical arguments for this view, refined to perfection by Nagarjuna and fully expressed in the Prasangika-Madhyamika expositions, are highly analytical and demand the development of a high degree of subtlety in abstract analysis.

But the analytical understanding of Emptiness is not sufficient to bring us to liberation from the "I" dynamic of suffering. The teaching is that it is necessary to gain non-conceptual insight into Emptiness through meditative practices, and to experience the direct realization of the state of Shunyata. Again, this cannot be achieved without the presence of a highly skilled teacher.

IMPERMANENCE, SUFFERING, NOT-SELF

These the Buddha called the three characteristics of Existence. The Pali Scriptures say that: "All formations are transient . . . and that which is transient is subject to suffering and change, and of that which is transient and subject to suffering and change, one cannot rightly say: This belongs to me; this am I; this is my ego."

The direct connection here is between the notion of transience and that of "not-self," or Emptiness (Shunyata) of self. Buddhism understands that nothing which is impermanent can be said to possess inherent existence. That which exists of itself must always have existed and always continue to exist changelessly, since it must exist outside of the laws of cause and effect (Karma). This again is a philosophical postulate that can only be grasped in a realized way by means of very close and subtle analysis. In this case too, penetrative meditation is of the highest importance.

THE FIVE AGGREGATES

The Five Aggregates (or groups of existence) were taught by the Buddha to be the five bases from which our imputation of inherent existence or "selfness" of ourselves, other beings, and all phenomena in general arises. Not discerning the interdependent and interoperative dynamics of the Five Aggregates, we perceive entities or "selves" rather than transient processes of conventional existence.

The five interdependent and interactive aggregates (or, Skandhas) are: form (or, corporeality), feeling, perception, mental formations, and consciousness. These are the products of our Karma, and the interaction of these aggregates gives rise to the mistaken notion of "I" and "it." Thus, we mistakenly speak of "my feelings," "my consciousness," "its form," and so forth, as though these were inherently existing entities in possession of such attributes.

To a large extent, the reason for these misapprehensions is that we consider our own conscious subjective experience to be "I." We say: "This consciousness which I experience must be my essential self." But the Buddha demonstrated that subjective consciousness also arises in dependence on the other Skandhas. Thus, in the absence of form, feeling, perception, and mental formations, consciousness itself cannot arise.

The temptation here is to take the obvious step in saying: "I am the sum total of the Skandhas; they are my attributes; I am constructed from them." But close analysis again reveals that anything or any being which arises in dependence on its parts cannot rightly be said to possess inherent existence. It is a process generated by the karmic law of becoming and is therefore characterized by impermanence, suffering, and not-self (or, the absence of an inherently existing self-entity).

COMPASSION

His Holiness the Dalai Lama has said that the first step in the practice of compassion is to recognize its usefulness. The life of an individual devoid of compassion cannot be happy. As Shantideva says: "The childish work for their own benefit; the Buddhas work for the benefit of others: just look at the difference between them!"

A compassionless society is prone to complete disaster. This is not merely a sentimentalist theory: we have seen and are still seeing today the negative results within societies with a history and tendency to function uncompassionately. In their midst is violence, crime, corruption, war, and economic hardship. It is impossible to doubt that there are strong links between compassion and prosperity in societies.

But there is a deeper and more transformative dimension to the practice of compassion in Mahayana Buddhism. Its essence is the willingness and wisdom to exchange one's own happiness for the suffering of others. In Western terms, this would be called the Mind of Christ, the attitude of ultimate self-sacrifice. In Buddhism, and more particularly in the Mahayana with its strong emphasis on the role of the Bodhisattva (The enlightened being of boundless compassion), the intention is to bring the practitioner to the understanding of Shunyata, beyond which there can be no suffering, since all attachment and aversion have ceased.

WISDOM-COMPASSION AND THE SIX PERFECTIONS

Mahayana Buddhism rests on the foundation of what might be termed the fusion of wisdom and compassion. The wisdom component lies in the right understanding of the empty nature of all beings and phenomena in the samsaric realm. The component of compassion is the motivation to rescue beings from samsaric suffering by leading them to the final liberation of Enlightenment. In this sense we could say that the final aim of our compassionate activity is to lead all sentient beings to the knowledge and realization (the making real in experiential terms) of Emptiness, and especially their own Emptiness. The aim, in other words, is to completely extinguish the suffering caused by the delusion of Samsara by leading all beings beyond Samsara. In the deepest sense, the intention is to put an end to cyclic existence itself.

Taking this thought to its extreme conclusion, this means that the ultimate solution to the problems and suffering of our world order and the human condition is to bring them to extinction through spiritual/mental practice.

In the meantime, Buddhism gives us six focal points on the path to the achievement of wisdom-compassion (Bodhicitta). These are the Six Perfections or Paramitas: The perfection of generosity, morality (or, discipline), patience, energy, meditation, and wisdom.

BODHICITTA AND SKILLFUL MEANS

In the awakening of Bodhicitta, the enlightenment thought, the Six Perfections play a profound role. It is they which enable us to progress from compassion to what may be called the perfection of compassion: from the aspiring Bodhicitta (the wish to attain Enlightenment in order to benefit all beings by leading them to Liberation), to the applied Bodhicitta (practicing with determination the methods for achieving Enlightenment). Cultivation of the Six Perfections is therefore central to our progress from aspiring practitioners to the attainment of ultimate Enlightenment with the compassionate wish to lead all sentient beings to that same state. For, unless we ourselves attain Enlightenment, we cannot fully liberate other beings. Bodhicitta, then, represents the ultimate altruism, not by self-sacrifice but by self-liberation.

Looking into the world around us, we have to acknowledge that Bodhicitta in its aspiring aspect is very rare among people, and even rarer in its applied aspect. Yet it seems the most beautiful and desirable of all attainments of which people are capable. Our deepest instincts yearn for it, and it lies at the heart of our inner cry to love and be loved completely, to be rescued from ourselves by the power and wisdom of Love. Since this is both our deepest need and our deepest potential, may we at least try to embrace the liberating powers of Bodhicitta.

THE BODHISATTVA

The Bodhisattva, the enlightened being of boundless compassion, represents the spiritual hope of all humanity and all sentient beings: The wish-fulfilling jewel. In Buddhist belief there are enlightened beings who choose to return to cyclic existence to help all beings to final liberation. From this point of view, all the great, powerful, compassionate teachers who have appeared in all religious traditions were Bodhisattvas working among sentient beings on earth. Certainly, there are Bodhisattvas working among us today.

THE INNER AND OUTER LAMA

It is taught that we can awaken (or become aware of) our inner teacher, the guiding voice which admonishes and corrects us on the path to Enlightenment. Of course, we are not speaking here merely of the human conscience. After all, the conscience is a highly conditioned process relying on input from our parents, peers, social conventions, religious doctrines, and so forth.

In Buddhism, and particularly in Tibetan Buddhism, the outer teacher or Lama is indispensable to our progress towards Enlightenment. It is therefore highly important that a "true" teacher be found; one who is learned, experienced, and full of integrity with regard not only to matters concerning Dharma, but in the complete experience of life.

STUDY AND PRACTICE

In Buddhism, as in all religions, the proper study and understanding of the doctrines and methods is important. But the mere intellectual or conceptual comprehension of these is not sufficient to transform our minds, even though they may instill a yearning to achieve the goals of which these teachings speak. Because they are conceptually presented and understood, they represent a challenge to go further rather than being an end in themselves.

Authentic spirituality requires much more effort than only becoming familiar with a particular doctrine. For working people it is difficult to find the necessary energy and time needed for effective spiritual practice. Their application and effort are sapped by the pace of the modern workplace and by the anxiety involved in dealing with financial and social pressures. People caught up in this cycle are continuously distracted by either pleasing or frightening prospects, and by the hope and fear which drives this system. Their responsibilities widen out from the needs and concerns of their families and dependents to their contribution to the society as a whole and, often unconsciously, to their role in the global economy.

Their religious practice is often thwarted by these factors, and progress is often slow and halting, involving in many cases periods of progress and regression. This is a problem particularly relevant to Buddhists in the West, where the supportive Sangha is relatively small in number, and there are few teachers, some of them incapable or even corrupt.

Perseverance on the path, no matter how seemingly slow or even irrelevant one's realization and achievements, is therefore vital.

THE VAJRAYANA

The Vajrayana or "Diamond Vehicle" is a set of tantric teachings and practices which, the masters tell us, constitute the quick path to Enlightenment. In essence, these practices lead us to an ever deeper and clearer view of our own emptiness (Shunyata) and provide methods for developing great compassion (Maha Karuna), purity, and a peaceful mind. They are based on developing unity between the realization of the emptiness of self (Anatman) and tutelary deities who are able to increase and stabilize the twin view of wisdom-compassion. In other words, they bring us into direct and tuitionary contact with highly accomplished enlightened beings.

Unfortunately, many of the Vajrayana teachings have been cheapened in the West, and there is a great deal of trifling curiosity and inexperienced experimentation that lead to greater self-delusion rather than to Liberation. It seems that, although Westerners prefer the quick path, they are often unwilling to pay the price which it demands.

Because of this trend, the question whether Western Buddhists are truly prepared for the Vajrayana needs to be posed, not merely as an academic enquiry, but as an enquiry into the preparedness of the average Western mind to surrender itself completely to "the way it is" (the Dharma).

VIEW, CONDUCT, MEDITATION

These three aspects of the Buddhist mental (or, spiritual) life are really the essential way out of delusion. They provide the key to escape from cyclic or samsaric existence, since they engage all the faculties that are the result of Karma in the pursuit of Liberation from Karma.

The first step out of delusion, or the delusory experience of reality, is to discover and cultivate the correct view (or, right view) of what that reality is. This view is cultivated through study and reflection and should rightly involve a high degree of close and relentless analysis. Without the employment of such analytical insight, one may end up with a religion based solely or mainly on faith. In such a case, one is called on to simply believe what the conventional mind is in fact incapable of believing. This leads to the faith/doubt dilemma, and to an increase of suffering. Thus, the Buddhist path is one of knowing, and of being able to demonstrate the basis of one's knowing, rather than simply believing what one has been taught from childhood onwards. This being the case, the Dharma is not a conviction, but a view. It is not the imagining of what may in some eternal way one day be seen, but the simple knowledge of what one has indisputably seen here and now.

In cultivating the right view, right conduct is a sine qua non. In this sense right conduct may be compared to the preparation of an accurate viewing device, such as a microscope. Any distortion in the device itself will lead to a "wrong view." The right conduct referred to here is the Noble Eightfold Path. These aspects may be seen as the necessary qualities of the viewing device (the mind), if the mind is to perceive "the way it is."

Meditation is the means by which the mind is enabled to cultivate right view, right understanding, and so forth. Without the practice of regular and insightful meditation the ordinary mind is likely to remain within the thought-feeling realm, that is, to remain in a state of distraction which prevents the true nature of mind from becoming manifest. For this and other reasons, it is almost impossible to attain to Liberation without the practice of meditation. Again, the instruction of a capable and righteous teacher is an indispensable factor here. There are dangers involved in meditation, dangers which stem from the untamed and impure imagination. The most important factor in this regard is that one's meditation remain both pure and realistic. What is being sought is the nature of mind, and the result of one's meditative practice should be that one find one's true mental nature rather than some pre-desired construct.

TAKING REFUGE

His Holiness the Dalai Lama has said that what differentiates Buddhists from other religious practitioners is the fact that Buddhists have taken refuge in the Three Jewels. These Jewels are the means by which Buddhists receive the blessing and aid to walk and complete the path to Liberation.

Generally the formula is: I go for refuge until I am Enlightened to the Buddha, the Dharma, and the Sangha. By the virtuous merit that I create through the practice of generosity and the other perfections, may I attain the state of a Buddha in order to benefit all sentient beings.

As the First Jewel, Buddhism recognizes the Buddha as the Teacher of supreme Truth. The Dharma, His Teaching, is acknowledged as the true and unavoidable path to Enlightenment. The Sangha is the fellowship of Buddhist practitioners which accompanies, assists, and encourages the aspirant to achieve the goal.

Taking refuge is not merely a statement of ingress. It must be an act of mental sincerity as well as an authentic appeal, and should involve a real desire for liberation from cyclic existence. In short, one should take refuge with all one's heart and mind.

The Dialogues

DR: Has anything really changed since the time of Prince Siddhartha? Have we really created a happier and more hopeful world by advances in technological and economic conditions? And can it be said that the experience of the Buddha is universal? What of those individuals who do experience (or claim to experience) life on earth with all its mundane entertainments as a very happy thing? Are they simply ignorant?

RINPOCHE: I think the basic question is the recognition of suffering as suffering. In the Buddha's first teaching in Sarnath he revealed his experience of the Four Great Truths, "Four Noble Truths," we usually say: The truth of suffering, the truth of the cause of suffering, the truth of the cessation of suffering, and the truth of the path to achieving cessation of suffering.

Worldly people do not recognize suffering as suffering. Many things are being taken for granted as pleasure or as happiness, and they do not understand that such pleasure and happiness are transitory, and are bound to come to an end. So, therefore, the Buddhist Canon classifies suffering into three categories. In speaking of the first two categories we list the suffering of suffering which simply means the usual things which everybody accepts as suffering, such as disease, old age, death, pain—nobody would call these pleasures—they are openly apparent discomforts, apparent pain; so everyone recognizes them as such.

The second suffering, or misery as we call it in Sanskrit and Tibetan, is the suffering of change. The suffering of change means that that which at first appears as pleasure eventually reveals itself, indeed, as the cause of a greater suffering. The youthfulness decays every second, every moment, and after ten years the youthful pleasure you experienced is no longer there. The decay is constant and irremediable—the medical and other sciences might be able to prolong the pleasurable aspects for a few years, but they cannot get rid of the seed of suffering. For instance, medical science may be able to increase one's lifespan, but until now nobody has promised a permanent life which never goes to death. I don't think anyone can promise or ever realize it, no matter how much science may advance. At least at this moment there is no such promise or possibility foreseen.

The suffering of change is apparent in daily experience. When you feel cold and go out to sit in the sun you feel pleasure because the discomfort of being cold is changing. But if you sit in the sun for a longer time, you feel uncomfortable again—you look for shade. This is because the feeling of warmth is not in itself a pleasure, but only seems pleasurable in contrast to the cold. But if you continue to consume or enjoy it, then it will become discomfort. Everything—eating or sleeping or whatever we do throughout the day or night: we cannot live with it forever as a pleasurable experience.

Similarly, sitting may be comfortable, but you cannot sit in one posture for four hours; it will become discomfort. Standing may be comfortable but you cannot stand for hours together, just as you cannot continue working for hours on end.

If whatever you feel is really and essentially comfortable, then the more you indulge in it, the more the comfort should be increased—but, in fact, it does not increase. It actually decreases and then finally it becomes discomfort.

One may be endlessly wealthy, and having wealth is considered to be a pleasure, but very often wealthy people need sleeping pills to sleep and they have no better health or peace of mind than the poor—and so on and so forth.

Aryadeva rightly said in a very short sentence: "Misery for the rich is mental, and misery for the poor is physical." People who are poor have more physical discomfort and rich people have more mental discomfort.

So if we examine the real nature of suffering we find that the causes of suffering have actually much increased since Siddhartha's time—and today everywhere there is discomfort, displeasure, suffering, and pain. You see them everywhere if you look deeply into the state of life. So rather than being only unchanged, there is more misery in the world today.

But there is a lot of illusion in terms of which misery is viewed as pleasure. When this illusion is penetrated, however, we must admit that pain and suffering today are much greater and more prevalent than in Siddhartha's time 2,500 years ago. Today they are greater.

DR: So those who claim to experience life as a happy thing are either lying to themselves and others, or are simply deluded?

RINPOCHE: I don't think they are lying. They are simply ignorant, and you should ask them what they have lost or whether they will eventually die. Then you can ask whether they experience these events and eventualities as pleasure and happiness, and at that moment they will realize.

As I said, in the moment we are often not able to recognize suffering as suffering. A prisoner who has been sentenced to death and who is going to hang tomorrow morning and yet still has all the worldly pleasures at his disposal: you can ask him, "How do you feel? Are you happy?"

And the fact is that nobody knows whether they will die tomorrow. There can be any kind of accident, any kind of cause can arise to cause a happy man to die abruptly, and at that moment all the worldly pleasures which he enjoyed will come tumbling down in the same way that anything can suddenly disappear.

If anybody really has happiness, such happiness should exhibit a form of permanence. Such happiness should not eventually result in misery.

DR: What of people whose entire experience of life, due to persistent poverty or illness or some other overwhelming tragedy, is one of endless misery? How can they be convinced that genuine happiness does not lie in wealth or health or indulgence in various mundane pleasures which they have never had the opportunity to know? This is not only a problem for afflicted individuals; there are whole nations and regions in the world whose daily existence is the experience of the miseries of hunger, poverty, disease, and hopelessness?

RINPOCHE: As I mentioned before, every living being has genuine natural needs, and those needs have to be fulfilled. Without fulfilling these needs you cannot convince them that happiness does not lie in the physical or material realm.

In the Pali Canon there is the story of a hungry man to whom Buddha would not give teaching. He said, "First you must feed him, and he must be satisfied. Only after that will he be in a comfortable position, then he will be able to listen to the teaching."

So, in the case of people who are consistently in poverty and misery, we need to address the immediate miseries first, and, thereafter, when these miseries have been removed, they should not be put in a position where unending physical or worldly pleasures can be pursued.

Only then can we tell them that, although poverty is bad, there are certain genuine needs which need to be fulfilled but not exceeded. Thereafter we can attempt to persuade them that happiness is to be found on the Middle Way between extremes, as Siddhartha taught. But without fulfilling the basic needs of the body, the mind is unable to get freedom from the painful demands of the body. This is a problem which lies in the nature of things, and we have to address it.

Earlier I mentioned the first two categories of suffering (the suffering of suffering, and the suffering of change), but I did not speak about the third category. This category is the more pervasive and most devastating. It arises from the compositeness of the body which is the vessel of all kinds of misery.

Although the physical body can be seen as the instrument for the enjoyment of so-called pleasures, it is actually the greatest limitation of the individual since the physical body is impure and dependent and has no freedom from the influence of defilements and karmic force. Kleshas (afflictions) are Karma: these two compose this physical body.

If one did not have a physical body there would be no ground for experiencing pain and suffering or disease and decay. But it is the vessel of defilement and suffering. Actually all worldly pleasure and pain is experienced through the transitory and impermanent body which is bound to decay and disappear, and the decay of so-called worldly happiness is the highest cause of suffering and pain.

So this needs to be discovered and realized. Unless it is realized, the tendency of humanity is to seek out transitory pleasure. Once you truly realize the transitoriness or impermanence of the basis of this pleasure, then that pleasure cannot persist. And the disappearance of that pleasure causes an even greater pain.

DR: Since most people conclude from their mundane experience that life is a mixture of pleasure and pain, they tend to place increasing emphasis on the creation of pleasures, content to enjoy them while they last, and to stoically endure periods of hardship. This view leads us ever-deeper into disaster, complacency, and apathetic acceptance of our limitations. We call this approach "realism." But, in fact, it is unrealistic, is it not? It denies our true potential and destiny?

RINPOCHE: Yes, I do agree with your premise and your question. We do not deny that life is a mixture of pleasure and pain. You have worldly pleasure and you have worldly pain, and most of your pain is due to absence of your so-called pleasure. And pleasure gives you pleasure, and when it goes away its absence gives you pain—and this is not realized by people. When you realize that there are these limitations on pleasure, that this reality of life has to be accepted, that both pleasure and pain are bound to come, and you conclude as a result that you should pursue pleasure as much as possible: that is the much bigger delusion which destroys the potential of life.

It is as though you say to yourself, "Whatever pleasure I am enjoying now, I should enjoy to the full without taking thought for tomorrow." And when tomorrow comes—and it certainly will come—then you suffer on two grounds. Firstly, you are simply suffering, you feel pain. The other suffering is that of regret: "Yesterday I could have done this or that to avoid today's pain, but I lost the time and therefore I am experiencing today's suffering."

So it is in the nature of human delusion that we pursue pleasure, and it is followed by pain, about which nothing can be done; so we convince ourselves that we have to accept this as the nature of life. But when the pain comes, we are not *actually* able to accept it.

And yet today, in this very life, particularly in the case of human life, you have the potential to get freedom from the bondage of Karma, the Kleshas, and the defilements—and you can achieve the never-ending Bliss, never-ending Peacefulness. You have that potential but are negating it by talking about the "reality of life." And you have very correctly said that this approach is actually unrealistic.

DR: People have often said to me: "I understand the value of compassion and morality, but what on earth can be the benefit of the realization of Emptiness?" To deny the entity, the "I," seems to them a nihilistic retreat from life. If there is no inherently existent "I," why bother with virtue and compassion? Why not simply surrender to nothingness and meaninglessness?

RINPOCHE: This is a very fundamental, profound question. I don't know how to simplify it. Not everything can be simplified: if something is not simple, it is not simple. There's no way to simplify it. But I will try to examine it.

Today when we talk about the Buddha's teaching of selflessness or the not-self or Shunyata, people mostly cannot comprehend the real connotations of these teachings. And they always fall into the error of negating the relative self. When you speak of selflessness, they take it to mean that they are completely devoid of self, that self does not exist at all.

It is only in Buddhism and in some non-Buddhist Indian traditions that the Truth is classified into two levels: the Ultimate Truth and the relative truth. And these two need to be understood at their respective levels. They are two sides of one coin, yet they differ vastly. The key point is that, if you deny the relative truth, then you cannot realize Shunyata, but will fall into nihilism instead: the negation of everything.

The Buddha does not negate the relative existence of anything, but teaches that whatever exists in the relative or conventional sense, exists interdependently and the common-sense of the interdependent nature of things cannot be denied by anyone. It is truth; it is a fact. Things do not exist as we view them in this moment, we who do not realize the true nature of existence. The ordinary person views phenomena as existing by their own nature, complete and independent in themselves. They impute the quality of inherent existence to these phenomena, as they do to the self. But the fact is that relative phenomena, including the self, exist in interdependence on each other and on a myriad bases. This quality of interdependence does not imply that relative phenomena simply do not exist at all, but only that their existence is not inherent to themselves. In simple terms, if you remove the interdependent factors of which phenomena consist, the phenomena themselves would disappear because they have no inherent existence of their own, or from their own side. So unless you clearly recognize what is to be negated and what is to be affirmed, there is every chance of descending into nihilism. In this case, what is to be negated is the notion that relative phenomena exist absolutely. On the other hand, it is equally important to affirm that they exist relatively or conventionally. It is important to take care and be very cautious about this; that you should not negate the relative existence of self. But the self which we conceive of now as an absolute entity having independent existence from its own side is to be negated.

So, unless you very profoundly see how you conceive yourself, you will fall into the error, either of absolutism or of nihilism. But if your understanding of self is profound, then you can very easily negate the notion of an inherently-existent "I," and that negation is Shunyata. The simple negation of inherent or independent existence is Shunyata.

The way we conceive of self, the way we conceive of phenomena, need to be very precisely and clearly recognized. Then you will realize that it is completely different from the real nature of the existence of self. So, it is quite a difficult process of analysis. But unless and until you realize what is to be negated, it is very dangerous to negate anything. You might negate the whole thing, and then you would fall down into nihilism.

So, it is very difficult to verbalize; but through meditation, through observation, you will realize how you conceive the self. It is not yourself which you negate, but that self of which you have formed a conception: that conception is to be negated.

At this moment, if somebody calls you or addresses you, you immediately conceive a self which is almost identical with body, mind, and speech: the gross combination. But you never conceive of self as something very subtle or very different than your conception of it.

Somebody hits you, and you feel that he has hit *you*, he abused *you*, he oppressed *you*: and at that time your conception of "I" is so gross, so monolithic, and so singular. There is the perception of the singularity of "I" which comes forward—a sense of the singular existence of "I," and that is a misconception, and that misconception is to be negated.

After negating that mode of existence, then you will automatically understand the transitory and interdependent existence of the relative self—and when you realize the relativity of self, it will cease to create attachment or hatred—and it will see, since it is in the right view of self-existence, and it will automatically give you the right view of the existence of others, and then compassion arising from that profound understanding of the equality of all beings will come out naturally.

So, the negation is not negation of the relatively existent self, but the negation is the negation of how we view ourselves right now. That view is to be negated.

In the Canon and in the teachings the self as a whole, as an entity per se, is negated—but at that time the teacher is addressing *you* directly, attacking, as it were, the way you perceive yourself. It is a method for finding that which indeed is to be negated. So it sometimes seems as though the teachings are negating the total relative self. But we need to separate the teaching technique from the object which it seeks to accomplish. We need to separate these two and identify the object which is to be negated. Only then can the reality of selflessness be realized.

DR: Even if I recognize that this "I" or ego is not myself as an inherently existing entity, can we speak of some other self or form of self that could be called my true or real self—a self without ignorance, attachment, or aversion?

RINPOCHE: Unless you recognize the present view of self (as an entity) and negate it through analytical inference, you cannot see the real interdependently originated self. You cannot see it because in that moment of experiencing self everything is clapped into one. That is why we need to negate the self itself as a first step in the process towards negating the misconceived self. We talk about the negation of self, but of course this does not mean the negation of the relative self. It is the negation of the self which you perceive yourself to be.

DR: Doesn't the view of not-self tend to a less functional, less motivated, less adaptive individual within society and, given the imperatives of our productive and creative world order, doesn't this view lead to a dysfunctional social group? It has been argued, for instance, that it was one of the reasons for Tibet's vulnerability.

RINPOCHE: I don't think so. Once the misconceived self is negated and one has the right view of the interdependently originated self which has no differentiation from the other, love and compassion are generated without any effort.

And in this way the universal responsibility of the individual will be realized. The right view of interdependent self will lead you to work much harder, to take much more responsibility because, speaking grossly, the realization of self in that nature of interdependence brings the knowledge that self is not there for selfish ends, self is for serving others, for sharing the wisdom of the relative "I" with others and performing all sorts of positive deeds. So society, I think, would become much more productive and creative.

The problem again is not realizing what has to be negated: people come to this kind of doubt: if self is negated, then why should there be productivity and creativity, and why, indeed, should we be motivated to do anything at all? This kind of thinking is a clear sign that the interdependent self is being negated, and this is a great error. What we have to negate is the independent, inherently existent self. This is not a negation of self itself.

But if you correctly differentiate between the self which is to be negated and the self which is to be affirmed, your view becomes legitimized. Then these sorts of doubts will have no place.

DR: The Buddha taught that the sure path to the cessation of suffering lies in the extinguishing of craving or desire. But, as has been said, our world order thrives on the dynamic of craving, especially in its socio-economic aspects. The mental work needed to extinguish craving requires the willingness to go deep, to employ intense concentration, discipline, and perseverance. How can we find the inclination, the motivation, and the time for these practices? Indeed, how can we find the initial impetus needed to motivate us in the first place? It comes back to a willingness to deeply contemplate the First Noble Truth and to test it in our own experience, does it not? But, before we can even make the attempt, we need to understand what the Second Noble Truth teaches us, that craving and the so-called "drives" are the result of a fundamental ignorance rather than a necessary fact of our individual and social nature?

RINPOCHE: Craving and motivation are two different things. In Sanskrit there are two different words, one for "craving," and the other meaning "motivation" or "determination" or "self-confidence": a different kind of driving force to go into the most difficult Bodhisattva activities.

So, craving need not be the only driving force. Craving comes out of the ignorance of the true nature of self, or, as we call it, Avidya. Avidya (not knowing, or ignorance) is centered in the self; a misconception in the view of self creates the craving because of the wrong view of self. This self needs so many things; this self needs a name, it needs fame, it needs pleasure, power, it needs all the rest of it—and therefore, restlessly, the craving comes: "I need this, I need that, I need that too."

And, therefore, whatever activity comes out of craving is necessarily self-serving, and mostly it becomes violence to others. The activity which arises out of craving does not see that it is violent or harmful to others, cannot distinguish whether it is something very negative. Craving says: "I shall have to achieve this by any and all means, right or wrong, whatever tactic is needed." That is the nature of craving.

But the nature of the positive driving force which realizes selflessness, whatever it does is for the benefit of others, not for the self. And it will not diminish in activeness, and it will not lead to dullness. But it will become increasingly unattached and unselfish, doing positive deeds very actively. So there is no chance of becoming inactive by removing craving. This is quite for sure.

But the social world order and the achievement of the cessation of suffering, these are two different things and should not be mixed up without analyzing or classifying them more properly and carefully.

I do not try to make the point that the perseverance for Nirvana or perseverance for the cessation of misery have nothing to do with the world order. I'm not saying that. It has very much to do with the world order. But from the viewpoint of cessation the world order is not something that depends on systems or governance or management. From the viewpoint of the cessation of suffering, the world order is something which is manifested in a purified self. Individual Enlightenment is the real source of orderly society. Therefore these two aspects can go together. But the world order which we see today, with all its ignorance, and the world order which can be brought about by spiritual practice and true understanding—these need to be differentiated.

In any case, the direct answer to your question is: The cessation of craving will, in fact, lead people to be motivated and to achieve more positive things. It will not make society non-productive.

DR: In today's world qualities of mental development are valued, but in a very limited and distorted way. Our discipline and morality have more to do with convention and social order than with purity and compassion. Our mental development is centered in the sharpening of our intellectual capacity and stops short of the meditative examination of mind. And, wisdom, for us, is generally worldly-wisdom, a form of shrewdness. But these fall far short of what the Buddha taught. How should we expand and deepen our understanding of what is really required of us with regard to these categories of development, if we hope to escape our stress and delusions?

RINPOCHE: In speaking of these and the other components of the Noble Eightfold Path, we should realize that there are two different ends. One is a worldly end; the other is beyond worldliness. Or, we could say that one is to achieve genuine contentment in this world, and the other is to go beyond the world and to achieve the cessation of all relative experience and to enter into Nirvana.

Discipline, concentration, and correct discernment or knowing correctly the way things are, are the three components necessary for human action if you need to perform something correctly. And this threefold education spoken of in Buddhism has these two levels, as I have said. One is for beginners who look only for worldly contentment, and the other is for those seeking cessation, to enter Nirvana, the Liberation.

So, for beginners, these components need not be a very high, very spiritual matter: they are really matters of common sense. To make a cup of tea, for instance, you need all three.

Firstly, you need to have a certain discipline: there are certain requirements for making a cup of tea. You need a heater or fire to boil the water, and you need the water itself, and a pot and tea leaves and so forth. You also cannot put the water beneath the fire. You have to put the water on the fire; only then can it boil. You have to follow these kinds of requirements. You can't act randomly.

And secondly, you have to concentrate on what you are doing. If you allow your mind to scatter, it will spoil the preparation of the tea.

And then you need to know how to make it: when the tea should be put in and how much to put in, and how much sugar is to be added, and how much milk is to be added or not added. You need the knowledge to discriminate in all these cases. Just for the preparation of tea or bread you need these three components. If these three components are acting in harmony you can produce good tea or good bread. If any of the three are neglected you may spoil the thing and may not be able to produce it at all.

Of course, in this case I am speaking about the principles of discipline, morality, and right knowing with regard to worldly competence, not in relation to the cessation of misery and entering into Nirvana. We are talking to people on the preliminary path who are only looking for a good worldly life. We are saying that even in this regard, moral conduct, implying discipline and knowledge, is absolutely essential.

DR: Speech has immense power and consequence. How can we learn the lesson that our speech should be exercised with wisdom and compassion? What important principles are we usually forgetting when we open our mouths to speak?

RINPOCHE: Speech is one of the most powerful gates of the expression of mind. We can express through words the maximum; more than in any other way we can express through words what we want to express. And therefore speech can mislead and it can threaten and it can lie.

Speech has so much potential: it can give correct information and increase of wisdom and knowledge, but it can also give misinformation, sow confusion, misleading and completely deceiving people. It is a powerful instrument. And this instrument, if you are not careful, if you are not cohesive with your mind and your speech, the possibility of misleading and lying is always there. And deception is a source of harming others. It can harm others and it can also harm the self. So therefore carefulness in speech, speaking with mindfulness, is absolutely necessary.

Speech should not become an instrument of propaganda or of indoctrination. Both of these belong to violence, to the actions of violence. They harm the other. Indoctrination harms the other for its own flowering of individual intelligence, and lying to and misleading people. This can lead to misery and harmful situations.

Today, with modern technology, communication has become very easy and very powerful, and therefore we need to mind our speech much more. In ancient times you could lie to 100 or perhaps 300 people at a time, but in the electronic age you can lie to and deceive hundreds of thousands of people within a short spell of time. The power of speech is much increased; therefore we should mind the discipline of speech much more.

DR: And how much greater is the responsibility for right speech in the case of our leaders and mentors?

RINPOCHE: Anybody who does not have the power and capability of right speech, he or she cannot be a leader. On the contrary, such a person would be a misleader. By wrongful speech the people would be misled, and we cannot say that a leader who misleads is a right leader.

DR: In many ways the principle of right living or right livelihood has actually revealed itself as the most important concern for global society today. It involves factors relating to social injustice, inequality of opportunity, ecological destruction, and increasing stress on the individual. How can we begin solving this problem in a realistic way? It seems obvious that labor, trade, industrial, and environmental laws are not adequate to the task of saving us from the really catastrophic consequences of ignorance and greed which we exhibit in our ways of earning a living.

What is the essential understanding which can help individuals to see clearly the importance of maintaining integrity and non-harmfulness in earning their livelihood?

RINPOCHE: In today's society right speech and right livelihood are perhaps the most important elements to producing a good social order, in the sense of society or worldly community. I do agree that in our complex world right livelihood is rather difficult to achieve.

We have prolonged, intensive discussions on how to achieve right livelihood in the complexity of our modern society. And sometimes it appears to be almost impossible.

But much more depends on mental attitude and intentions than on what actually happens in the material world. By the means of intention we can prove that right livelihood is still possible if someone were to embrace the intentions of right livelihood, even in today's world.

Right livelihood means that one should produce those things that fulfill the real needs of an individual to lead a good life; and the production of one's needs should not involve violent action. Non-violently earned materials are right livelihood.

A farmer working on the fields and producing his own food and clothing without harming any other living beings is considered to be a very pure form of right livelihood. And if one is not a farmer but a businessman, do business with all moral and ethical requirements. Earning a moral, reasonable profit without harming any other person is also right livelihood.

A laborer, a carpenter, an artist, a teller—whosoever it may be—they do their own physical work, and on that basis a reasonable wage is earned, and that reasonable wage is used for their food, clothing, and other genuine needs. This is right livelihood. But not affluence, not misuse. Income should be kept non-accumulative.

Gandhi was of the opinion that a person who keeps more than his real needs is holding onto a material that is not his share: someone else's share is being kept by that person. So, accumulation is also not a right livelihood.

Right livelihood is consistent earning and consistent utilization in a way which does not exploit anyone else. This kind of right livelihood will bring social equity, and there will be no difference between poor and wealthy. If everybody is capable of producing their own needs, and no-one holds onto what is not his real need—in that way a proper distribution of wealth will be possible and nobody will be deprived of their share.

So, this is, generally speaking, the way to right livelihood. It also will not lead to the extraction of unneeded natural resources, and the environment will be protected.

The question is: will this be possible in the modern economic world? We use money and we keep money in the banks, and the banks use our money for all kinds of harmful exploitation and harmful businesses, and we are contributing to those financial transactions, and then we draw money from the same banks and we purchase from the market, and so forth. Also, money is very easy to accumulate: it is not like clothing or green food—you don't need any space to keep it; you can just put it in the bank unlimitedly.

So within this paradigm, the banks are among the most powerful institutions for structural violence. And they give financing to all kinds of harmful modern industry and so forth, and sometimes they provide financing for wars and killing and such things.

For instance, the meat industry is killing animals and harmful big industries are destroying the environment, and using up natural resources and so on—it is very difficult.

Then, coming back to the factor of intention: even if you are using impure means of livelihood but your own way of earning and your own way of using is not intended to encourage structural violence; you are not keeping your money in the bank with the intention of financing the sinful industries but just for safekeeping of your money, and you are quite innocent in that way, and you use whatever you earn by your own efforts, and you do not accumulate, and even if there is accumulation, you are ready to share it with whoever is in need of it—in this way I think even today we can practice right livelihood if the intentions are right.

DR: With regard to right action our own conventions and laws make distinctions between cases where right action may sometimes be wrong, and vice-versa. For instance, in times of war the soldier is expected to kill, and there are many economic laws today which seem to constitute a form of legitimized theft. Our mores, too, are constantly shifting: what was considered sexually illicit 50 years ago is today seen as acceptable, and people are ostracized and even punished by law for so-called prejudiced views and discrimination against what were previously viewed as unacceptable practices. How are we to gain more clarity and consistency with regard to right action?

And can the practice of right action in the face of injustice; for instance, a non-violent response to violence, not also be viewed as a form of uninterestedness and even cowardice? And, at this point, can we investigate the role of motivation in the practice of the Eightfold Path?

RINPOCHE: Right action depends on right view. If you have a right view, then your action cannot be a wrong action. Unless and until you achieve right view, you have to regulate yourself through your own analytical discriminating mind and with the help of spiritual teachings.

I don't think killing can be justified in any way. Killing is killing, and putting a life to an end, putting a living being to death, whether it is in self-defense, whether it is imposed by law—the death sentence, for example—whether it is in defense of a nation, I don't think there is any way that killing can be justified under any circumstances.

But there are some exceptions in the Buddhist Canon as well. There is a Jataka story you might have heard: When a Bodhisattva became the captain of a ship that carried more than 500 people, merchants, and there was a robber who had the intention to kill all 500 merchants and loot their wealth, the captain had no other alternative but to kill the robber. And with a great compassionate mind to save the robber from the sinful act, and to suffer himself in consequence of killing the robber, he killed that robber. And for that act he himself also suffered, but he was ready to take on the suffering. But it was not considered a wrong act. In this way, there is sometimes debate on mercy killing: an animal or some person is greatly suffering, and in order to put that suffering to an end by injection or some other method, the living being is killed. I don't know whether it really helps to end the misery; nobody knows what the Karma of that being will be in the next life.

So what I'm trying to express is that killing cannot be justified in any way, but there are some few exceptions if the killer is absolutely compassionate towards the person to be killed, to the object of the killing, and in that way there may be some exceptions which can be classified as right action. Otherwise killing is not justifiable.

Stealing is also not justifiable, but there may also be exceptions depending on intention, circumstances, and the final result of the theft.

Sexual misconduct is largely an act which depends on social systems, and also individual likes and dislikes. Harmful or not harmful, violent or non-violent, it largely depends on individuals and on social acceptability. So this might vary from time to time and some of these acts may be justifiable as well.

But there are many forms of sexual misconduct which are absolutely unjustifiable. For example, sexual relations with one's own parents or one's own children, or sexual misconduct with spiritually elevated persons: Arahantas. In such cases, even if they are socially accepted, they can never be viewed as right actions. But the other usual acts of sexual misconduct may depend upon social or individual acceptability and so on and so forth.

So we have to deal with each one of the gross misconducts and, of course, right action does not mean that in the absence of these three gross misconducts, all other actions are right. But these are the gross wrong actions which might be committed by someone, and are classified as such. But there are so many other actions which are directly or indirectly harmful to others. These are all considered to be wrong actions.

I definitely agree that acceptance of injustice is also an injustice. Acceptance of violence is definitely violence. The Buddha explained very explicitly on many occasions how violence is committed: you do violence by yourself, you encourage someone to do a violent act, or you appreciate an act of violence. All of these three are equally wrong conduct, and there's not much difference between them.

So, therefore, it is our responsibility to dissociate ourselves from acts of violence. If a nation is waging war, we should express our disagreement: by not expressing our disagreement we become, so to speak, citizens of that nation and in doing so become party to that war, and we become the killers of whoever is killed during that war.

And all injustice must be opposed. Not opposing an injustice is a kind of silent agreement with, or support for, the doers of injustice. So we must oppose it. But the opposition must be right action. Killing the killer is not right action. Stopping a thief by counter-theft is not right action. Violence is to be stopped by compassionate non-violent action, and non-violent action is also very difficult. Unless you have a compassionate mind and are not influenced by anger and hatred, your mere physical non-violence is not non-violence. So whatever we have to oppose, it must be opposed by genuine non-violence with a compassionate mind.

DR: It is clear that the absence of right mindfulness has greatly reduced compassion in our world. On a global scale the protracted history of unmindful activity is steadily leading towards destruction of our planet. From this perspective can we not say that the practice of mindfulness is today a vital part of the necessary responsibility of every person, rather than only a religious practice. How can we teach ourselves to be more mindful? What are the benefits?

RINPOCHE: Of course I entirely agree with your question. Mindfulness is absolutely necessary for everything. Even in the case of unholy actions: if there's mindfulness, that unholy action can be much reduced or much lighter in its effects.

Mindfulness is necessary for leading a good worldly life as well. If a person is mindful of personal feelings, matter, and phenomena, there is every chance to avoid many sufferings and every chance to accumulate many so-called worldly conveniences. Through mindfulness we can have much better health, and a mindful person, a student, for example, can study with much more success than the other students.

And particularly for the spiritual life, mindfulness is the key. One of the Kadampa Geshes said, "I have nothing to do but to keep my mindfulness and to watch my own mental activities, and that is the whole of my spiritual practice." And in a way that is true. If you achieve mindfulness, it can always be converted into right action.

DR: So far as right effort is concerned there is the problem of the flux of what may be considered wholesome and unwholesome at different times and in differing circumstances, a flux which leaves the unskillful confused. Are there absolutes in this regard, whose cultivation will result in tranquility at all times and in all circumstances? How can we find the energy needed to cultivate right effort?

RINPOCHE: As you have already explained, right effort is of four kinds, and that is true. But real right effort, if I interpret it a little differently from the Canon, is aimed at achieving all action effortlessly— the achievement of effortlessness is the ultimate aim of right effort.

Any action which depends on effort may go wrong or be less productive, showing less perfection and so forth. So, whenever we make an effort, that effort must be accompanied by mindfulness, and mindfulness leads your effort in the right direction. Such effort helps you to bring about the arising of many positive things, to maintain these positive things, to destroy the negative things, and so forth.

And gradually the effort becomes a kind of spontaneity or effort-lessness. This aspect I consider mostly relevant for spiritual practice. It may have less relevance to worldly endeavors and the social order.

Nevertheless it also has some relevance in ordinary or worldly life. We produce so many defective products and we are not able to accomplish a project or an action with excellence due to defective effort. There may not be shortcomings in your intentions, there may not be shortcomings in the other conditions, but due to shortcomings in your effort, the result will be something defective.

To avoid this it is necessary to practice full and right effort, to cultivate it in one's own mind. And I think that "effort" is not really a very accurate translation of the Sanskrit word. In English it may convey something a little different. But it should be understood to be the strength of one's completely abiding with the action without any desire or craving. Without craving, to remain with whatever one is doing.

DR: Generally we understand mind only at the shallowest levels, those of modern psychology and neurology. Our idea of right concentration is concentration applied at the ratiocinative, interpretative level, with the utilitarian purpose of making accurate relations between mental objects, whether abstract or substantive. But this is not right concentration, is it?

RINPOCHE: I was told by some neurologists that the human being functions using only a very small portion of the brain, and that a vast portion of the human brain is non-functional or not being used by the person, which reminded me that this can equally be applied to the mind: we can roughly say that the average person uses less than 1%; 99% of our mind remains inactive or idle, doing nothing.

Shamatha and Vipashyana meditation; these are the basic methods for developing towards using 100% of the potential of mind, and Shamatha comes first. Shamatha means: to let the mind settle down peacefully. The mind should settle down peacefully on any object, no matter whether the object is inner or outer. If you are able to peace-fully settle the mind 100% on the object, that is the achievement of Shamatha. At that time your mind is obedient to your commands. You command your mind to be concentrated on one point; 100% of your mind is concentrated on that object, and nothing else comes to your

mind. So that is the full utilization of one's mind, and the full utilization of one's mind is beneficial not only on the spiritual path but also
in modern worldly works as well.

You might have heard that these days a lot of companies in India
sponsor their employees to attend ten-day meditation courses, and
they pay full salary and allowances for this period. They are not interested in spirituality; they are interested in increasing the efficiency
and performance of their workers. Industry owners are sending their
people so that the quality of their work can be improved, carpenters
can produce better products, and so forth.

So, concentration of mind is very necessary, indispensable to
achieving mental wisdom, and to see selflessness or Shunyata: without
a concentrated mind you cannot reach that stage.

And for modern matters also, concentration is helpful and important: so whether your objective is spiritual attainment or efficiency in
worldly matters, concentration is absolutely necessary.

Modern psychology and the sciences still do not have the comprehension of the possibility of settling the mind down 100% on an
object. And perhaps this can only be realized by meditative practice.
Only a meditative practitioner, once he achieves that state, can realize
it: otherwise it cannot be explained or talked about without achieving
it. Because at this moment our mind is so scattered, and we don't
know the extent to which it is scattered. We also do not know how
small a portion of our mind is employed or aware. For purposes of
knowledge or thinking or creation, the portion we use is too small. Yet
the perfect concentration of mind is achievable.

DR: What is the minimum of right understanding needed to make us
truly beneficial or, at least, harmless in the world? And, what degree
of understanding is needed to accomplish our Liberation?

RINPOCHE: Understanding has so many different levels. And, also,
there may be a right understanding which is right at one level, while
at another level it may well be misunderstanding and would need to
be eradicated. Understanding is relative to the inner mental development of the individual.

The minimum right understanding for right action or, for that
matter, practice of all the other paths, is a correct discrimination
between right and wrong. That discrimination should be based on any

action which directly or indirectly involves violence, or any action which does not directly or indirectly involve violence—and, more than that, whether the action is beneficial to others. This is the basic discrimination of good and evil: whether it is violent, non-violent or beneficial.

So, this understanding, this kind of right understanding at the minimum level is necessary for all kinds of spiritual practice and also for understanding the other paths of the Eightfold Path. And it is not difficult to cultivate if you have a certain degree of analytical mind and rationality.

Understanding is different from belief. Belief can be cultivated without any rationality, but understanding must proceed from logic and reasoning and the understanding or power of discrimination between good and evil. That is the minimum level of the requirement of right understanding.

DR: Right thinking is a very subtle component of the Eightfold Path. Yet without the practice of right thinking we are left without skill in our dealings with others and with phenomena, as well as in our ability to correctly analyze and solve both spiritual and mundane problems. What are the essential qualities of right thinking?

RINPOCHE: Yes, "right thinking" is a little "loose" as a translation. The phrase in Sanskrit means a kind of analyzing, not only thinking as such: it actively involves analyzing.

Right thinking is the prerequisite for right understanding. Right understanding can be cultivated if you have right thinking. Right thinking creates right understanding. And, as I have said, right thinking is not only thinking; it is analyzing, reasoning, and researching whatever appears to your mind or your conception or your thought: not to accept it just because it is apparent, not simply to believe it, but to analyze it: consider whether it is reality or not reality, whether the apparent and the actual are one or whether there are differences, or whether it is right or wrong. This kind of analytical approach is necessary, and it is what is termed right thinking.

And right thinking and right understanding are necessary not only for the spiritual life but also for social coherence. Today most of the social conflicts are based on misunderstanding and misconceptions. Wrong thinking creates misunderstanding and misunderstanding creates suspicion and non-trust, and these create a lot of social conflict, not only within communities but also among the nations.

So, right thinking and right understanding will help a great deal towards the establishment of cohesiveness in social relationships. Relationships largely depend upon understanding between persons, and that understanding can be created through right thought.

DR: The Eightfold Path is a seamless process or practice of development in which the eight components are tightly interdependent. Each contains the seed and fruit of every one of the others. If one or more are absent, those which have arisen in our mental domain will seek them out, call for them, and inevitably find them because, unless they are all active, we cannot travel any further on the path to Truth. The Eightfold Path, in other words, can become in us a spontaneous process?

RINPOCHE: Yes, of course. The preliminary Eightfold Path can be cultivated or practiced separately, one by one. But at the time of awakening, when someone enters into the path of seeing, all the eight components will become part of one wisdom. That is the path of seeing: in itself all eight components are present.

And unless the Eightfold Path becomes as one whole, spontaneously, a part of one wisdom, it will not be able to eradicate the opposition of ignorance. So, in order to eradicate ignorance and, further, to eradicate the influence and the very seeds of ignorance, to achieve the complete cessation of misery, you need that powerful perception of the Truth with all the components of the Eightfold Path. This is called the Path of the Aryas.

DR: Surely the practice of the Eightfold Path, or even only some of its components, would be of great value even in our mundane endeavors?

RINPOCHE: Yes, as I mentioned before, the real Eightfold Path is the composite of one wisdom, and that is the Arya Path. But it can be cultivated separately in a sequence. And in the mundane world, particularly in our social structures, if anyone could cultivate or achieve even *one* aspect of the Eightfold Path, his or her outlook on the world and their relation to the other would definitely be different—not as we experience it today.

Some people do not have the right view and, therefore, due to ignorance, they do all the wrong actions. Then there are many people who have the right view in a certain way, but their view is not accompanied by or associated with mindfulness or right thinking and right understanding—they are not able to put their right view into action or to implement it.

For example, there are a number of scientists or scholars who know very well the condition of the environment on this earth and they also know the dangerous results of the degradation of the environment, and that we should be doing something to correct or restore it right now. So, they have that necessary view or vision, but due to lack of mindfulness and understanding they are not able to change their lifestyle.

I read somewhere many years back a statement—quite a famous statement—that the environment is very important, but that the American lifestyle cannot be compromised. So, the importance of the environment is realized, and that is a form of right view, but there's no right understanding and mindfulness, so they are not able to change their lifestyle. We can say that in these areas almost every part of the Eightfold Path is needed.

DR: Buddhist teaching is often not clear on the subject of Karma. The question is often left unanswered: how is it that beings whose true nature is Emptiness or voidness (Shunyata) can at the same time be called owners of their Karma—for there is no self-existent being which can be the heir of their own Karma. How can one explain this—the conjunction of Emptiness and the law of cause and effect or becoming?

And it is taught that Karma is also the force which shapes our ordinary or ego-mind: the reason we see ourselves, others, and the phenomena of our realm the way we do is the result of mental karmic formation. Can you expand on this?

RINPOCHE: This is a very big and complex question. I don't know how to answer it in a short, compact statement. But I will try to deal with the question through a few steps.

Firstly, I would say that the Buddhist theory of Karma is very clear, unambiguous, and understandable in a very clear way. Causality is possible only because things exist interdependently. If things existed by their own nature, then there could not be any causality; there cannot be any transaction, there cannot be relationship between the cause and the effect. The cause, if at all there were a cause, would remain a static cause giving no effect because it would exist by its own inherent nature. If there were any effect, it would remain a static effect because it would exist by its own inherent nature.

Causality only exists when things are of Shunyata. That's why the famous sentence was spoken by Nagarjuna: "If Shunyata is possible, then everything is possible. If Shunyata is not possible, then nothing is possible." Nothing will happen if things exist by their own inherent nature. There cannot be transition and change and momentariness. Everything would be static.

I repeat so that you can clearly understand: things do not exist statically by their own nature. Until you conceive this, and realize and understand their true nature, it will be very difficult to explain cause and effect. Things are interdependent, they are apparent, and they are transitory. Therefore causality is not only possible, but actually becomes the law of nature. All composite things come into existence by causes and conditions, and without causes and conditions nothing can happen.

When causes and conditions are present, the effects will certainly happen. There can be no doubt: when causes and conditions are completed there cannot be an absence of effect; this cannot happen. This is a certainty. Both are in fact certain: without causes and conditions nothing can happen, but when causes and conditions come into being then the result is absolutely certain. So, this is the law of causality. This law of causality is justifiable and obvious because nothing exists by its own inherent identity, or inherently by its own nature. Therefore the laws of interdependence come into functionality. This is the general view of causality.

Then, causality of Karma and the result of Karma: action and its effect. That is also very clear in the Buddhist teaching. First we have to understand the force of Karma. You do something, and you do it with the causes and conditions in completeness; then it creates a certain forceful karmic reality or karmic entity, and once that karmic entity is created it will not go without a result unless you destroy it by an opposite force or wisdom: accumulation of good deeds or something like that. So, it is certain—just as when a seed of weed is preserved in good condition and sown back into the earth it will certainly come up in the form of a weed again. But if that seed is destroyed by something like fire, then this will not be the result.

This does not mean that there is no potential of giving the result, but the potential is being destroyed by another force and is therefore different. So the certainty of karmic result exists, but there is also a remedy to avoid any karmic force from giving its result. Both possibilities are present.

The Buddhist literature also teaches how a certain Karma can become so powerful that it is certain of result. There is need of four or five conditions, but we can stick to four. The first is object, the second is intention, the third is understanding, and the fourth is the accomplishment of the action. The fourth can be divided into two: to act, and to complete the action. These four conditions are necessary.

For example, there is a living being which is to be the object of killing, and secondly, the intention of killing is aroused in the killer's mind. Thirdly, the killer knows that this is a cow or a man or whatever, and I am going to kill it. The fourth step is the action, by firing with a gun or stabbing with a knife or whatever weapon: acting on the intention brings the intention to completion. Death has come into being. That is the completion of the action.

In this case everything has been brought to completion. In such a case the act of killing will create a force which is certain to give its result unless it is destroyed in-between by an opposite force. Or some element may be lacking. A small insect may be dying under your feet, but you had no intention, or you had no understanding of the object as a living being, or you did not do the action on purpose. The small creature died accidentally. A life has been put to an end and death has come into being but it doesn't create a karmic force because the other components have not been completed.

In such a case, you may realize later that something has been killed, and you may feel carelessness or even appreciation. These attitudes will influence the karmic force. If you are happy that you have killed a wasp, it becomes a more forceful Karma. Yet it is not entirely completed. For example: the intention was absent. It is a subtle matter. If you are moving on the road with a sense of carelessness: "If anything comes under my feet I don't care"; if this kind of mind is present, then it will again become a more powerful karmic force.

So the object, the intention, the understanding, the act, and its accomplishment: when these are all there in totality, then the karmic force is created. This is the means of creating a karmic force.

For example, if you perform an act of killing with all these four components, then you have created a very powerful negative karmic force of killing and you are bound to experience the result of it.

But you can also create an opposite force. Your objective might be a good deed, and you have repentance that you have killed some creature: you realize it was terrible and bad and you should not have done it, and you resolve not to do it in future. Establishing this kind of mind, and praying and doing charitable work or whatever good deeds you do: the karmic force created by this resolve and such actions can destroy the karmic force created by the act of killing. So all this goes together.

Then comes the giving of a result by a karmic force. You may find a person who is very crooked and doing all kinds of evil things, but during his lifetime he always prospers, he always meets with good fortune and he never experiences any result of bad Karma. On the other hand, you may come across a very righteous and religious-minded person, yet his whole life is suffering. This does not immediately represent the causal law of Karma and the result of Karma. Remember: Karma goes across many births and lifetimes.

If someone does not believe in rebirth, then, of course, for them, everything should have its results in this very lifetime. But Buddhists believe that the stream of consciousness has no beginning or end: it goes on and on. So, you die in this body, and you have to be reborn in some other body, or in some other realm. By this way the karmic force accumulated in this lifetime does not necessarily give its result in this lifetime, unless it is very powerful.

Thus, the result of Karma is divided into three categories: very powerful, which may give its result in this lifetime; less powerful, which gives its result in the immediately succeeding lifetime; and the third karmic force which will give its result in any consequent lifetime—there may be hundreds of births having taken place in-between, but the karmic force remains there undestroyed and it will give its result, perhaps only after hundreds of thousands of years.

This is quite possible. Therefore a crooked person might prosper: he is consuming the result of a good karmic force accumulated in a previous lifetime, and whatever bad karmic force he accumulates in this lifetime is in "storage," and it will give its result in some subsequent lifetime.

So, this apparent contradiction does not negate the principle of good Karma giving a good result, and bad Karma giving a bad result. It is a matter of understanding the endlessness of the stream of consciousness. Then there is no contradiction of karmic force.

DR: Can we speak of a collective Karma? A social and global Karma? In our socio-political affairs we employ strategies which obviously relate to cause and effect: we adopt policies in order to achieve definite ends, and we do so collectively. But the implications of Karma are completely ignored in our decision-making processes. Why? And with what results?

RINPOCHE: Collective Karma is a very important theory in Buddhist doctrine. Almost all Karma is accomplished in a collective way, involving more than one person or being. It is almost unlikely that a single person, not dependent on any other, should accomplish a forceful Karma.

If you need to accomplish a good Karma, you need to do something beneficial to others. It always depends on the other: if there's no other, you cannot give, you cannot forgive, you cannot help. It is due to the presence of other sentient beings that you are in a position to do something beneficial or, on the other hand, something harmful.

In fact, the accumulation of bad Karma depends on other sentient beings. Whether you are killing or stealing or indulging in sexual misconduct, it always depends on the presence of other sentient beings. If there is no other living being, you can't kill anyone. When you kill somebody the karmic force is individual as well as collective: individual because the actual act of killing is being done by you alone; in this regard it is an individual Karma. But it is also collective. For example, the person you have killed or harmed might have wronged you in a previous life. Therefore, the act of harming that person is not "free": the person being harmed has some contribution from a previous lifetime. Or it can be a matter of usefulness: most animals are killed for their meat or their hides, and the perceived necessity for meat and hides are relative to each other and to the killer and to the killed animal, and in this way a collective karmic force is established.

And with regard to the nations, the universe, everywhere, each individual has a collective Karma without which the person cannot be born into this realm. We are all living in this universe and this universe is created by collective Karma. Unless I have a share in the collective Karma of all living beings in this universe, I will not be able to perceive or use this universe and its facilities. In order to be able to utilize this universe and its phenomena, for instance, both of us using this table, we need to share in the collective Karma which enables us to do so. That is why we are able to use this table equally: we share that particular collective Karma. Otherwise, if you don't have a collective share, you would not be able to use this table. If I did not have my collective share, I would not be able to use it or even to perceive it.

It is a vast and complex dynamic: all sentient beings on this earth share a collective Karma for the creation of this earth. And, of course, there is also individual Karma: I am using my share which is not going to you, which does not mean the same to you, which is not substantially the same to you. If the same glass of water were used by a man, a Deva or a being of a higher realm, or by a ghost, that same glass of water would have differing tastes to each. But all three have a share of collective Karma to that glass of water; therefore it can be used by all three classes of being.

And also there is individual Karma, as I have said. With regard to the glass of water: the human being is destined to taste it as ordinary water, the higher being perceives it as a kind of nectar, and the ghost (Preta) would experience it as a very bad tasting poison. So, there is a collective Karma insofar as all these beings can use the water, but there is also the individual Karma which characterizes the quality of the water for all these different beings. Thus, individual and collective Karma are conjoined, yet presented differently to differing beings.

So, there can be absolutely individual Karma, but it is very rare. The Karma of each individual is mostly related to someone else, to other sentient beings. For this reason we may say that it is both individual and collective. For example, if one hundred people all contribute to the killing of one person, and each of the hundred acquire the completion of the act of killing, even though only one person has been killed, the karmic force will be that of killing 100 people. Each individual of that group will have accomplished a complete act of killing.

So, the theory of individual and collective Karma is a little complex, and it is difficult to differentiate very categorically into watertight compartments: it is always interrelated and fluid.

And therefore the result affects those individuals who share in the collective karmic force, and passes by those individuals who have no collective share. This is quite obvious in many things we see. Sometimes you have a major air-accident with many people killed, and by a "miracle" one or two survive because they do not share in the collective Karma to die on that day.

DR: Again, since the teaching states that there is no self-existent "I," what exactly is it that is being reborn into Samsara in consequence of the law of becoming?

RINPOCHE: I think we have discussed this earlier also. The inherently existing self, an independent existence of "I" does not exist; it is to be negated, it is just an illusion. It is only after such negation that the relative "I" is able to attain to discipline or can reach the experience of happiness which accumulates the relevant Karma, which experiences suffering or enjoyment as the result of that karmic force.

To reiterate, the person, the "I" or the "You," is an interdependently originated nature, and this mode of existence is real, and it is there.

We are not negating the interdependent existence when we are negating the "I." In other words, we are not negating the "I" which does exist relatively. Who, after all, is the negator which negates the inherently existent "I"? If that negator is not present then how will the inheritently existent "I" be negated, or who will negate it? So, the existence of the interdependent "I" is never negated by Buddhism.

DR: But does this belief have any socio-political value? For instance, can we make the simple statement that, if more people were to practice Dharma in this generation, the following generation would be closer to Enlightenment, and so on? Can we validly simplify in this way?

RINPOCHE: I don't know how to answer this question. Individuals either act badly or practice Dharma, and this is always a matter of individual choice. A father who is a very good practitioner of Dharma cannot give his mind of Dharma or his accumulated merit as a genetic inheritance to his son or daughter. It is entirely his own action, proceeding from and relating to his own Karma.

But, born in a religiously-minded practitioner's house, the children will naturally have a social and cultural influence during their childhood and adolescence in association with their parents. Good or bad parental influence is undeniable.

But it is not correct to state that the father, or the parents, will share their merit with their children. That is not possible. The familial, environmental, and social influence will definitely be present and operational. It is in this way that the practice of Dharma by the present generation can influence the next. But to say that the karmic fruit will be enjoyed by the next generation: I would definitely say no. It cannot be.

But the present culture of this generation will have a positive influence on the next generation, and the next generation will be better than the previous generation due to the effects of this positive education and positive influence: these will definitely be passed on to the next generation.

DR: Please give us some insight into the path of seeing: that is, the point at which one knows without doubt that the Dharma, or any spiritual path based on wisdom and compassion, is the true destiny of all sentient beings, and especially of humanity, the being which can grasp and practice the Eightfold Path, or any other path leading to the fruits of Bodhicitta.

RINPOCHE: On the path of seeing you achieve the confirmation of your Buddha-wisdom, and there is no possibility of losing that wisdom. You are confirmed in that path and you are confirmed in that wisdom, and this wisdom eradicates some of the defilements which are to be dispelled by this path.

Now it is a path of the Arya, a path of the elevated one, elevated because you see the Truth through perception and you remove the duality of Shunyata. So, now you are in a position to go ahead unfettered on the spiritual path.

The path of seeing enables you to rid yourself of the mental defilements, which are divided in Buddhist teaching into several modes of "gross" and "subtle." Any serious student of Buddhism will discover these at the right time.

Then, following the principles and the Truth of the Five Paths, the subtle residues of the mental defilements will be eradicated. These are the last three stages of the meditative path: they eradicate the subtle residue of mental defilements which are a hindrance for the direct perception of all phenomena.

Finally, as you eradicate the subtle residues of these hindrances, there is no more defective principle influencing your mind, and you are awakened and you enter into Buddhahood, and this state of Buddhahood is eternal. This is called the Path of No More Learning, because nothing remains which has to be learned. Everything is clear to the awakened mind. The Buddha-Nature is all-pervasive, and enters into Dharmakaya.

This is a very gross explanation, and I would encourage students of Dharma to study these matters much more closely, but, more especially, to combine their study with daily meditation and practice.

DR: Is it possible to reach our enlightened destination relying only on the inner teacher? In other words, is it vital to have an outer teacher to guide us through the possibilities of self-deception which can arise from listening only to the inner voice? Can we be deceived by our inner teacher? If so, how can this happen?

RINPOCHE: You cannot be deceived by your inner teacher. That is for sure. But you may deceive yourself several times in the process of awakening or recognizing the inner teacher. You may not have awakened your inner teacher, you may mistake something else as your inner teacher, and that voice will deceive you.

For very beginners, I don't think that without external guidance or without the transmission of an outer teacher, you can simply rely on books or your "inner teacher." You need an outer teacher, but you need not depend on an outer teacher for a long time. You may have an outer teacher or a guide for a short spell of time. For instance, an outer teacher might guide you with regard to the books you ought to read. It is a matter of human connectedness during which a kind of transmission or a kind of lineage is established, and thereafter a book can be your teacher.

Before the Buddha died he told his Sangha: "Until now I was your teacher, your path-pointer, and I am entering Mahaparinirvana, and henceforth the *Vinaya Pitaka*, the Book of Conduct, will be your teacher." It is not only a teaching, but is also a teacher: a combination of teacher and teaching. So you are able to learn transformatively from these kinds of books.

But still you need someone to rely upon whenever you have doubts in interpreting or understanding the writings. You should not insist that you are capable of solving the problems presented by these scriptures. At certain times there should be someone to refer to: "I do not understand this or I am understanding it incorrectly; what is the true way in which to understand this?" Nowadays this can be done through correspondence or email or telephone, or the many other channels of communication we have today. It is not as difficult as it was in the past. There are many ways to establish communication with a teacher.

Awakening the inner teacher requires a high level of spiritual attainment. And I think that for the Bodhisattvas it comes in the middle of the second path, and not until they attain that path are they able to depend on the inner teacher completely. But I would not presume to establish a criterion or a science for correctly interpreting the voice of the inner teacher. But I would caution that there is a lot of danger in not recognizing the inner teacher correctly. But once you have correctly identified it, then it is completely dependable.

In the meantime, a book is probably more dependable than an "unconformed" inner teacher to whom you may be listening. [Laughter]

DR: The practice of religion presents a much greater challenge than the study of its teachings, especially for the people caught up in the secular, working life. They face the twin difficulties of the exhaustion of their energies as well as of their time. They often struggle with the anxiety and stress associated with simply earning a living in the modern world. At every turn they face distractions in the form of rewards and threats.

Besides the practice of the Eightfold Path, there are more refined analytical and meditative techniques taught by Mahayana Gurus.

Can we make the sweeping statement that it is all too much for the modern "householder"? That the attempt to faithfully adhere to these manifold, intricate, and demanding practices must necessarily end in a cycle of frustration and regret? What specific practices would you consider suitable for people in this situation? And, can we realistically hope that the limited study and practice we are able to achieve in this lifetime, under these conditions, will find some form of continuity in a subsequent lifetime?

RINPOCHE: These are very practical and important questions. I hope to deal with them at greater length in the future, but I will deal with them briefly now.

I think we should provide a means of guidance, a small booklet by means of which the beginners of Dharma practice, who are totally involved in the modern economic world, can find a source of spiritual survival, as well as the inspiration to practice. I think there should be some guidance for such people.

But here I would also say that nothing is too much as far as teaching and learning are concerned. Whether it be teaching of Bodhicitta, teaching of the Six Perfections, or even more difficult teachings. There's no harm in listening to them or reading them. Whatever is suitable for you will go into you, and whatever is too much will simply go over your head. [Laughter]

But having heard the teachings once, twice, three times, they will go deeper and deeper into you. Even if you think that it is too much now, and you will never arrive there—you should simply deal with what you think is too much or too little. There is no harm in receiving high-level teaching; there's no harm. Each time you hear them, these teachings will make a small, small impression or impact on your mind—and they are a kind of seed which you can safely allow to remain there. If one planted a seed five months earlier and there was no moisture and no rain and no conducive climate, the seed would remain present but dormant. Then one day it rains, and the sun shines, and the seed grows. It will grow. So nothing is too much.

But there should be a properly structured way of practice. In the case of an individual who has a good teacher, that teacher will bring it to fruition. But even if there is no adequate teacher, one can make progress by oneself: one can make it happen. There is always a way to make it happen.

And there are a few points I would like to mention here. Firstly, you will never find sufficient time for Dharma practice. Whatever you do, you will never find sufficient time for Dharma practice. Therefore Dharma practice should not be made into a separate timetable. Whether sleeping, driving, working, bathing, talking—in every situation you should maintain the continuity of your Dharma mind. Here again mindfulness is absolutely important. You may simply be driving down the road being mindful of others, mindful of the insects which cross or fly across the road, mindful of the flying insects which might collide with your windshield, mindfulness of your total surrounding, and keeping a compassionate mind. In this case you are practicing Dharma.

Whether you are talking with your friends or arguing with your employer, keep calm and mindful. So, your lifestyle, your life-conduct, your life itself should be a Dharma practice. Otherwise, if you confine your practice to half an hour in the morning and forty minutes in the evening, and sometimes you are not even able to keep to that timetable, it will not bring you any progress.

You can set aside time for prayer or making offerings or performing some other rituals. You can make a timetable for these things, and even five minutes is enough. But consistent mindful exercise, that should go on day and night, and should be made a part of your life. This is true regular practice. So, this is one thing to bear in mind.

And the other thing is that you should recognize your needs and those of your family, and you should be in a position and holding to the intention just to fulfill those genuine needs. And all the artificial needs must be cut down. This attitude and practice will help you both in your secular and religious life. If your needs and wants keep increasing and you are not able to obtain them, then you will not remain with Dharma practice. So, want and need should be differentiated; need and greed should be differentiated. Your needs may be a little high—that is alright—but some reasonable need must be recognized, and you aim a little above that. And beyond that you should not be under stress, running and competing with others: "He has two cars; why do I not have three cars?" Or, "He has four cars, therefore I should have five." On such a way, the mind will never return to practice of Dharma. It is important to know this.

And the third important element I would mention is that the Western lifestyle allows for frequent vacations, and these vacations should be used for Dharma practice. It need not be a long vacation: three days are enough. If you use this time fully, you will find yourself refreshed in your motivation. It will refresh you in other ways as well.

Finally, you should have good Dharma friends with whom you can talk about Dharma, with whom you can talk about spirituality, and share with each other. These are a few things which will be helpful to Western practitioners.

After all, these are logical and reasonable methods for making progress towards the goal of final Liberation.

CONCLUSION

To pretend to conclude the teachings of Samdhong Rinpoche would seem both presumptuous and superfluous. To attempt a summary would be nothing short of ridiculous, since they are living and transformative. They cannot be reduced to the level of the academic, to a set of rules or precepts.

Nevertheless, I would like to conclude this book by offering to the reader a selection of reading material which may be helpful in clarifying certain points, and, more importantly, in stimulating the motivation necessary for a life of wisdom-compassion.

I would recommend the following:

1. Sogyal Rinpoche, *The Tibetan Book of Living and Dying* (Random House);
2. H.H. the Dalai Lama, *A Simple Path* (Thorsons);
3. Lama Thubten Yeshe, *Make Your Mind An Ocean* (Lama Yeshe Wisdom Archive);
4. Jeffrey Hopkins, *Meditation on Emptiness* (Wisdom Publications);
5. John. F. Avedon, *In Exile From the Land of Snows* (Michael Joseph).

Of course, books and articles on Tibetan Buddhism are abundant, and the titles given above are only meant as introductory material. It is the author's wish that all may find the Path that leads to inner peace, non-violence, and a truth that is illumined by the clarity of reason.

May all sentient beings benefit from this small work.

The Venerable Samdhong Rinpoche

GLOSSARY OF TERMS

Bodhicitta: Lit., "Enlightenment thought," i.e., the fusion of wisdom and great compassion.

Bodhisattvacarya: Discourses on the Way of the Bodhisattva.

Darshana: The "suchness" of things; the way things really are when viewed more penetratively than at the level of appearance only.

Dharma: With a capital "D," the Truth of the Way It Is, the Ultimate Truth as taught by the Buddha; with a small "d," the essential nature or true way of being of phenomena and beings, e.g., the dharma of a cat, the dharma of the moon, etc.

Four Kinds of Birth: Egg-born (Andaja), Womb-born (Jalabuja), Moisture-born (Sansedaja), Spontaneous birth (Opapatika).

Geshe: Tibetan title, equivalent to Doctor of Buddhist Philosophy; a degree attained in monastic training.

Jatakas: Lit., "Birth Tales"; a collection of mythological stories or parables illustrating the teachings of the Buddha.

Kushala Karma: Wholesome Karma, achieved by wholesome deeds; the opposite of Akushala Karma or unwholesome Karma, generated by unwholesome or non-virtuous deeds (or thought or speech).

Lama: One who is on the Path; a title given to accomplished or distinguished monks or practitioners.

Mahaparinirvana: Lit., "The Great Utter Passing Beyond" (i.e., of Samsara and duality).

Mahayana: One of the three "yanas" or vehicles of Buddhism. The earliest vehicle is the Hinayana or Lesser Vehicle, nowadays more politely called the Theravada or School of the Elders. The Mahayana is the Greater Vehicle. The Vajrayana is the Tantric Vehicle, which developed from the Mahayana. The basic difference between Hinayana and Mahayana is that in the former one practices to achieve Enlightenment for oneself, whereas in the latter one practices to attain Enlightenment in order to liberate others. The Vajrayana teachings are largely secret because they are dangerous in the hands of non-adepts.

Paramita: Perfection, or going beyond the ordinary. The Six Perfections are: Giving, Moral Discipline, Patience, Energy, Meditation, Wisdom.

Pramanavarrtika: A commentary by Dharmakirti on Dignaga's *Compendium of Valid Cognition*.

Rinpoche: An honorific title meaning "Precious One."

Sangha: Fellowship of Buddhist practitioners.

Sangha-Karma: Action or decision taken by the Sangha as a whole.

Six Worlds/Six Realms: Samsaric or cyclic realms, characterized by suffering, impermanence, and not-self, and by constant rebirth. The six realms are: The unfortunate realms, i.e., (1) the hell realms; (2) the hungry ghost (Preta) realms; and (3) the animal realms. The fortunate realms, i.e., (4) the human realm; (5) the demi-god realm; and (6) the god realm.

Ten Evil Deeds: 1. Of the body: killing, stealing, sexual misconduct. 2. Of speech: lying, slandering, harsh speech, frivolous talk. 3. Of the mind: covetousness, ill-will, wrong views.

Vinaya Pitaka: One of the three "baskets" of the Buddhist canon. The baskets are: *Abidharma Pitaka* (The Basket of Philosophy), *Vinaya Pitaka* (The Basket of Monastic Rules), and *Sutra Pitaka* (The Basket of the Buddha's Discourses).

BIOGRAPHICAL NOTES

SAMDHONG RINPOCHE was born as Samdhong Lobsang Tenzin in 1939, in the Tibetan province of Kham. At age five, he was recognized and enthroned as the reincarnation of the fourth Samdhong Rinpoche. He began his monastic studies at age 12 and eventually obtained a Doctorate in Buddhist sciences at the University of Drepung in Tibet in 1970. In 1959, Rinpoche fled to India to escape the repressive Chinese government in Tibet. There, he was commissioned by His Holiness the Dalai Lama to serve as a teacher to monks in exile. He was appointed director of the Central Institute for Higher Tibetan Studies in Varanasi in 1988 and remained there until 2001. On July 29, 2001, Rinpoche was named Kalon Tripa, or Prime Minister of the Tibetan Exile Government, the first political leader to be directly elected by the people in exile.

DONOVAN ROEBERT is the founder and coordinator of the South African Friends of Tibet. Born in East London, South Africa, he is a painter whose works are sold internationally. A devoted practitioner of Mahayana Buddhism for over a decade, he has also written several religious and philosophical articles on reconciling the new physics and neurosciences with the subjective human religious experience. He lives in Broederstroom, South Africa.

H.H. THE DALAI LAMA is the spiritual and temporal leader of the Tibetan people. Following the invasion of Tibet by the communist-inspired Chinese Army in 1959 and the impending threat on his life, he escaped into exile and has since resided in Dharamsala, the seat of the Tibetan Government-in-exile. He is a recipient of the Nobel Peace Prize and an author of numerous books and essays, including *Kindness, Clarity, and Insight, A Human Approach to World Peace*, and *Ocean of Wisdom*.

Donovan Roebert

INDEX

Absolute Reality, 26, 44
Absolute Truth, 34, 41, 44, 164, 169-170
Absolutism, 203
Activism, 164, 173-174
Age of Decay, 72
Ahimsa, 109-110, 141, 144, 152, 161, 164, 172
Ahimsak, 164
Amdo, 116, 127, 130, 131
Anatman, 65, 68-69, 195
Arahantas, 213
Arya, 37, 218, 226
Atman, 69
Attainment, 18, 29, 36, 39, 184, 192, 216, 228
Avidya, 18, 206

Benevolence, 19
Bodhicitta, 192-193, 226, 229
Bodhisattva, 18, 191, 193, 206, 212
Bodhisattvacarya, 28
Bodhisattvas, 193, 228
Buddha (Shakyamuni), 37-38, 176
Buddhadharma, 37, 179
Buddhahood, 18, 227
Buddhas, 38, 191
Buddhists, 8, 31, 39, 70, 194-196, 222

Capitalism, 71
Capitalists, 22
Chamdo, 156
Christianity, 35, 68, 163
Colonialism, 89
Commodities, 20, 24-25, 50, 92
Communism, 71, 139

Conflicts, 17, 19, 52, 71-72, 111, 158, 217
Conformity, 4-5, 66
Constitution, 80, 132, 134, 164
Creator, 8, 54
Cuba, 110
Cultures, 13, 16-17, 22, 35, 40
Customs, 16, 35-36, 41, 117-118

Dalai-clique, 135-136
Dalai Lama, 44, 66, 71, 105, 109, 115-121, 124, 132-139, 154-156, 164, 191, 196, 233
Darshana, 32, 34,
Death-rates, 130
Decollectivization, 119
Deforestation, 127-129
Dehumanization, 93, 144
Deities, 35, 195
Delusion, 17-18, 46, 65, 79, 94, 185, 192, 195, 201
Demilitarization, 110
Democracies, 19, 80, 84
Determinism, 43
Dharamsala, 108
Dharmakaya, 227
Dharmakirti, 49
Dignaga, 23
Disarmament, 110
Discrimination, 52, 123, 131, 211, 216-217
Diversity, 5, 16, 22, 58, 109, 169
Doctrine, 8, 79, 93, 187, 194, 223
Dogma, 9, 73
Drepung, 122

Economics, 20-21, 145

Economy, 20, 22, 50, 55, 81, 128, 146, 150, 194
Ecosystem, 106, 110, 151
Educationists, 43
Ego, 182, 187-188, 190, 204
Ego-identity, 186
Ego-mind, 188, 219
Emptiness, 187, 189-190, 192, 195, 202, 219, 233
Enlightened One, 47
Escapism, 5-6, 48-49, 182
Evolutionary, 9-10, 12, 16, 38, 41, 44
Exile, 117-119, 142-143, 155, 171, 233
Existentialism, 30

Faith, 70, 88-89, 91, 97, 172, 195
Family, 12-13, 18, 80, 123, 136, 173, 230
Famine, 118, 128
5-Point Peace Plan, 109, 110, 119, 133, 134
Four Kinds of Birth, 28
Four Noble Truths, 167, 187, 197
Fourth Refuge of Dharma, 144

Gandhi, Mohandas K., 19, 54-55, 98, 111, 164, 166-169, 210
Gandhian, 20, 103, 163, 168
Gandhiji, 163, 168
Genocide, 115, 117, 133
Gita, 163
Globalization, 20-22, 79, 91-92, 150
God, 8
Goddesses, 45
Gods, 45
Gotama, Siddhartha, 181
Governance, 6, 18, 20, 29, 80, 138, 140, 145, 206
Government of Tibet, 120, 132-134

Health, 11, 14, 105, 125, 131, 147-148, 198-199, 214
Healthcare, 92, 123
Healthy-mindedness, 85
Himsa, 172
Hindu, 36, 88, 145, 163
Hiroshima, 54
Holocaust, 11
Hong Kong, 120, 151-152
Humankind, 10, 26, 41, 67, 77, 152
Hussein, Saddam, 108

Ideas, 27-28, 33, 45, 54, 63, 67-68, 82-83, 117, 144, 146, 163, 169
Ideologies, 28
Ideology, 91, 124, 128
Individualism, 67-68
Indoctrination, 3, 90-91, 93, 208-209
Industrialization, 24, 127, 129
Industries, 23, 25, 147-148, 211
Intellectualism, 182
Intelligence, 22, 209
International Commission of Jurists (ICJ), 117, 122, 125, 132-133
International Committee of Lawyers, 137
International Law, 80, 102-103, 132-133, 137
International Relations, 120, 137, 139, 152
Iraq, 15, 81-82, 102, 107
Israel, 158

Jainism, 44
Japanese, 54
Jatakas, 170
Jesus, 83, 169
Jinpa, 126
Judiciary, 29, 134, 151-152
Jung, 67
Jurists, 116-117, 137

Kadampa, 214
Kali Yuga, 72
Karma, 8, 12, 39, 58, 97, 105, 137,
    140, 188-190, 195, 200-201, 212,
    219-226
Kashag, 140
Kashmir, 158
Kham, 116, 127-128
Khyentse, 5
Kleshas, 200-201
Krishnamurti, 73
Kuiyan, Chen, 124-125
Kushala Karma, 39, 137
Kyoto Protocol, 107-108

Lamas, 116-117, 138
Legislation, 66, 79, 82, 102
Liberation, 43, 116, 181, 184-185,
    189-190, 192-193, 195-197, 207,
    216, 231
Lifestyle, 87, 105, 108, 150, 219,
    230
Love, 5, 15, 29, 53, 63, 68, 109,
    124-125, 140, 167, 176, 193, 205
Loving-kindness, 18

Madhyamika, 31-32
Mahaparinirvana, 228
Mahayana Buddhism, 28, 191-192,
    228
Maitreya, 38
Manchuria, 131, 138
Mandala, 47
Mao, 116-118, 132
Maoists, 94
Marxist, 125
Mechanization, 23
Media, 3-4, 24, 100, 115, 185
Medicine, Medicines, 30, 36, 88,
    92, 94, 123, 148
Michungri, 123
Monasteries, 117-118, 124-125,

139, 143, 148-149
Morals, 30
Multicultural, 13, 80
Multiethnic, 13, 80
Multinational, 23, 150

Nagarjuna, 189, 220
Nagchuka, 130
Nationalism, 14, 119
Nationhood, 13-14
Nepal, 94, 127, 140, 143, 146
Nihilism, 202-203
Nirvana, 104, 206-208
Noble Eightfold Path, 73, 181, 196,
    207
Non-harm, Non-harmfulness, 133,
    144-145, 146-147, 161, 172, 185,
    209
Non-Violence, 40, 82, 109, 130,
    141, 145, 155-159, 163-164, 166,
    174-176, 213, 233
Nunneries, 124, 149
Nuns, 123-125, 149
Nyidron, 125

Pakistan, 25, 95, 97, 127, 158
Pali, 190, 200
Paramita, Paramitas, 18, 28-29, 192
Path of No More Learning, 227
Path of Truth, 175
Philosophies, 30-32
Prajna Paramita, 29
Pramanavarrtika, 49
Prasangika-Madhyamika, 189
Preta, 224

Race, Races, 13, 36, 53, 67, 86, 138
Realism, 201
Rebirth, 7, 85, 104, 189, 222
Religions, 8, 35-36, 39, 145, 168-
    169, 194
Renaissance, 46

Revolution, 23-24, 74, 117-118, 133, 135
Righteousness, 83-84, 137

Samadhi, 29
Samsara, 77, 79, 104, 182, 188, 192, 225
Sangha, 28, 36-37, 194, 196-197, 228
Sangha-Karma, 28
Satya Yuga, 72
Satyagraha Movement, 173-175
Satyagrahi, 163, 166, 171-172
Sautantrika, 32
Self-entity, 64, 191
Selflessness, 30, 53, 66, 68-70, 202, 204, 206, 216
Self-view, 66-67
Self-worth, 184
17-Point Agreement, 116, 117, 132, 133, 156
Shakyamuni, 38
Shakyamuni Dharma, 37
Shayatavada, 44
Shunyata, 189-191, 195, 202-203, 216, 219-220, 226
Siddhartha Gautama, 168, 170, 181, 197-200
Six Perfections, 192, 229
Six Realms, 189
Six Worlds, 28
Skandhas, 190-191
Socialism, 27, 124
Sovereignty, 103, 119, 135, 140
Spirit, 29, 35, 43, 45
Splittism, 120, 136
Survival, 22, 34, 45, 67, 127, 132, 229
Survivalist, 18, 39, 45, 84
Suzerainty, 135
Swaraj, 19-20, 55, 103

Taiwan, 141-142, 165
Tantric, 194, 236
Tibetan Autonomous Region (TAR), 117, 127, 128, 130, 131
Teilhard du Chardin, 9
Ten Evil Deeds, 28
Terlingkha, 130
Terrorism, 25
Tibetan Government-in-Exile (TGIE), 118-119, 134-135, 137, 157-158, 164
Thamzing, 118
Thoreau, Henry David, 19, 163, 168-169
Tibetan Buddhism, 124, 193, 233
Tolstoy, Leo, 163, 168-169
Transformation, 56, 66, 72, 74, 104, 116, 133, 152
Transitory, 29, 197, 200, 203, 220
Tribal, 18, 39, 67
Tribes, 12-13
Truthfulness, 81
Truth-insistence, 68, 81, 161, 167
Truths, 71, 167, 169, 181, 187, 197
Truth-vision, 170
Tsaidam, 129-130
Turkestan, 131

Ultimate Truth, 202
Ultra-behaviorism, 63
Unity, 120, 124, 195
Utopia, 104
Utopianism, 104

Vaibashika, 32
Vajrayana, 194-195
Vijnanavada, 32
Vinaya Pitaka, 228
Vipashyana, 215
Voidness, 183, 219

Warfare, 55, 89, 96-97, 115

Well-being, 22, 28-29, 183
Westerners, 195
Wisdom-compassion, 192, 195, 233
Wisdom-realization, 37
Worldliness, 104, 207

Xijang, 130
Xinhua, 130

Yoga, 46-47, 148

For a glossary of all key foreign words used in books published by
World Wisdom, including metaphysical terms in English, consult:
www.DictionaryofSpiritualTerms.org.
This on-line Dictionary of Spiritual Terms provides extensive
definitions, examples and related terms in other languages.

Titles in the Spiritual Masters: East & West Series by World Wisdom

The Essential Sri Anandamayi Ma: Illustrated,
by Alexander Lipsky, 2007

The Essential Swami Ramdas: Commemorative Edition,
compiled by Susunaga Weeraperuma, 2005

The Essentials of Shinran: The Path of True Entrusting,
edited by Alfred Bloom, 2006

The Golden Age of Zen: Zen Masters of the T'ang Dynasty,
by John C.H. Wu, 2003

Honen the Buddhist Saint: Essential Writings and Official Biography,
edited by Joseph A. Fitzgerald, 2006

Introduction to Hindu Dharma: The 68th Jagadguru of Kanchipuram,
edited by Michael Oren Fitzgerald, 2007

The Laughing Buddha of Tofukuji:
The Life of Zen Master Keido Fukushima,
by Ishwar C. Harris, 2004

Messenger of the Heart: The Book of Angelus Silesius,
by Frederick Franck, 2005

Paths to Transcendence: According to
Shankara, Ibn Arabi, and Meister Eckhart,
by Reza Shah-Kazemi, 2006

Samdhong Rinpoche, Uncompromising Truth
for a Compromised World:
Tibetan Buddhism and Today's World,
edited by Donovan Roebert, 2006

The Sufi Doctrine of Rumi: Illustrated Edition,
by William C. Chittick, 2005

Tierno Bokar: The Sufi Sage from Mali,
by Amadou Hampaté Ba, translated by Fatima Jane Casewit, 2008

Timeless in Time: Sri Ramana Maharshi,
by A. R. Natarajan, 2006